MONTANA

DISASTERS

TRUE STORIES OF **TREASURE STATE**
TRAGEDIES AND TRIUMPHS

BUTCH LARCOMBE

FARCOUNTRY
PRESS

To Jane, Matt, Ben, and Harry.

ISBN: 978-1-56037-776-4

© 2021 by James E. "Butch" Larcombe

Front cover: Helena train explosion photograph by Gene Fischer,
© 1989 *Helena Independent Record*.

Back cover: Rescuers at the Custer Creek train wreck photograph courtesy of Terry Gunther.

For more information about our books, write Farcountry Press,
P.O. Box 5630, Helena, MT 59604; call (800) 821-3874;
or visit www.farcountrypress.com.

Library of Congress Cataloging-in-Publication Data on file.

Produced and printed in the United States of America.

25   24   23   22   21   1   2   3   4   5   6

From earthquakes to plane crashes,
Larcombe writes compellingly about some
of Montana's most devastating disasters.
His passion for history and compassion for
the victims is apparent in the turn of every page.
—**Diana L. Di Stefano**, editor,
Montana The Magazine of Western History

Butch Larcombe's riveting new book,
Montana Disasters, *recounts many well-known*
tragic events in the Treasure State's history
but also some long-forgotten ones. The book
is much more than just a listing of the disasters
that killed thousands of Montanans. Larcombe,
a former top Montana journalist, tells
a compelling story about each disaster,
quotes contemporary accounts of survivors
and witnesses, and does some fresh reporting
by interviewing descendants of the victims.
The book is packed with amazing photos.
—**Chuck Johnson**,
retired Montana news reporter

From childhood memories to cairns
marking the path to remembering, the author
presents a host of striking Montana tragedies.
"Planes, trains, and automobiles, Oh My."
Montana's human-caused
and natural disasters flow forth.
—**Ken Robison**, Montana author and historian.

Montana is no stranger to disaster.
There have been many tragic events
in the state's history, from train wrecks,
floods, and earthquakes to plane crashes,
catastrophic explosions, and mine disasters.
These and many others are documented
in this comprehensive and informative look
into the destructive side of the state's history.
Butch Larcombe has, for the first time,
compiled these heart-breaking events into
this one captivating volume that is
an important addition to the chronicles
of Montana's colorful history.
—**Jon Axline**, Montana author
and Cultural Resource Specialist/Historian
at the Montana Department of Transportation

In Montana, where a small population
is scattered across a huge and sometimes
menacing landscape, disasters are inevitable.
But Butch Larcombe's careful and compelling
dissection of some of the most remarkable
events leaves the reader with vivid memories
and deeper understanding of what
went right and what went wrong.
—**Scott McMillion**, editor,
Montana Quarterly magazine

CONTENTS

ACKNOWLEDGMENTS

THERE ARE MANY PEOPLE WHO HELPED IN ONE WAY OR ANOTHER IN the research for these stories. I have a deep debt of gratitude to the following people who shared insight, stories, memories, and photographs:

Roberta McConnell, Bill Kuebler, Wade Bilbrey, Eric Spragg, Steve Karkanen, Tom Bauer, Chris Peterson, Matthew Levitan, Shirley Anderson Harrison, George Ostrom, Terry Kennedy, Sean Logan, David Poor, John Shontz, J.R. Feucht, Amy Andreas, Aaron LaFromboise, John Paull, Ellen Crain, Earl Old Person, Jeff McNeish, Charles Palmer, Nancy Thornton, Todd Harwell, Steven Helgerson, Ken Robison, Larry Krattiger, Mike Stickney, Lu Besel, Terry Gunther, Lori Taylor, Kristi Dunks, Matt Lindberg, Claudia Rapkoch, Anita Fasbender, and David McCumber.

A special thanks to Pam Larcombe Coffman, my sister, for her early editing and proofreading.

Thanks are due also to these entities for their assistance and contributions: the Montana Historical Society Research Center, Browning High School, Blackfeet Community College, the National Museum of Forest Service History, Rocky Mountain Laboratories, Great Northern Railway Historical Society, the Helena *Independent Record*, *The Billings Gazette*, Carbon County Historical Society, Stumptown Historical Society, Butte-Silver Bow Public Archives, Phillips County Museum, the Special Collections and Archives at the University of Montana, National Park Service, U.S. Geological Survey, and the Air Force Historical Research Agency.

To those who I have failed to mention, my sincere apologies.

INTRODUCTION

"Nothing is ever really lost to us as long as we remember it."
—Lucy Maud Montgomery

THIS ALL STARTED WITH CHILDHOOD MEMORIES.

A faded, framed photograph of a man at a podium, on the wall of a cluttered office in a small-town Montana newspaper. A hazy recollection of a vacation trip across the Hi-Line, the family station wagon navigating around Glacier National Park on muddy, hastily constructed roads and over shaky temporary bridges.

The man in the photo, I was told by my newspaper publisher father, was Montana governor Donald Nutter, who died in a plane crash. The muddy roads and makeshift bridges were the result of a big flood, according to a similarly sparse account provided by my mother, who was at the helm of the station wagon. The gathering of pertinent details, in both cases, was left to me.

The first version of my story on the Flood of 1964 appeared in *Montana Quarterly* magazine a few years ago. Later, the magazine's editor, Scott McMillion, in a weak moment, consented to the publication of yet another "disaster" story, this one about a 1938 train wreck out in the sage-studded prairie east of Miles City.

More than five decades after I pondered those childhood questions, this book is my attempt to explain what happened in the plane crash and the flood, and provide similar details surrounding several dozen additional disastrous events.

This book isn't an attempt to construct a list of the worst disasters in Montana history. Such a list would be highly subjective and perhaps not as compelling as what I've aimed to do here. Instead, to the degree possible, this book tells the stories about some of the people who experienced the floods, trains wrecks, and other tragic occurrences that dot the Montana decades.

In writing about the Mann Gulch fire, author Norman Maclean noted his desire to build "a monument of knowledge" to those who died on that steep, smoky slope above the Missouri River in 1949. The stories on these pages may not be monumental, but I hope they can serve at least as cairns that mark a path to remembering.

TRAIN WRECKS

IN THE AGE BEFORE THE AUTOMOBILE CHANGED THE WORLD AND commercial air travel ferried Americans long distances, trains ruled the transportation world, and Montana was no exception.

At one point, three transcontinental railroads bisected the state, connecting Chicago with Seattle and bringing freight and passenger service to cities and towns across Montana. The flagship passenger trains carried colorful names like the *Olympian*, the *Empire Builder*, and the *North Coast Limited*.

For decades, passenger trains were part of the fabric of Montana life. But a gradual decline in ridership began during the Great Depression and accelerated into the 1950s, despite the debut of spiffy, comfortable "streamliners" and dome cars that could get passengers from the Midwest to Puget Sound in as little as forty-five hours and provide a grand view along the way.

But with improved automobiles, the web of interstate highways, and the public's embrace of air travel, it was clear by the 1960s that the rail passenger service offered by the Great Northern Railway, the Northern Pacific Railway, and the Chicago, Milwaukee and St. Paul Railroad was nearing the end of the line.

Montana's railroad-owned passenger trains stopped running in 1971, and Amtrak, the federally owned passenger service, began service on the

3

northern Montana route built by James J. Hill, the creator and namesake of the *Empire Builder*.

Today, two Amtrak trains cross Montana's Hi-Line each day, one headed east, the other west, and they represent one of the most popular long-distance rail routes in the United States. While the golden age of train travel is long gone, the trains of the past served up colorful—but sometimes tragic—slices of Montana history.

NYACK TRAIN COLLISION, 1901

WEEPING IN HELPLESS MISERY

The Great Northern Railway completed laying track through the Rocky Mountains of Montana, the spine of North America, in 1892. It was a big step as the fledgling railroad pounded its way west toward the Pacific Ocean.

The Great Northern route snakes its way through the canyon of the Middle Fork of the Flathead River. In the early days, progress for eastbound trains was measured by stations at Belton, Nyack, Garry, Paola, Essex, and Java before reaching the Continental Divide and Marias Pass at 5,236 feet.

Mountain Type Locomotive for Passenger Service on the Great Northern

Great Northern locomotives like this one pulled passenger and freight trains across the Continental Divide at Marias Pass east of Nyack siding.
PHOTOGRAPH COURTESY OF *RAILWAY AGE*, 1914.

The siding at Essex.
PHOTOGRAPH COURTESY OF THE STUMPTOWN HISTORICAL SOCIETY.

It was an arduous climb. In the early days of the railway, locomotives made frequent stops to take on coal and water to generate enough steam for the push up the mountain pass.

It was almost certainly a tough haul for the eastbound freight train, pulled by one locomotive and pushed by another helper engine, that chugged into Essex, seventeen miles west of the pass, late in the day on August 30, 1901. After pulling onto a siding, the two engines were disconnected from the train to take on water. The crew of the freight, except for a lone brakeman, left the train to prepare for the run over the Continental Divide.

It is likely that the members of the freight crews paid little attention to another train, the westbound passenger train known as Great Northern's No. 3, as it lumbered through Essex westbound on the mainline. But when the freight crew returned to the siding, they made an alarming discovery: the freight cars they had hauled uphill for miles, all twenty-eight cars, were gone.

The brakes had somehow come loose, investigators were later told. With no locomotives to stop or even slow them, the freight cars, heavily loaded with lumber and wooden shingles, began to roll down the hill, picking up speed quickly, barreling toward Nyack sixteen miles down the line.

Investigators later marveled at the fact that the freight cars, reaching speeds of 80 to 100 miles per hour, managed to negotiate the many curves between Essex and Nyack without leaving the tracks.

The westbound train, the No. 3, had just left the Nyack station and was accelerating when sharp warning whistles sounded from another train, a freight stopped on a siding at Nyack. The locomotive engineer on the No. 3 reported hearing the warning whistles and said he "threw open his throttle." But it was too late. The runaway cars overtook the departing train in gathering darkness at about 8:30 P.M.

A vivid account of the collision appeared in the *Kalispell Bee* newspaper the next day. "Coming down the steep mountain grade like a meteor," the *Bee* reported, the runaway cars crashed into the rear of the passenger train. The heavy freight cars sheared off the roofs of the last two cars on the No. 3 and came to a stop atop them, creating a pile of wreckage witnesses estimated to be at least forty feet high.

The runaway freight cars also clipped a portion of the other freight train standing on the siding, hitting its caboose with enough force to overturn it. Oil lamps in the caboose ignited the wreckage. The fire, fueled by the lumber and shingles, was so intense that some would-be rescuers were rendered helpless, allowed only to witness an inferno. The *Bee* account described the blaze as "a funeral pyre for the men caught and pinioned in the ruins of the cars."

An account in the *Dupuyer Acantha* a few days after the collision noted that witnesses reported that some victims were burned alive, "in sight of help and making the mountains ring with their piteous cries for help as they slowly roasted to death . . . the night was such to cause strong men to weep in helpless misery."

There was no lack of will to try to help those injured. Several of the passengers on the No. 3, most of whom were uninjured, tried to help those less fortunate, aided by crew members of the second freight train and others at Nyack.

While the intense flames and heat kept many would-be rescuers at bay, Kalispell resident Jack Kendall, a passenger on the passenger train and a railroader himself, was credited with somehow hefting large pieces of wreckage that allowed others to pull two injured men from the wreckage. Kendall later needed medical help after being overcome by smoke and heat.

The last car on the passenger train carried railroad laborers, many of them recent arrivals from Scandinavian countries who had signed on with the Great Northern in Duluth, Minnesota. Much of the labor crew was bound for Jennings, a small community east of Libby, Montana, where they were to help construct new rail line. It is likely many died quickly under the crushing weight of the freight cars that landed on them.

The coach car the laborers rode in carried forty-six men, according to initial reports. Just thirteen survived the collision and fire. Investigators needed hiring records shipped from Minnesota days later to learn the names of the dead laborers.

The identities of the occupants of the car just ahead of the demolished coach were easily determined. The private car carried P. T Downs, the assistant general superintendent of the railroad's western division, and his son, Kirk, and a cook, Henry Blair. Downs oversaw the Great Northern operations in an area that stretched from Minot, North Dakota, to Spokane, Washington. He was believed to have been on a tour, with his son, who was in his early twenties, acting as a secretary.

It was unclear if the three occupants of the private car were killed in the collision or the flames that followed. The body of Blair, a father of thirteen, was found and removed from burned wreckage the day following the collision, while those of Downs and his son were last seen in the inferno, "but they were beyond earthly help and they were soon lost to sight," the *Bee* reported.

The body of the younger Downs was never recovered or identified. His father's charred remains were only identified when morgue workers found a watch attached to an arm, the railroad executive's name inscribed on the back of the watch case. The face of the watch, its crystal damaged, read 8:27, consistent with the estimated time of the collision.

In the aftermath of the crash, crews detached the locomotive from the No. 3 and sent it west from Nyack to Belton, where rail operators telegraphed news of the fiery wreck to Kalispell at about 9:30 P.M. Another undamaged car was loaded with the injured and bodies of some of those killed.

In Kalispell, a rescue train was quickly assembled and every doctor in town was summoned. The train returned from Nyack between 2:30 and 3 A.M., its cargo described by the *Bee* as "a gruesome load of dead and bleeding humanity." By the time the rescue train arrived, a throng of residents had gathered. Some were awaiting word on passengers, while others helped carry the injured to the hospital and bodies to the morgue.

The initial death toll was thirty-six: thirty-three laborers and the three men in the private car. But accounts vary about the precise number of people killed and injured. The car carrying the laborers was added at Havre, and its occupants were not listed on the train's passenger list. Later, railroad officials said some of the laborers got off the train in Shelby and Cut Bank.

Another thirteen laborers and crew members were reported to be injured, some of whom were expected to die. A detailed story in the *Great Falls Daily Tribune* on September 1, 1901, noted that Great Northern officials proclaimed the accident to be the worst in the railroad's history "and one of the worst in the annals of American railroading." (Claims about the worst train wrecks in American history should be regarded with caution. While the Nyack wreck may have been one of the deadliest in 1901, a wreck just a few years later near Pueblo, Colorado, killed ninety-seven. The exact number of deaths at Nyack is difficult to determine. It could be the second deadliest rail incident in Montana history, behind a 1938 wreck east of Miles City at Custer Creek. A head-on collision at

Youngs Point near Park City, Montana, in 1908 killed twenty-one people and would also rank high on the list.)

Despite the ferocity of the collision, the deaths and injuries were limited to the occupants of the last two cars, sparing the train's regular passengers, a fact that surprised observers and investigators.

The odd configuration of the No. 3 likely played a significant role in shielding the passengers. Railroad crews would typically ride in a car closer to the front of a train, often just behind the baggage car. But in this case, the car carrying the laborers was added to the rear of the train in Havre, Montana. The presence of the private car also added a buffer between the passengers and the runaway freight cars.

For one Kalispell-bound passenger on the No. 3, the ill-fated trip included what the *Tribune* described as "a narrow escape from death." John O'Brien, the superintendent of the Somers Lumber Company, which provided lumber and railroad ties to the Great Northern at the time, was returning from Minnesota on the train. He had received an invitation to join Downs for dinner.

When O'Brien went to the car, he found the door locked. Confused, he returned to his sleeper car further forward on the train. He was in the sleeper when the collision killed all the occupants of the private car.

In the days after the collision, questions about how the cars broke loose were abundant. An editorial in the *Tribune* on September 3, 1901, alleged that the deadly collision was caused "by the criminal negligence of the train crew." The editorial also took the railroad to task for not having a telegraph operator stationed in Nyack to receive word of the runaway cars. Given warning, the passenger train could have been moved off the mainline, and nothing worse than "a few ditched freight cars would have resulted," the editorial asserted.

At an inquest in Kalispell on September 4, 1901, a coroner's jury heard from members of the freight crew, including the brakeman, who was thrown from the runaway freight as it collided with the passenger train and somehow was uninjured. The brakeman said he set eight brakes on the cars before they rolled away. Other crew members reported seeing the brakeman performing his required duties. The jury concluded that the crew had not acted negligently but arrived at no explanation for the tragic collision.

Today, many freight trains

Cork Hill and John Fraley placed a memorial plaque at the site of the Nyack train wreck. PHOTOGRAPH BY CHRIS PETERSON, COURTESY OF *HUNGRY HORSE NEWS*.

and a passenger train known as the *Empire Builder* traverse the route daily across the mountains near Glacier National Park. While many of the stations and depots developed in the line's early days are long gone, the rail route remains largely unchanged.

In the fall of 2018, Nyack resident Cork Hill and Flathead Valley author John Fraley placed a memorial plaque at the site of the deadly collision. The plaque recounts the collision and notes that many of those killed were buried in a mass grave on the site. It reads, in part: "Even now, some will say that the ghosts of the wreck still haunt the sleepy Nyack Valley."

CUSTER CREEK TRAIN WRECK, 1938

"THEY WERE TRAPPED LIKE RATS."

Florence Maguire climbed aboard the *Olympian* in Milwaukee, Wisconsin, bound for Montana. Her sister in Miles City was getting married, and the smooth-riding train, the flagship of the Chicago, Milwaukee, St. Paul and Pacific line, offered a comfortable means of reaching the small town out west.

A muddy Custer Creek roils around derailed train cars.
PHOTOGRAPH COURTESY OF TERRY GUNTHER.

When the train reached Montana many hours later, rain pounded the prairie and lightning pierced the darkness. "There was," Maguire would recall later, "a feeling of wildness about it."

As the *Olympian* rumbled across a trestle that spanned Custer Creek near Saugus, a speck of a town about twenty-five miles east of Miles City, a wild night turned tragic. The intense rain, collected by the coulees and ravines that led to the creek bottom, formed a torrent that ate at the concrete piers supporting the trestle. As the train crossed the trestle, the locomotive and forward cars derailed. "The cars followed each other like bullets from a machine gun," a railroad official said later. The locomotive and tender lodged into the opposite bank, while other cars, including several carrying passengers, fell into the raging creek. Several passenger cars at the rear of the train miraculously remained on the track.

The train cars plummeted into the creek at about 12:35 A.M. on June 19, 1938. Even though dawn was hours away, the dark reality that dozens were likely drowned or killed in the crash itself was immediately apparent to survivors and rescuers.

Maguire, moments before the crash, was standing in the lavatory getting ready to disembark in Miles City. The train seemed to come to a sudden stop. She realized the trouble was serious when water entered the lavatory and rapidly rose. Grabbing a towel rack to stay above the water, she kicked at a window and eventually it gave way, allowing her to reach the top of the rail car, where a train porter and others helped her to safety.

In a detailed account in the *Miles City Daily Star* the day after the crash, Maguire, who suffered only cuts and bruises in her escape, shared a haunting account of the fate of those trapped in the passenger cars, first filled with rushing water and, later, heavy silt.

Crawling on the top of a partially submerged sleeper car, "I could hear some of the them tapping on the windows and could hear over the roar of the wind and rush of the water the faint cries for help," she said. "There seemed to be no way to get to those people who were trapped in the car. No doors could be opened. It was terrible, but we who were on top of the cars could not stop, the water was liable to wash us off the path over the wrecked coaches and other cars."

Another passenger, riding in a car near the rear of the train, one of just a few that didn't plunge into the creek, confirmed the futility of most rescue efforts. "The most pitiful thing about it was that we couldn't do anything

A sleeper car rests in Custer Creek.
PHOTOGRAPH COURTESY OF TERRY GUNTHER.

to help those down in the river," Isadore Orenstein of Chicago told a *Star* reporter. "The water was roaring just like Niagara Falls around the coaches."

William Shearer, a veteran Milwaukee locomotive engineer, was one of several railroad employees on the train "deadheading" to their homes in Miles City. Initially, he recalled thinking the train had landed in the Yellowstone River. "It was a few minutes before I found out it was Custer Creek," he told investigators. "Why, I've put a train over these tracks a thousand times and I never saw [more than] a bucket of water in that creek at once."

Just two hours before the trestle collapsed, a Milwaukee Road worker dispatched to check the condition of the track in the area of the trestle— a routine duty during heavy rain—reported the creek carrying about four feet of water. In the days after the wreck, investigators speculated that the water in Custer Creek may have reached a depth of twenty feet during the deluge.

Shearer said he and his fellow railroaders crawled out of the watery coach and saw the locomotive, mail car, and others "piled up every which way. We crawled along the pile like monkeys, wondering how anyone could be alive," he said. While a couple of the railroaders climbed the creek bank and went to Saugus to telephone for help, Shearer and another man crawled back into the wreckage hoping to find survivors.

"I knew the boys in the locomotive must be dead," Shearer said. "We saw a woman jump out of a window she smashed. She floated down against a pile of wreckage and I think she must have drowned. Her husband yelled at us to help her, but it was no use."

As word of the wreck washed over Miles City, residents of the town of about 7,100 quickly responded. According to the *Star*, four doctors and five nurses hopped onto an emergency train sent to the crash site to

Wreckage rests in a swollen Custer Creek.
PHOTOGRAPH COURTESY OF TERRY GUNTHER.

13

Men search for victims in a partially submerged car.
PHOTOGRAPH COURTESY OF TERRY GUNTHER.

render first aid and ferry the injured to Holy Rosary Hospital. About thirty of the most seriously injured arrived in Miles City at about 5:30 A.M. All told, more than sixty-five passengers would be treated for injuries, with just one succumbing at the hospital.

A morgue was established at Graves Funeral Home (named for the former owner, James E. Graves). As the death toll mounted in the days after the crash, the newspaper described the funeral home as "a scene of intolerable sadness" as relatives arrived, often relying on jewelry or bodily scars to confirm the identity of their loved ones.

Word of the tragedy spread across the nation, and the Miles City telephone exchange was overwhelmed with the desperate calls of distant relatives trying to determine the fate of loved ones who were traveling on the *Olympian*. Railroad officials estimated that the number of dead would top forty. In the days to come, those estimates proved to be reasonably accurate. The railroad officially pegged the death toll at forty-seven. Others, including Terry Gunther, a Milwaukee Road rail buff who grew up in Miles City and now lives in Billings, think forty-eight people were killed.

He contends that a fourteen-month-old baby, the daughter of a woman who died in the crash, has never been recovered. Gunther, the descendant of a line of Milwaukee Road employees, has done extensive research into the wreck, combing official railroad reports and tracking down survivors. When it comes to the tally of deaths, he said, "Every story you read or hear, there are different numbers."

It is possible that the railroad never had a firm count of the passengers due to a failure to capture the names of those who boarded the train as it was en route to the West Coast. Other accounts note that passenger records may have been in a train employee's valise that was lost in the crash.

And there was the storm itself. So much water pounded down Custer Creek and other tributaries that the Yellowstone River was likely flowing at an unimaginable pace. Indeed, late on the day of the early morning crash, the body of a female passenger was recovered near Glendive, forty miles downstream from where Custer Creek, typically dry for months at a time, meets the Yellowstone. In the days to come, the bodies of other passengers were found near Fallon and even further downstream near Sidney.

Stories of grief and familial loss filled the *Star*'s pages after the wreck. One young passenger lost his twin brother. Three young children, none older than ten, were orphaned when both their parents were swept away, the mother pulled from the arms of one of her children.

The train that plunged off the trestle included a locomotive, a tender, and twelve other cars, many of them carrying passengers. All but four—a diner, two sleepers, and an observation car—went into the creek. The four others remained on the damaged trestle and the east bank of the creek. Many passengers in those cars were not immediately aware of the crash. Some slept for several more hours, oblivious to the unfolding tragedy.

Warren "Buck" Jones was one of the passengers in the rear cars, traveling from his home in Wisconsin to spend a summer on a ranch owned by his family near Two Dot, Montana. The seventeen-year-old was traveling with his ten-year-old cousin, John Baxter.

In an interview with *The Billings Gazette* nearly seven decades later, Jones noted the wreck was "in what was about as deserted a chunk of Montana as you can find." As the cars sat near the trestle, he recalled a period of eerie silence and the unmistakable smell of sagebrush. "I didn't have any sense of being in an impact accident. I just became aware of the fact that it had gotten awfully quiet."

As dawn broke, he grabbed a camera and snapped a dozen photos of the crash scene and later sent the film to his father for processing. It's believed that these images were among the first taken of the historic crash.

In the first days after the wreck, the *Star* published several stories, recapping efforts to recover bodies of missing passengers and remove the rail cars from the creek bed. To the east, railroad officials scrambled to piece together the events that led to the first passenger deaths on the railroad in two decades. The railroad also attempted to quell rumors about the wreck, including claims that several innovations—the steel frames that replaced the wood chassis of the passenger cars and the more tightly sealed windows that allowed the cars to be cooled—made it more difficult for passengers to escape or be rescued.

People look on as Custer Creek surges by the wrecked train.
PHOTOGRAPH BY WARREN JONES, COURTESY OF TERRY GUNTHER.

Railroad official K. F. Nystrom described the impact of the cars tumbling into the creek as similar to an air crash and said the windows were not sealed. "They didn't have a chance," Nystrom said of those who died in a story published by the *Milwaukee Journal* about a week after the wreck. "They were trapped like rats." He added, "If a car is under water it makes no difference what kind of glass is in the windows; you're trapped."

The *Journal* also noted the railroad's interest in developing a better signal system and possibly some sort of method that could alert train crews to damaged track like that encountered at Custer Creek, where, according to Nystrom, "the tragedy happened so fast that the engineer was still in his seat, hand on the throttle, when rescuers found him pinned there in death."

The Prairie County coroner held an inquest into the deaths and heard testimony from six witnesses, most of them Milwaukee employees who survived the crash. The nine-man jury concluded that the rain, not the railroad, was at fault for the deadly wreck. The first funerals were held on June 22. The Milwaukee Road began repairs on the trestle the next day and ran trains on Northern Pacific Railway lines between Terry and Miles City until the work was finished.

Initial accounts of the wreck claimed that the trestle collapsed as the train passed over it. Milwaukee Road officials later concluded that a portion of the 180-foot-long trestle had washed away before the train arrived. The accident report released by the Interstate Commerce Commission in August 1938 concluded the train had derailed as it crossed the trestle due to shifting of rails caused by erosion around the base of several piers during the cloudburst.

Tragedy involving the *Olympian* didn't end at Custer Creek, however. Six days after the trestle incident, the westbound *Olympian* collided head-on with an eastbound train carrying members of the Civilian Conservation Corps from Spokane to Fort Dix, New Jersey. The collision occurred at about 3:35 A.M. near Ingomar, Montana, about 125 miles west of Custer Creek. Miraculously, there was just one death and less than twenty injuries

LIFE

Vol. 5 No. 1

JULY 4, 1938

ODQUIST TOOK THIS PICTURE AT 4 A.M. HEADLIGHTS OF THE FIRST HOSPITAL TRAIN FROM MILES CITY BLINK ABOVE THE WRECK

A SURVIVOR PHOTOGRAPHS THE WORST AMERICAN TRAIN WRECK SINCE 1887

Maurice V. Odquist (*right*) is a top-notch salesman, head of the marketing division of American Can Co. He is also an amateur camera enthusiast. In Chicago on the evening of June 17 he boarded the *Olympian*, crack Chicago-Tacoma express of the Chicago, Milwaukee, St. Paul & Pacific R. R. ("The Milwaukee Road"). By midnight of the second day, with some 160 passengers, the train, unchecked by a sudden cloudburst, was gathering speed across the high, thinly-settled plains of eastern Montana.

Ahead of the train lay a 180-ft. trestle of steel and concrete over Custer Creek, named for the hero of the famous Last Stand, 26 miles east of Miles City, Mont. It had been built in 1913, when The Milwaukee Road was being completed in the last great thrust of American transcontinental railroad building. Ordinarily Custer Creek carries only a trickle of water down to the Yellowstone River. But the same cloudburst which pelted the *Olympian* had now filled it to brimming, sending a roaring, 30-ft. wall of water—what Westerners call a "flash

flood"—to batter the supports of the 25-year-old trestle.

At 12:34 a.m. Mr. Odquist was shaken by a heart-sickening jolt as his car, which had been traveling about 50 m.p.h., suddenly stopped dead. Snatching his bag and camera, he scrambled out into the storm and forward with other frightened passengers to the east bank of roaring Custer Creek. There, by lightning flashes, he and they stared in helpless horror on an awful scene. The center span of the trestle was gone. Across the creek on the west bank the *Olympian*'s locomotive and five cars were piled in a shambles of crumpled steel. Two other cars lay deep in the roaring creek. There were screams aplenty, but Mr. Odquist did not hear them. "The river was making too much noise for that, thank God," he said afterward. Retiring to his Pullman, one of the four rear cars left safely on the rails, he waited until dawn brought the first rescue train to the isolated spot. Then he emerged to take the first pictures, here printed exclusively by LIFE, of the worst American train wreck since 1887.

Maurice V. Odquist was the *Olympian* surv who took these first pictures of the wr

Life magazine covered the wreck with passenger Maurice Odquist's images.
PHOTOGRAPH COURTESY OF TERRY GUNTHER.

stemming from the collision, which was blamed on the *Olympian* engineer's failure to follow orders.

While news of the Custer Creek wreck made headlines across the nation, the story also unfolded on the glossy pages of *Life* magazine. Maurice Odquist, another passenger in the rear cars of the *Olympian*, also snapped photos of the wreck as light allowed on June 19. A salesman for the American Can Company, Odquist contacted *Life* as soon as he arrived in Miles City. The magazine ran the story on July 4, 1938, under the headline, *A Survivor Photographs The Worst American Train Wreck Since 1887.*

Jones, who sent his film to his father in Milwaukee after he arrived safely in Harlowton, later graduated from college and made his way back to Montana, where he helped operate the family ranch, was involved in banking, and raised a family. He lived most of his life in the Harlowton area before moving to Billings in his final years. He died in 2008.

"We didn't know anything about it when we were kids," said Bill Jones, one of Warren's children. "For a long time, he was busy with the ranch and interested in other things, and he just wasn't interested in talking about it." After retiring, the elder Jones began to research the crash and connected with others with similar interest, including Gunther. He didn't venture back to Custer Creek until 2004, sixty-six years after the crash, joined by his son. When the elder Jones talked of the wreck, he described himself as a spectator, not a survivor.

But his son suspects his father was deeply affected by the wreck and a decision by his own father, who in 1938 bought the train tickets for Jones and his cousin. The initial tickets were for seats in a car ahead of the dining car, one that went into the water at Custer Creek, trapping many passengers.

"For some reason, a couple of days before they were going to leave, my grandfather went down to the train station and got the tickets changed to the car behind the dining car," Bill Jones said, noting that his grandfather never could explain why he sought the change. "Those sorts of things seem to happen in life. I think it probably took awhile for that to really sink in with my dad, how fortunate he really was."

EVARO TRAIN WRECK, 1962
CULPABLE HUMAN FAILURE

On June 9, 1962, the *North Coast Limited*, the premier passenger train of the Northern Pacific Railway, left Seattle at about 1:30 P.M. and headed east, loaded with passengers toting fresh memories of the Space Needle, the monorail, and other futuristic elements of the World's Fair under way in the city's center.

The passenger list also included five members of a young family hoping to create a new life in Montana. The Yates family had taken a local passenger train from their home in Centralia, Washington, to Seattle, where they boarded the *North Coast Limited*. Freshly discharged from the military after being stationed at Fort Lewis, Washington, Jim Yates was taking his new wife, Dauretta, and their three daughters east to Billings, where family members would meet them and take them to Ekalaka.

"When he was discharged, we were moving back to Montana," Roberta McConnell, the oldest daughter, recalled nearly six decades later. "He was born in Montana."

About fourteen hours after leaving Seattle, the *North Coast Limited* pulled into Paradise, a little town in western Montana along the Clark Fork River that was a crew-change point. Late in the evening, the engine crew (an engineer and fireman in the locomotive) and three trainmen (a conductor, head-end brakeman, and rear brakeman-flagman) had guided the westbound version of the train from Missoula to Paradise, turned the train over to another crew, and waited to meet the eastbound version about six hours later and take it into Missoula.

As railroad jobs go, it was a good one, offering a regular short run from Missoula to Paradise, a five- to six-hour rest period, and then the trip back, passing through Ravalli and Arlee before climbing to Evaro and making the descent into the Missoula Valley. Elden Lynn, the Missoula-based locomotive engineer at the helm the morning of June 10, had nearly three decades of experience and had been making the trip to Paradise and back for several years.

In the wee hours of that morning, the Yates family had nestled into the lower level in one of the *North Coast Limited*'s Vista-Dome coaches as the train rolled through the darkness, likely lulled to sleep by the gentle rocking of the car.

There was a thirty-five-mile-per-hour speed limit for passenger trains as they approached the Evaro summit. Over the crest of the summit, the speed limit for such trains dropped to thirty miles per hour due to the steep downhill grade, numerous curves, and a trestle, the highest on the Northern Pacific line, carrying the tracks 226 feet above the ground.

According to a speed-recording tape in one of the locomotive units, the train passed the summit at fifty-four miles per hour and began its downhill run. After negotiating several curves, even as it gained speed, the train left the tracks as it encountered a left curve about 1.6 miles below Evaro. The tape showed the train was moving at eighty-seven miles per hour when it derailed.

The locomotive unit carrying Lynn and fireman Gerry Haines tipped as it left the track and slid on its side for more than 400 feet. Other locomotive units followed, as did other cars carrying baggage and people.

Passenger cars spilled down the embankment onto the highway.
PHOTOGRAPH COURTESY OF ARCHIVES AND SPECIAL COLLECTIONS,
MANSFIELD LIBRARY, THE UNIVERSITY OF MONTANA.

All told, all four locomotive units and fifteen of the train's seventeen cars derailed to the right of the track, some slamming into the highway embankment below. (That highway is now U.S. Highway 93, the major north-south conduit through western Montana.)

The Willig family lived across the highway from the scene of the derailment, which happened as dawn was approaching. "I have never heard a noise like that before," recalled Carl Willig, the family patriarch. His wife told an interviewer: "The house shook so hard that I thought it might be an earthquake."

Because the derailment tore up telephone lines, Carl Willig drove down the highway to find a functioning telephone to report the derailment and summon help. He returned to help the train passengers and crew and at one point drove some of those injured to hospitals in Missoula.

Margie Swenson, a passenger in the Vista-Dome car that carried the Yates family, offered a vivid account to a reporter from the *Missoulian* newspaper in the hours after the accident. "I was sleeping," she said. "There was a terrible jolt. I fell into the aisle and I kept rolling and rolling. It was awful. The dirt came into the end of the car. Two little girls were buried in it. We could only see their feet."

The two little girls were Roberta McConnell's younger sisters, Jacqueline and Teresa Ann. They had been riding in a seat in front of their older sister, who was just a few days short of her fifth birthday.

"I can remember the feeling of the car coming off the rails and sliding down the embankment. When everything stopped, I started crying and asking for my mom and dad."

She sat near a teenage girl while others, including her mother and stepfather, worked to free the girls in the mud and debris. "They pretty much dug until their hands were raw and bleeding."

The rescuers were able to free Jackie—"she was pretty much buried alive for that short amount of time," recalled Roberta. After a time, Roberta, Jackie, and her mother were taken to St. Patrick Hospital in Missoula. Her stepfather stayed at the scene to help in the effort to free Teresa Ann, the youngest of the girls.

All told, 282 of the 338 passengers, including 25 workers on the train, were injured in the derailment. Some were hospitalized at St. Patrick Hospital, the nearby Northern Pacific hospital, or at Community Hospital. Many others were treated and released throughout the day on June 10. More than 150 passengers found shelter at the Florence Hotel in Missoula.

The *Missoulian* reported that the Sunday-morning scene at local hospitals was chaotic. "Sirens screamed intermittently for three hours as scores of

Rescuers help lower a passenger to safety.
PHOTOGRAPH COURTESY OF ARCHIVES AND SPECIAL COLLECTIONS,
MANSFIELD LIBRARY, THE UNIVERSITY OF MONTANA.

passengers injured in the Northern Pacific train wreck were brought in by ambulance, private cars, trucks, and buses. All doctors, nurses, student nurses, hospital employees, and Red Cross workers were called into action," reporter Evelyn King wrote.

There was just one person killed in the spectacular derailment, young Teresa Ann, whose body was pulled from the mud and debris in the first of the four Vista-Dome cars. Initial reports said she died of suffocation. But a coroner determined the girl died after suffering a broken neck in the derailment. The death of the two-and-one-half-year-old is the only passenger death in the seventy-one-year history of the *North Coast Limited*. (The *North Coast Limited* began service in 1900 and continued until 1971, when the Northern Pacific and other railroads were merged into what became the Burlington Northern Railroad. Amtrak took over operation of passenger trains in May 1971 and the *North Coast Limited* name disappeared. Previous fatal accidents did not involve passengers. In March 1962, just a few months before the Evaro derailment, two engine crew members were killed and numerous passengers were injured when the westbound *North Coast Limited* derailed near Granite, Idaho. About two miles below the site of the June 1962 derailment, a freight train loaded with lumber "ran wild coming down Evaro Hill" on April 29, 1906. The engineer, fireman, and several transients were killed in that wreck and resulting fire, according to the *Missoulian*. Brake failure was the apparent cause of the derailment.)

Suffering only minor injuries, Lynn, the engineer, and Haines, the fireman, were able to exit the locomotive and were spotted walking away from the derailment scene. In early statements, the railroad noted the train's

The train's excessive speed flung passenger cars down the hillside.
PHOTOGRAPH COURTESY OF ARCHIVES AND SPECIAL COLLECTIONS, MANSFIELD LIBRARY, THE UNIVERSITY OF MONTANA.

high speed and the possibility of brake failure and speculated that recent rain could have softened the railbed, which may have caused the heavy locomotive to derail on the curve.

But within two days of the derailment, Northern Pacific officials publicly narrowed the list of possible causes, noting it had found no sign of brake malfunction, mechanical failure, or any issues with the railbed at the accident site. "There is every indication the accident was caused by excessive speed," Robert McFarlane, Northern Pacific's president, said in a statement.

Shortly thereafter, a lawyer hired by Lynn held a press conference, and said the locomotive engineer had done "everything humanely possible" to prevent the derailment, denied any negligence, and questioned the conduct of the conductor and brakemen.

The Northern Pacific held a closed-door inquiry in Missoula about two weeks after the accident but did not publicly disclose any conclusions. But details surrounding the derailment emerged a few weeks later when the Interstate Commerce Commission, the federal agency charged with regulating the nation's railroads, held a public hearing in Missoula that drew more than 100 spectators.

At the hearing, the ICC included the testimony of the enginemen and the rest of the train crew given during the closed Northern Pacific inquiry. The key element involved the activities of Lynn and Haines during the "rest period" in Paradise.

While the others said they went to rented rooms to sleep, the two men met up with others and headed to the Legion Bar in Paradise. After having at least one beer, the group bought a six-pack of beer and drove north to Hot Springs, where a community celebration was taking place.

Lynn and Haines acknowledged visiting the Cowboy Bar in Hot Springs and drinking more beer. Several witnesses at the bar told the ICC that the two men did not appear drunk. But another witness recalled speaking with Lynn at the bar, telling him he should leave the bar and sober up before driving the train. According to the witness, Lynn responded,

"Don't worry, you don't have to steer the train; you just push buttons, and I can do that that in my sleep."

While the men claimed to have had just a few beers in Paradise and Hot Springs and getting sleep before boarding the train, blood-alcohol tests performed in a Missoula hospital more than five hours after the derailment told a different story. Factoring in the rate that alcohol dissipates from the body, the physician who performed the tests concluded that Lynn likely had a blood-alcohol level of 0.153 at the time of the derailment, high enough to be legally drunk, while Haines was at 0.088.

The ICC concluded the two men likely drank more than they admitted during the rest period. They also noted that the throttle of the train was in the wide-open position at the time of the derailment, and there was no evidence that anyone responsible for operating the train—the enginemen or train crew—took any action to slow or stop the train.

The investigators concluded that the engine crew "relaxed into a condition of somnolence" as the train climbed toward Evaro. The bottom line was that "culpable human failure and not mechanical failure was the primary cause of this accident."

While the ICC report didn't delve into the actions and roles of Lynn, Haines, and the train crew, others concluded that Lynn may have been sleeping on the floor of the locomotive while Haines operated the locomotive. Bill Kuebler, a Northern Pacific historian, past president of the Northern Pacific Railway Historical Association, and author of two books related to the railway, said he interviewed members of the crew in the years after the derailment and learned that Lynn was likely sleeping at the time of the accident. Haines may have also been lulled to sleep as the train approached Evaro.

"I am confident that is what happened," Kuebler said, noting that while alcohol played a clear role in the derailment, other factors, including the failure of the rear brakeman to conduct a running brake test at Evaro, as regulations required, along with the fact that Haines was a last-minute replacement for another fireman, were also issues. "When these accidents happen, they are almost never caused by just one thing," Kuebler said. "It's almost always a chain of events that lead up to an accident." Kuebler noted that interviews with the other Northern Pacific employees who worked with Lynn over the years revealed that Lynn had issues with alcohol consumption and would often visit taverns during stops at Paradise, then rely on a fireman to drive the train back to Missoula. According to the ICC report, Lynn admitted to drinking beer before reporting to work in Missoula on June 9, 1962.

Shortly after the ICC hearing, Lynn and Haines were fired by the Northern Pacific. Railway regulations clearly prohibited workers from being on duty while under the influence of alcohol or drugs.

While a coroner's jury found no criminal intent in the death of the young girl, Missoula County Attorney H. J. Pinsoneault later charged Lynn with involuntary manslaughter and during the 1963 trial accused the engineer of "inalertness, ineptness, and negligence," contending he was asleep in the cab of the locomotive when the train left the tracks. A jury deliberated for about twenty-nine hours before returning a not-guilty verdict.

While Haines left Missoula after the derailment and "disappeared into a different life," according to Kuebler, Lynn remained in the Garden City. He died about eight years after the Evaro derailment.

After the death and burial of Teresa Ann, the young Yates family completed its move to Ekalaka and lived there and in Miles City for several years before moving back to Washington state. But questions about the derailment and death lingered through the decades.

Despite being very young—her fifth birthday arrived while she was hospitalized in Missoula after the derailment—Roberta McConnell said, "It's not something I have ever forgotten. It was traumatizing, and it got worse as the years went by."

Prowling the Internet, she found the name of Kuebler in a forum discussing the Evaro incident. She contacted him in search of more information in 2010, the year after her mother died and forty-eight years after the train wreck.

"He filled in a lot of the blanks that Jackie and I had as far as the accident was concerned," McConnell said. They first met Kuebler in Spokane at a gathering of the Northern Pacific history group, and later she, her stepfather, and Kuebler traveled to Missoula. The trio visited Elden Lynn's grave and went to the derailment site and placed roses in memory of Teresa Ann.

"It was the first time I had been back since the accident. It was emotional for me," said McConnell, who lives in western Washington. The knowledge and sad truths were painful but "kind of helped bring closure to me, my dad, and my sister," she said. "Now, we have answers and it makes it easier to come to terms with what happened that day."

SOURCES

Nyack Train Collision

Billings Weekly Gazette. September 3, 1901.

Dupuyer Acantha. Early September 1901 (exact date unavailable).

Goeser, Bruce and Tim Victor, contributors. Essex Reference Sheet. Great Northern Railway Historical Society, St. Paul, Minnesota. June 2010.

Great Falls Daily Tribune. September 1–5, 1901.

Kalispell Bee. August 31, 1901.

Custer Creek Train Wreck

Billing Gazette. June 20–24, 1938.

Billings Gazette. "Survivor recalls the worst train wreck in Montana history." April 10, 2006.

Gunther, Terry. Personal interview. March 2017.

Interstate Commerce Commission. "Accident on the Chicago, Milwaukee, St. Paul and Pacific Railroad, Saugus, MT, June 1938." Investigation No. 2278, Report on August 9, 1938.

Jones, Bill. Personal interview. March 2017.

Life. "A Survivor Photographs the Worst American Train Wreck Since 1887."
   July 4, 1938.

Miles City Daily Star. June 20–28, 1938.

Wilkerson, Bill. "Ingomar Wreck." *MilWest Dispatch.* Vol. 5, Issue No. 3, July 1992.

Evaro Train Wreck

Interstate Commerce Commission. Railroad Accident Investigation, Ex Parte No.
   229, Northern Pacific Railway Company, Evaro, Montana. June 10, 1962.

Kuebler, William "Bill." Personal interview. July 2019.

McConnell, Roberta. Personal interview. July 2019.

Missoulian. June 11–July 22, 1962.

Missoulian. "ICC Says 'Human Failure' Caused NP Train Wreck."
   September 11, 1962.

Missoulian. "Jury Acquits Lynn After Deliberation of Nearly 29 Hours."
   June 14, 1963.

Northern Pacific Railway Historical Association. www.nprha.org.

The Spokane Chronicle. "Missoula Coroner's Jury Hears Rail Death Details."
   August 15, 1962.

WILDFIRES

VAST FORESTS COVER MUCH OF THE MOUNTAINOUS WESTERN THIRD of Montana, while islands of forests dot the central and southeastern regions of the nation's fourth-largest state. These forests, and adjoining large swaths of grasslands, when mixed with a relatively dry climate and typically hot summers, offer a reliable recipe for wildfires.

Fire seasons in Montana and across the West have become more intense, increasing the challenges and risks faced by the women and men who fight the blazes. While wildland firefighting doesn't land on the lists of most-dangerous jobs, it does encompass elements of some of the deadliest occupations, including logging, truck driving, flying aircraft, and manual labor.

In Montana, there have been forty-seven wildland firefighting deaths, according to the National Interagency Fire Center. That number is likely inaccurate, given that it doesn't include any Montana deaths from the fires of 1910, or the three deaths incurred during a forest fire in the Little Rocky Mountains southwest of Malta in 1936.

The causes of wildland firefighter deaths in Montana vary, ranging from vehicle accidents and aircraft crashes to falling trees, rolling rocks, and, in at least one case, hypothermia. Some workers have suffered heart attacks or strokes on the fire line, while others have been similarly stricken during training exercises.

But by a wide margin, the most wildland firefighter deaths in Montana have involved flames. Labeled as "burnovers" or "entrapment" in the statistics, fire itself has killed twenty-five wildland firefighters in Montana, according to the National Interagency Fire Center. While the fires and deaths fit neatly into the lists maintained by the agencies, the numbers fall far short of telling the stories of the lives lost and the limits of our efforts to honor or remember them.

The four events recounted here occurred under varying circumstances, but they demonstrate a common truth about the danger of trying to outrun a raging wildfire.

THE FIRES OF 1910

WHEN THE MOUNTAINS ROARED

In the first decade of the twentieth century, the Chicago, Milwaukee, St. Paul and Pacific Railroad was pursuing its plan to stay competitive with other railroads, including the Northern Pacific and Great Northern Railways. This meant connecting its lines in the Midwest with the Pacific Coast. At staggering cost (the total to reach the coast was estimated at $1.7 billion in today's dollars), the "Milwaukee Road" built its way west across Montana, with progress measured tie by tie, mile by mile.

In 1907, the ambitious railroad reached the base of the Bitterroot Mountains west of Missoula. The steep canyons ahead presented a formidable list of demands: bridges, trestles, and tunnels, and the strong backs to build them.

The task was daunting but not undoable. About two decades earlier, the Northern Pacific had completed a line that linked Missoula and northern Idaho following a course to the north along the Clark Fork River.

Along the Milwaukee route, towns sprang up, some fueled by rail construction, others also driven by earlier mining and timber cutting.

With names such as Saltese, De Borgia, Haugan, and Taft, they were often ramshackle, ragged, even wretched places, none more so than Taft.

Just a handful of miles from the Idaho border and near a series of tunnels and trestles that required intensive labor, Taft and Grand Forks, a community of similar nature just over the Bitterroot crest in Idaho, quickly developed legendary reputations, as home not only to rail laborers but also to pimps, prostitutes, and murderers.

Taft quickly grew to about 3,000 thirsty, lusty souls. According to an account from the Spokane Historical Society, "if a working man had an appetite for vice, he was sure to get his fill in Taft."

One account described Taft as being home to twenty-three saloons and "300 women and only one decent one." It wasn't a safe place, with spring's warmer temperatures revealing bodies that had rested undiscovered in deep snow for weeks or maybe months. By some accounts, the snowbank body count in the spring of 1910 reached seventeen.

The raucous reputation spread quickly. When William H. Taft stopped in the then-unnamed town in 1907, the man who would become the U.S. president just a few years later, speaking from a Northern Pacific train, described the town as "a sewer of sin," and "a sore on the otherwise beautiful national forest."

Liquor barrels line the sidewalk on Taft's aptly named Saloon Street, circa 1909.
PHOTOGRAPH COURTESY OF MONTANA HISTORICAL SOCIETY RESEARCH CENTER.

The locals apparently were not offended by the characterizations offered by Taft, then the nation's secretary of war. They soon named the town after him, possibly an act of mocking celebration.

The town's reputation was cemented when a *Chicago Tribune* reporter, in 1909, dubbed it "the wickedest city in America," even though there were plenty of rivals for that distinction among the mining, timber, and cattle towns across the western United States.

A century later, Jim Kershner, a reporter for *The Spokesman Review* newspaper in Spokane, Washington, wrote, "Back in 1910, respectable folks believed the wild, debauched towns of Taft and Grand Forks deserved to burn in hell." And burn they did, in a thirty-six-hour period that left indelible human and physical scars in Idaho and Montana and cast a pall across the nation.

There was plenty of snow during the winter of 1910 in the inland Northwest, but as spring unfolded, the typical rains didn't materialize. News accounts pinpoint the first wildfire in northwest Montana in late April of that year.

By June, the U.S. Forest Service was reporting fires all over the region. By mid-July, more than 3,000 men were working as Forest Service firefighters, with raw, largely untrained recruits being drawn from Missoula, Butte, and Spokane. By the middle of August, they had battled more than 3,000 fires in the region, including about 90 large blazes, which Forest Service officials claimed to have controlled, in part with the assistance of Army troops ordered to the region by Taft, now the president and commander in chief.

By August 19, many fires still burned across western Montana and northern Idaho, but the situation looked less dire. There were news reports that some firefighters in the Missoula area might be released from duty.

But then the winds came, slowly at first, but then rising to a howling gale by late afternoon on August 20. Small flames became big flames, and small fires were soon large ones. In the days and weeks after what had become known as the "Big Blowup," the "Big Burn," and more broadly as the "Great Fires of 1910," witnesses described fire behavior seemingly beyond human experience.

The fires, Idaho ranger Edward Stahl recalled, were "fanned by a tornadic wind so violent that flames flattened out ahead, swooping to earth in great, darting curves, truly a veritable red demon from hell."

The trouble started in Idaho, but within hours state borders were rendered irrelevant as flames, smoke, and destruction quickly spread to the east, driven by strong winds.

A Forest Service report titled *When the Mountains Roared: Stories of the 1910 Fire*, describes the afternoon of August 20, 1910. "Fires lines which had been held for days melted away under the fierce blast," the report reads. "The sky turned a ghastly yellow, and at four o'clock, it was dark ahead of advancing flames. One observer said the air felt electric, as though the whole world was ready to go up in spontaneous combustion."

In the coming hours, flames in some areas would spread thirty to fifty miles, jumping creeks and rivers and spanning mountain ranges. The largest community in the heart of the conflagration was Wallace, Idaho. As firefighters and other able-bodied souls worked to battle the fire that appeared to encircle the town, others scrambled aboard trains to flee.

While about one-third of Wallace would burn or be heavily damaged, early news accounts predicted an even more dire outcome. The *Daily Missoulian*, on August 21, carried a series of headlines telling of the devastating fires on the Idaho side of the mountains. "Flames Envelop Wallace . . . Entire City is Doomed."

That day's newspaper also reported that flames had surrounded Mullan, Idaho, east of Wallace, and that over the hill in Montana, fire had crept close to Taft, prompting evacuations in the early hours of August 21. Relying on telegraph and telephone updates, the newspaper said that a train operated by the Northern Pacific, on the Milwaukee rails, was bringing about 300 refugees from Wallace, Mullan, and Taft to Missoula and was

Residents of Wallace, Idaho, take stock of what remains after the fires swept through town.
BARNARD-STOCKBRIDGE PHOTOGRAPH COLLECTION, DIGITAL INITIATIVES,
UNIVERSITY OF IDAHO LIBRARY.

expected to arrive at about 7 A.M. "Missoula will do all she can for the relief of others," the paper reported.

By August 22, the *Daily Missoulian* reporting took on a more apocalyptic tone, with the lead headline noting that "death and destruction" was a certainty in the wake of the widespread fires. The paper, which had relied on telegraph and telephone reports to share news of the fires in previous days, noted that both had been lost to the flames, elevating concern "for the safety of many."

While details of what was happening between Wallace and St. Regis were initially hazy, it was clear that a major disaster was unfolding in the Pacific Northwest.

Smoke from the fires out West soon smudged the horizon in New York City and Boston, and soot from the fires was reported in Greenland. In Southern California, the *Los Angeles Herald* devoted many columns of newsprint to the fires in Montana, Idaho, and eastern Washington, but also to those scattered broadly across the West.

In a story with a Butte dateline on August 23, 1910, the *Herald* reported that "volcano-like smoke" was hanging over Montana, not only from the big fires near the border but dozens of others across the state. "[T]he entire state," the newspaper said, "prairie and forest, is like tinder, and no one can tell what town will go next."

The Big Blowup has since been defined as a roughly thirty-six-hour period starting on August 20 and continuing through August 21. While fires continued to burn for weeks and sometimes longer, a change in wind direction and spike in humidity put a damper on their explosive spread, starting in the first hours of August 22. News accounts from that day reported rain and even high-elevation snow.

While the flames subsided, details about the horrific scene left behind came into focus. The fires of 1910 burned more than 3 million acres of public and private land (officials estimate that about 75 percent of that area burned in the thirty-six-hour blowup) and an estimated 7.5 billion board feet of timber. The fire area, comprising many individual blazes, spanned the Montana-Idaho border in a region that stretched from west of Hamilton, Montana, north to near Libby.

The flames took a heavy human toll. Most historical accounts put the number killed in the main thirty-six-hour firestorm at about eighty-five,

A burned area on the Lolo National Forest.
PHOTOGRAPH BY ROLLIN H. MCKAY, COURTESY OF THE U.S. FOREST SERVICE.

with total deaths in the nineties. Because of the scope of the fires and how quickly they spread, however, there is little certainty in the numbers.

In *Year of the Fires: The Story of the Great Fires of 1910*, historian Steven J. Pyne wrote that "the tedious, often futile accounting of those injured and killed [was] an exercise that exposed the ramshackle process by which the men had been hired and shipped to the fire lines."

Even as bodies were discovered, their identities remained a mystery. "In most instances," Pyne wrote, "the deceased left no identifying papers. Rumors, reported friendships, fragments of letters, telegrams thrust into pockets, all provided clues."

The majority of the firefighters killed in the fires died in Idaho. A website created as the 100th anniversary of the Big Blowup approached, www.1910fire.com, includes a detailed list of those known to have died and their burial sites. It also notes the existence of unmarked graves and the ongoing search for other possible victims. According to the site, deaths occurred at twenty-one distinct locations, many on the Big Creek and Storm Creek fires. The largest number of deaths in a single fire, twenty-eight, occurred in Setzer Creek near Avery, Idaho, which served as a supply center for a number of fire camps.

The website creator, Wade Bilbrey, began work around 2001 to locate gravesites and record their location. A former Forest Service employee and later postmaster in Avery, Idaho, Bilbrey was close to the human epicenter of the 1910 tragedy. A cemetery in nearby St. Maries, Idaho, holds graves of fifty-seven of the estimated ninety-four known victims of the 1910 fires and is home to the St. Maries 1910 Fire Memorial, known locally as the Firefighters' Circle. "That left me about thirty-seven to find," Bilbrey said in an interview in the spring of 2019.

Using coroners' reports as a launching point, Bilbrey traveled widely over Idaho, eastern Washington, and Montana in search of possible gravesites. As the 100th anniversary of the fires approached, he worked to record and memorialize his discoveries on the website.

While he has devoted little time to the project since 2010, Bilbrey readily acknowledges that there are likely more fire victims than have been documented. "I'm confident of that," he said, noting that based on informal accounts and "folklore," he has pursued reports of remote, unmarked graves of possible additional victims across the three-state region. "There were likely firefighters who decided to make a run for it on their own that were overcome by fire and ended up who knows where."

While fewer in number, the Montana deaths offer a glimpse of the human tragedy of that August long ago.

Andrew Christ, age forty, lived in a cabin in Copper Gulch near the Bull River with another man, John Erickson. As the fire suddenly and rapidly approached, both men bolted from the cabin and ran toward the river. At some point, Christ turned and returned to the cabin to retrieve a suitcase. Erickson survived. Christ didn't.

"They found Andy about 300 feet from the cabin," a man named Frank Berray recounted in *Behind These Mountains*, published by Mona Leeson Vanek in 1986. "He got the suitcase because you could see the iron frame and the ashes shaped from it. He was on his hands and knees. He tried to crawl, I guess." A pocketbook found under the charred body held items that identified Christ, who is buried in Thompson Falls.

The Tuscor Fire, in the Swamp Creek drainage near Trout Creek, claimed the lives of four members of a fifteen-man fire crew, some who had recently joined the fight in Thompson Falls, enticed by Forest Service pay of 25 cents per hour.

The men were fighting a fire in a gulch when another blaze raced up from behind them. While details are unclear, the four who died—Andrew Bourret, George Strong, Edw. Williams, and George Fease—may have tried to flee the approaching fire.

According to an account in the Sandpoint, Idaho, *Pend d'Oreille Review* on August 26, 1910, "four of the party lost their heads and all four were burned. The others saved their lives by crouching low to the ground."

Strong was just sixteen, while Bourret was due to be married in just a few weeks. An obituary in the *Sparta Herald*, in Wisconsin where Fease had lived, hinted at his inexperience. "He went West a year ago last spring and appears to have only recently gone to the place where he met his death." Few details about Williams are known. A headstone on his grave in St. Maries, Idaho, notes only an "August 1910" date of death at Noxon, Montana.

Along with the extensive damage to Wallace and the obliteration of Grand Forks, Idaho, the fire's rapid run also destroyed bridges, trestles, mining shacks, and ranger stations. There are harrowing accounts from railroaders of burning bridges and trestles in Idaho and Montana. John Mackedon, a locomotive engineer, recalled crossing one bridge at the helm of a train loaded with evacuees. "Why, all you could see was a wall of flame, but we crossed it," he said. "We expected that every minute would be our last on Earth."

The series of rail tunnels that brought so many laborers to the region offered a place of refuge from the inferno. More than 400 people survived the 1910 fires by huddling in the nearly 1.7-mile St. Paul Pass Tunnel, just two miles from Taft. To the west, a smaller group spent eight days in a tunnel waiting for the flames to subside and for bridges and trestles to be repaired, allowing the train they rode to move safely.

U.S. Forest Service photographers Rollin H. McKay (left) and Joe B. Halm (right) documented the aftermath of the 1910 fires.
PHOTOGRAPH COURTESY OF THE NATIONAL MUSEUM OF FOREST SERVICE HISTORY.

In the wide swath of charred destruction were De Borgia, Haugan, and Taft, the Montana towns nearest the crest of the Bitterroots.

While Taft had been damaged by fire previously in its short life, the intensity of the 1910 fire there was unprecedented. The town was largely consumed by the flames, and the town's reputation was further tarnished by the desire of some residents to drink rather than help fight the fire. Ranger Frank Haun reported trying to enlist recruits from saloons and residences. "Instead of readying for retreat or defense, instead of digging fire lines or packing clothes or belongings, instead of watering down roofs or gathering shovels and picks, the people of Taft went to work hoarding and then consuming their entire whiskey supply." Elers Koch, the Lolo National Forest supervisor, told other officials, "The Taft denizens decided if they were going to be burned to death in an inferno that engulfed the Bitterroots, they would go down drunk." Ultimately, most residents did leave the town, many on trains headed for Missoula.

As the fires advanced, William McKay, a forty-five-year-old carpenter, was paid to stay in Taft as a watchman out of concern for possible looting. According to news accounts, McKay and another man only left the town after their shack caught fire. McKay suffered burns from head to foot, but his companion was able to help him escape and they made their way to neighboring Saltese. McKay died soon thereafter, reportedly after bandages on his burns caught fire from an oil lamp. He is believed to be the only resident of Taft to die in the 1910 blaze. McKay's brother in Anaconda tried to retrieve William's body for burial there, but fire conditions prevented him from traveling beyond Missoula.

In Taft, just three or four structures remained standing after the fire, but they withered away in ensuing years. The construction of Interstate 90 in the 1960s wiped out most remaining traces of the town. Today, there is a Taft exit sign off the four-lane highway but little else. *Montana Place Names: From Alzada to Zortman*, produced by the Montana Historical Society, includes entries for neighboring Saltese, De Borgia, and Haugan, but it lacks an entry for that most reviled town, Taft.

The 1910 fires devastated the U.S. Forest Service Savenac Nursery
near Haugan, which had been established by Elers Koch only four years earlier.
Tree-growing operations were later moved to Coeur d'Alene.
PHOTOGRAPH COURTESY OF THE NATIONAL MUSEUM OF FOREST SERVICE HISTORY.

In the summer of 2018, John Shontz, a retired Helena attorney and Milwaukee railroad historian, was joined by a Forest Service archaeologist and a handful of others on several trips to Taft to search for the site of the town's cemetery. A year later, armed with a powerful metal detector, the searchers eventually located buried buttons, buckles, bullets, and pieces of iron that might have been nails used in coffins. They found these items in an overgrown area about 250 yards above Interstate 90. It is likely the cemetery. Missing are grave markers of any sort. The great fire that consumed the "wickedest" of towns burned with such hellish intensity that it gobbled up the wooden crosses in the cemetery.

WALDRON CREEK FIRE, 1931

A SMALL BUT VICIOUS FIRE

Tucked along Montana's Rocky Mountain Front west of Choteau, the Waldron Creek drainage was long known by locals for its remoteness, steepness, and thick stands of timber unusual in this grand but often dry, windy region.

Fighting the Waldron Creek fire.
PHOTOGRAPH COURTESY OF THE NATIONAL MUSEUM OF FOREST SERVICE HISTORY.

When a lightning-sparked fire broke out in Waldron Creek near the North Fork of the Teton River late in August 1931, the initial *Choteau Acantha* account noted the "destructive" nature of the blaze.

"Those familiar with the territory report that some of the best timber on this part of the Lewis and Clark Forest is on Waldron Creek and that the fire is raging in the heart of it," the weekly newspaper reported in its August 27, 1931, issue.

The remote fire, with ample fuel, grew quickly and kicked up a huge column of smoke visible in Choteau, more than thirty-five miles away. The search for firefighters, who were scarce in what had already been a hot, smoky summer in the Northwest, took on added urgency. Forest officials turned to Great Falls, where they reportedly "scoured every tavern and hotel, the unemployment office and the soup kitchens to man the fire crews," the *Acantha* reported decades later.

A twenty-man crew from Great Falls headed to the fire, first by train to Choteau and then deposited by cars and trucks at the mouth of the Teton Canyon. From there, it was a twelve-mile hike to the fire line. A local man, Franklin Fellers, described as an experienced woodsman and firefighter, led the way into the smoky terrain on the afternoon of August 25, 1931.

The crew, likely able-bodied but lacking firefighting training or experience, stopped at a roughly twenty-acre burned area about one-quarter mile from the active fire line, where Fellers instructed them to wait while he made contact with a crew boss in the area.

A precise accounting of events in the coming minutes and hours can only be left to speculation. According to accounts shared days later, the nearby fire began to grow, and flames spread in the crowns of trees. The fire began to descend a hill toward the burned area and the crew. Some wanted to seek safety deeper in the burned area. Others advocated fleeing the area, away from the approaching flames.

Ultimately, five of the Great Falls recruits—Herb Novotny, twenty; Frank Williamson, twenty-four; Hjalmer "Harry" Gunnarson, thirty-nine; Charles Allen, thirty-seven; and Ted Bierchen, forty-seven—left the burned area that afternoon. Their bodies were found in the next few days,

Men gather for a meal at fire camp on the Waldron Creek fire.
PHOTOGRAPH COURTESY OF THE NATIONAL MUSEUM OF FOREST SERVICE HISTORY.

their identities determined only by scraps of clothing or items in pockets not destroyed by the flames and intense heat. The freshly minted firefighters had survived less than a day in the employ of the U.S. Forest Service in the fiery cauldron of Waldron Creek.

Four of the bodies were found in close proximity, while the body of Novotny, the youngest, was found about seventy-five yards uphill from the others. No one witnessed the deaths. It is speculated that the five men headed down the gulch, thinking they were avoiding the encroaching flames only to be confronted by more fire rapidly moving uphill toward them. Several of the men were discovered to have broken legs and other injuries, possibly incurred as they ran over rocky slopes and fallen logs ahead of charging flames.

On September 3, 1931, the *Acantha* labeled the deaths a tragedy, the result of a "small but vicious fire."

Members of the remaining fifteen-man crew told officials that as the five departed, the others moved deeper into the burned area and eventually made it to the top of a ridge and ultimately found their way to a fire camp by following a fork of the Teton River. A roll call at the camp attached names to the missing men.

Forest Service officials issued a statement shortly after the discovery of the bodies, recapping the statements of three crew members who had made it to fire camp. Instead of joining with those who eventually escaped, the statement said, "the five went down the slope toward the fire and were overtaken by it, causing their deaths. It is our opinion that all possible precautions were taken by those in charge of the fire to provide for our safety."

There is no evidence that the Forest Service conducted a thorough investigation into the deaths of the firefighters or that an official report was completed.

Charles G. Roberts, the Teton County coroner and operator of a Choteau funeral parlor, took part in the crew interviews. He speculated

Smoke permeates the Waldron Creek fire camp.
PHOTOGRAPH COURTESY OF THE NATIONAL MUSEUM OF FOREST SERVICE HISTORY.

that the five killed may have succumbed to exhaustion, heat, and smoke rather than the flames. No inquest into the deaths was held.

In the official death register, the place of death for each was simply listed as "37 miles northwest of Choteau." The cause: "Came to his death by being trapped in a forest fire. No one to blame but himself."

News of the perished firefighters did not reach the pages of the *Great Falls Tribune* until four days after their deaths. Despite the dramatic loss of the local men, the news took second billing on the newspaper's front page to the record-setting fair attendance the previous day. In ensuing issues, short articles outlined funeral plans for Williamson, once a cook, and noted that Novotny, who had worked as a truck driver, was survived by a wife, two children, his parents, four sisters, and three brothers. Both would be buried in Highland Cemetery in Great Falls.

Relatives of Bierchen were located in Chicago, and his body was shipped there for burial. The bodies of Allen and Gunnarson were buried in Choteau. When he signed on with the fire crew, Allen had given an address for his mother in Pittsburgh, Pennsylvania, but officials were unable to contact her.

Gunnarson had lived in Canada shortly before arriving in Great Falls. A sister in Manitoba asked that his body be shipped to her for burial, but the Forest Service declined. An article in the *Acantha* explained that "the government will pay the expense of shipping bodies of men whose lives were lost in fighting forest fire to any place in the United States but will not pay the expense into foreign countries."

A "simple but impressive" funeral service for the two men, attended by a few local people and some Forest Service officials, was held in early September 1931. An editorial written by E. L. Jourdonnais, the *Acantha* publisher, noted the men, while not area residents, had died in the line of duty and deserved to be regarded as "real heroes," and that their "lifeless forms are entitled to the caresses of Old Glory."

With the burials completed, news accounts of the fire focused on the amount of timber burned and the potential for salvage. The words of heroic praise in the *Acantha* editorial appeared to have been carried away by the wind.

More than seventy years later, the research and writing of Nancy Thornton, an *Acantha* reporter and local history buff, rekindled interest in the fire. Within a few years, the men who died in 1931 would gain a measure of posthumous fame as the "Forgotten Five." Thornton found a story about the fire while paging through old issues of the *Acantha*. The discovery was simply serendipity.

In June 2003, the Choteau newspaper published an in-depth story written by Thornton about the Waldron Creek fire. The story recapped the fire, the seeming bureaucratic indifference to the tragedy, and the fact that just one of the fire victims, Frank Williamson, was buried in a grave marked by a headstone.

While Thornton was able to track down relatives of two of the men who died in 1931, she also found a lack of local knowledge about the event. "I was just amazed," she said. "Nobody even at the [local] Forest Service office knew about this. There is not even a monument up there."

The *Acantha* is a small weekly newspaper with little circulation beyond Teton County, but Thornton's article about the fire caught the eye of Charles Palmer, a former wildland firefighter and smokejumper, then fire researcher, and eventual associate professor in the department of Health and Human Performance at the University of Montana. Since 2006, Palmer has taught courses in sports psychology and conducted research into wildland firefighter performance and decision making.

Palmer started researching the fire and deaths, driven largely by curiosity. "I just became absolutely fascinated with the story she told," Palmer said. "I started my research as a quest to answer some questions I had. I've always been interested in fatality fire."

Over the course of a decade of on-again, off-again digging and sifting for information about the fire and its victims, whom he came to refer to as the "Forgotten Five," Palmer completed a book about the little-known fire titled *Montana's Waldron Creek Fire: The 1931 Tragedy and the Forgotten Five*.

While the college professor developed theories about some aspects of the fire and deaths, he was unable to unearth any sort of official report or evidence of thorough investigation on the part of the Forest Service, despite filing federal Freedom of Information Act requests.

There is no marker or detailed description of the location. The same general area was burned in 1917, fourteen years before the 1931 fire. Signs of those blazes remain, but the forest has regrown. With only the vague, seven-decades-old descriptions from surviving crew members as a guide, the search for the location where the Forgotten Five died has been fruitless. "Nobody knows that spot," Palmer said. "We don't know exactly where the bodies came down."

Palmer faults the Forest Service for failing to investigate the deaths and for the apparently callous treatment of the victims. But he tempers any criticism of the agency, noting the fire occurred during the Great

Depression and financial realities played into many decisions and actions. "That's the way things were done then," he said. "Life was tough, and people died."

Also lacking is a sound explanation of why the five men chose to leave the crew, which likely led to their deaths. Palmer cites several factors that likely played into their fateful decision, including their hasty recruitment, a lack of training, poor communication, no apparent leadership, fatigue from a twelve-mile hike to the fire line, and that most understandable human emotion, fear. "I've never come to any understanding of why they felt that 'we just have to get out of here,'" Palmer said.

Pursuit of the facts surrounding the fire was driven by Palmer's professional interest, but other pieces of the story became more personal for the college professor. Frank Williamson's family paid for a headstone at the time of his burial. Herb Novotny, Charles Allen, and Hjalmer Gunnarson, however, were buried in unmarked graves, and that gnawed at Palmer. With help from residents of Choteau and a high school friend in the monument business in Great Falls and others, Palmer personally paid for headstones for the three men.

Palmer also worked to track down relatives of the men who died, a process that proved time-consuming and challenging, especially in the case of Novotny, whose wife remarried not long after the fire. While Palmer was eventually able to locate and communicate with a daughter, who was just two years old when her father died, he also had to gently share pieces of her family history that the daughter had not known. "Her mom had never told her the story of her biological father," Palmer said.

Some family members were able to attend a 2011 ceremony for the placement of Novotny's headstone on his grave in Highland Cemetery. That same year, the Great Falls City Commission issued a proclamation honoring the five men.

While the story of the Forgotten Five has become better known, there remains one unlocated, unmarked grave. The body of Ted Bierchen was

The grave marker for Hjalmer Gunnarson.
PHOTOGRAPH COURTESY OF THE NATIONAL MUSEUM OF FOREST SERVICE HISTORY.

The grave marker for Charles Allen.
PHOTOGRAPH COURTESY OF THE NATIONAL MUSEUM OF FOREST SERVICE HISTORY.

shipped to Chicago and is believed to have been buried in St. Henry Catholic Cemetery, which sits north of the city center not far from Lake Michigan. But relatives and Palmer have been unable to find the grave.

"Unfortunately, there is one guy left who doesn't have a headstone," Palmer said, a fact that leaves an unfinished chapter in a story with many unexplained elements and unanswered questions. "In some ways, it seems fitting that this is left unresolved."

LODGE POLE FIRE, 1936

The spring and summer of 1936 were dreadfully dry across much of the nation's northern tier, including in much of Montana. The United States and Montana were in the deepest depths of the Great Depression and the "dirty thirties."

That season's first wildfire in the Little Rockies, an island mountain range southwest of Malta, came early in July and hinted at what lay ahead. Later that month, the forest in the mountains was tinder dry. A fire that started on July 25, 1936, near Lodge Pole, a town on the Fort Belknap Indian Reservation at the north end of the Little Rockies, spread quickly up a canyon, racing south toward Zortman, which along with neighboring Landusky was the hub of gold and silver mining in the region.

As wind-driven flames spread on that Saturday, hastily assembled fire crews from the reservation, nearby ranches, and the mines, along with all available men in Malta, Harlem, Dodson, and Fort Belknap, rushed to fight the blaze. Among the untrained fire crews were members of a U.S. Geological Survey team working in the area, headed by Dr. Maxwell Knechtel, who lived in Washington, D.C., but had spent several summers in the Little Rockies doing fieldwork.

The Geological Survey crew, based in Landusky, joined others to form a roughly twenty-person crew and hit the fire line at about 3 A.M.

Smoke billows from the Lodge Pole fire in the Little Rockies.
PHOTOGRAPH COURTESY OF LU SEAFORD BESEL.

on Monday, July 27. By day's end, some were dead, others were burned, and all who survived suffered from "smoke, heat and fright," according to a newspaper story.

Knechtel, who was burned and briefly hospitalized in Malta, provided an account of the event published in the *Great Falls Tribune* a few days after the fire. He said the crew was working on a ridge when the wind suddenly shifted at midday from the east to the west, "whipping the fire into a blazing inferno." The fire leapt into the crowns of the trees and moved quickly, leaving the crew feeling trapped.

In intense smoke and heat, the crew sought safer ground. The men became scattered, and the group with Knechtel eventually found a limestone outcropping on the ridge. But as the fire came closer, the group decided to flee and eventually stumbled into what was described as a small cave or fissure in a rock outcropping.

Exactly how many of the men made it into the cave is unclear, although accounts seem to agree that those who were deepest in the cave survived, while those near the entrance, or those who may have tried to run from the cave, perished.

One of the survivors, Art Tiedemann, recalled there being five or six men in the cave when three more appeared at the entrance, but the intense flames created a vacuum that somehow prevented them from getting inside. Tiedemann recalled seeing the form of a man, likely John Roles, just outside the cave "being tossed about in the furnace-like heat like a piece of paper." (The names of the survivors and victims of the fire are spelled in a variety of ways. Art Piederman, in some statewide news accounts, is identified as Art Tiedermann, a Malta-area resident, in the *Phillips County News*. Research by the author indicates that his actual last name might be Tiedemann. Statewide accounts name John Rowles as a victim, but he appears as John Roles in the local weekly newspaper. A death certificate spells his name Rolles.)

Along with Knechtel and Tiedemann, the cave survivors were Curtis Miller, Francis Williams, and Edgar Palmer, all from Landusky. The badly burned bodies of Roles, a Landusky miner, and Cameron Baker, twenty-four, a member of the Geological Survey crew from the Havre area, were found near the entrance to the cave. The third fire victim, Sawyer R. Brockunier, also part of the Geological Survey crew, was found alive but severely burned.

All three men were found by Andrew Whitehorse, a fire crew leader, who left to retrieve water and food for the crew, and learned of the fire blowup and scramble to the cave from other crew members. He rode a horse up the ridge to search for the missing men and soon spotted the bodies of Baker and Roles, and then found Brockunier about one-quarter mile away.

"He was still alive," Whitehorse said, according to an account in the *Great Falls Tribune*. "His clothes were still on fire. I cut the burning clothing from his body. We didn't dare touch the burned man's flesh. It came away in our hands."

The circumstances of how the three men were burned are hazy.

"It was an inferno and we scarcely knew what happened for a while, so thick and terrible was the smoke and heat," said Knechtel, in an Associated Press account. "I saw Baker and Brockunier come in, and that's all I remember."

One unnamed survivor was quoted as saying Baker and Roles, nearest the cave entrance, were seared by flames and "apparently crazed by the fire and heat, they ran out." Witnesses in the cave said Brockunier tried to stop Baker from leaving and was likely burned in the attempt.

There were others burned or treated for smoke inhalation in the fire that Sunday afternoon, including Otis Pewitt, the brother of James Pewitt, the lead Forest Service ranger in the Little Rockies, where the non-reservation public lands were then part of the Lewis and Clark National Forest.

The Lodge Pole fire drew nationwide news coverage and brought hundreds of trained firefighters, equipment, and Forest Service officials to the Little Rockies. But before the smoke had cleared on the deadly fire, another blaze broke out nearby. The second fire, the Mission Peak fire, also burned thousands of acres and prompted the evacuation of Zortman, Landusky, Hays, and the nearby St. Paul's Mission.

For more than a week, the Little Rockies were pummeled by intense fire activity. At one point, more than 1,000 men were on fire lines. News accounts made mention of possible causes of the fires, including lightning, neglected campfires, a careless toss of a cigarette, and, based largely on rumor, the possibility that the deadly first fire was deliberately set by "pyromaniacs" or some type of "incendiarist." The latter suspicion was fueled by

The Landusky store burns during
the Lodge Pole fire in 1936.
PHOTOGRAPH COURTESY OF LU SEAFORD BESEL.

reports that "two strange men" had been spotted in Zortman the day the Lodge Pole fire started.

R. L. Campbell, the Phillips County sheriff, checked out the possibility that the fires were deliberately set, but no suspects were publicly identified, nor were charges filed, according to news accounts.

But as the smoke cleared, it became evident that the Little Rockies had been deeply scarred by wildfire. Pilot C. B. Sutliff flew over the mountain range on August 1, 1936, and shared this observation with Forest Service officials in Missoula that supported pulling out firefighters and equipment: "There is little likelihood of further damage, as there is nothing left to burn."

During the Mission Peak fire, the publisher of the *Phillips County News* in Malta drove to the Little Rockies to observe the firefighting effort and damage. He supplied an account of what he saw to the United Press, a news wire service. The publisher, J. Russell Larcombe, the grandfather of this book's author, described haggard firefighters, many of them farmers, miners, or "schoolboys." On the fire line, he described seeing the Mission Peak fire leap across gullies and canyons "at a dizzy speed," covering at least six miles and charring the mountains. And he noted the fires and deaths were a heavy blow to a region already locked in drought's grip.

"Foundation herds of cattle are on the move over grassless prairie once lush with rich food," he wrote. "Sheep trail waterless to the railroad for shipment to market. Farmers and ranchers are broken in spirit. And now, the one attractive recreational spot left in the area had to go up in smoke. It's very discouraging."

There is no sign that any government agency investigated the deadly fire or produced a formal report. Along with filing a Freedom of Information Act request with the Forest Service, the author also contacted the National Interagency Fire Center, the Bureau of Indian Affairs, and the U.S. Geological Survey in search of an official report on the fire and deaths. The 1936 annual report from the director of the Geological Survey makes no mention of the deaths or the fire. A 1936 fire record maintained by the Lewis and Clark National Forest shows that crews were dispatched to the fires in the Little Rockies but provides no details. A coroner's jury, called due to the deaths of Roles and Baker, found no evidence of wrong-doing. The men "met death by fire over which they had no control," the jury concluded.

Roles, according to death certificate information, was forty-four and was born in Saint Leo, Minnesota. His official cause of death was given as "Caught in a forest fire. Burned to death." He was initially buried in Malta on July 29, 1936. Later, his body was reburied in Saint Leo.

Baker, a member of the Geological Survey crew headed by Knechtel, had parents living in the Laredo area and attended school in nearby Havre. He also attended college there and was working for the Geological Survey during a break from a teaching fellowship at Northwestern University near Chicago, where he was pursuing an advanced degree in geology. At the time of his death, Baker was engaged to Elizabeth McCoy, a Havre resident. In a story published by the *Great Falls Tribune* on July 31, 1936, McCoy told of having a dream that her fiancé would die fighting the fire. The dream occurred two nights before he was killed. Along with pleading with Baker to leave the fire crew, McCoy reportedly traveled to Landusky and sought out mine manager P. A. Wickham to keep Baker from returning to the fire line. "Please stop him," she is said to have told Wickham. "Don't let him go into that fire."

Reverend John B. Stuart, a longtime friend of Baker, eulogized the twenty-four-year-old, describing him as an earnest, respectful only child. "It was just like him to be the last one to enter the cave," Stuart said. Baker is buried in Highland Cemetery in Havre.

Brockunier, the third fire victim, was able to walk to a car and was taken to a hospital at the Fort Belknap Agency near Harlem. He had recently completed his Ph.D. in geology at Yale University, with his dissertation focusing on the geology of the Little Rockies. One news account noted

MONTANA WEATHER
Generally fair Tuesday and Wednesday; little change in temperature.

WYOMING WEATHER
Partly cloudy Tuesday and Wednesday; warmer southeast portion Tuesday.

The Billings Gazette

FINAL MORNING EDITION

VOL. XLVIII.—NO. 267.   UNITED PRESS   BILLINGS, MONTANA, TUESDAY, JULY 28, 1936.   ASSOCIATED PRESS   PRICE FIVE CENTS

TRIO IS TRAPPED, KILLED IN FOREST FIRE

U. S. AMBASSADOR QUITS SPAIN TODAY

The Great Game of Politics
By FRANK R. KENT

WILL TRANSFER TO COAST GUARD CUTTER CAYUGA

Plans Move to Keep Abreast of Developments in Revolution Cruising on Coast.

REFUGEES FLEE MADRID MONDAY

Government, Rebels Resume Battle in Mountain Passes; Evacuate Americans

FOUND GUILTY

GORMAN WINS AUDITOR RACE OVER SWEENEY

Official Canvass of Primary Vote Shows Error by Judges in South Side Precinct.

MIDDLE WEST GETS MOISTURE BUT LOSS GREAT

Iowa, Illinois and Wisconsin Reveal Production Losses Due to Dry Period.

MIDDLE WEST GETS MOISTURE

Teacher Paints His Dwelling and Does a 'Sweet Job'

LOCAL INFANT DROWNS MONDAY

Searchers Find Body Along Edge of Ditch Near Pompeys Pillar

ALVIN KARPIS IS GIVEN LIFE TERM IN KIDNAP AFFAIR

Fitzgerald Receives Similar Sentence in Hamm Abduction at Trial in St. Paul.

BOTH DECLARE PEIFER INNOCENT

Pair Is to Be Committed to Leavenworth Penitentiary, Sanford Bates Says.

STORMS STRIKE GULF OF MEXICO AREAS MONDAY

Tropical Disturbances Accompanied by Winds of Gale Intensity; Warn Shipping

LOUISIANA IS FEELING BLOW

Other Is Moving by Slow Stages Through Bahamas; Residents Move Inland Quickly

LAMSON WEDS WRITER

RED LODGE BOY IS FOUND AFTER LENGTHY SEARCH

John Alden, 6, Strays Away From Picnic Party Sunday Held in the Beartooths.

ROOSEVELT FOES SCHEDULE MEET

Notable Democrats to Consider Plans to Defeat President.

MARLAND, LEE HURL CHARGES

Oklahoma Run-Off Primary Is Slated to Be Held Today.

SURVEY PARTY'S MEMBERS DIE IN MONTANA BLAZE

Little Rockies Conflagration Is Scene of Tragedy Monday Night; Seek Leader.

ONE IN HOSPITAL; PAIR IS MISSING

Mobilize All Available Men in Harlem, Malta and Ft. Belknap Areas for Duty.

COMPLETE WORK AT FAIRGROUNDS AS START NEARS

$10,000 Is Expended in Oiling, Remodeling of Buildings for 19th Annual Event.

22 Are Injured In Bus Accident

Plane Falls, Pilot Clears in Parachute

REPORT FIRST CHILDBIRTH BY HYPNOTISM IN MIDWEST

BUY LESS AND SELL MORE IS NEW AIM OF RUSSIANS

Brockunier had worked in the mountain range for several years prior to his death and likely knew more about the topography and geology in that area "than any other man in the United States." He was an assistant geologist with the federal agency.

Brockunier died within hours of being hospitalized. Shortly before his death and despite intense pain from third-degree burns, the hospital workers reported that the twenty-five-year-old insisted on calling his mother, Elizabeth, in Massachusetts to tell her of his dire situation. He is buried in Lowell, Massachusetts.

MANN GULCH FIRE, 1949
A SPECIAL TRAGEDY

Getting to Mann Gulch isn't easy. For most, the journey requires a boat, a good pair of hiking boots, and a desire to understand an event that has haunted families, firefighters, fire agencies, and many others for more than seventy years.

With each step, first through stands of pine and fir, and later on a very steep slope of grass and rock, the haunting story of the wildfire that took the lives of thirteen young firefighters and consumed the last years of one of Montana's best-known authors roars to life in the hearth of the imagination.

Late in the afternoon of August 5, 1949, a load of smokejumpers from Missoula was summoned to Mann Gulch, in the steep and rugged Gates of the Mountains Wild Area (now Wilderness) about twenty miles north of Helena, to fight a fire sparked by lightning.

From the open door of the C-47 jump plane, the fire looked small and routine to a young, confident sixteen-member squad of smokejumpers, regarded as some of the best firefighters in the U.S. Forest Service. At about 4 P.M., all but one of the sixteen jumpers left the plane. On a day of record

Strong winds rapidly expanded the Mann Gulch fire,
seen here from a U.S. Forest Service airplane.
PHOTOGRAPH COURTESY OF THE U.S. FOREST SERVICE.

heat and unstable air, the turbulent flight from Missoula had sickened a number of the jumpers, leaving one too ill to make the jump. That was Merle Stratton, who apparently quit the smokejumper program shortly after the plane returned to Missoula.

Less than two hours later, twelve of the fifteen men who made the jump, along with a Forest Service recreation guard from the nearby Meriwether Campground, were dead. They perished in a "blowup" fire that would make national headlines, scar the Forest Service's reputation, and fuel controversy, lawsuits, and decades of debate.

The Mann Gulch victims, while not the first smokejumpers to die, represented the worst firefighting tragedy in the United States for many decades. Even today, the deaths continue to poke at the soul of the tightly knit community of former and current smokejumpers. (The first smokejumper death occurred in Oregon, almost exactly four years earlier than the Mann Gulch fire, when a jumper landed in a tree then fell onto rocks while attempting to climb down.)

More than forty years after the Mann Gulch fire, Norman Maclean, a Missoula native, retired University of Chicago English professor, and former wildland firefighter, in his book, *Young Men and Fire*, noted, "Although Mann Gulch occurred early in the history of the smokejumpers, it is still their special tragedy."

The crew that left the jump plane was indeed young. Many were World War II veterans, and a number of them were forestry students at the University of Montana. While most had some experience with the Forest Service and firefighting, nine of the Mann Gulch crew were in their first season in a program that started in 1939 and was still officially labeled "the parachute project."

R. Wagner "Wag" Dodge, thirty-three years old, was the oldest member of the crew. As the foreman, he had sixteen years of combined firefighting and smoke-jumping experience. The oldest rank-and-file member was David Navon, a twenty-nine-year-old former U.S. Army paratrooper who earned a forestry degree just a few months before the fire. Bill Hellman, the squad leader from Kalispell, had a newborn son and turned twenty-four just two days before heading to Mann Gulch.

Most of the crew were in their early twenties. According to Forest Service records, the youngest crew member was Eldon Diettert, a University of Montana student who was summoned from his nineteenth birthday celebration to report to the jump base. Years later, it was revealed that the youngest crew member was actually Robert Sallee. The native of Willow Creek, Montana, was seventeen, having lied about his age on the smokejumper application.

Just three of the men who jumped into Mann Gulch that day lived to see another birthday: Dodge, Sallee, and Walter Rumsey.

Before the crew exited the plane, Dodge and spotter Earl Cooley, a pioneer in smokejumping and a leader of the program, agreed upon a landing spot above the fire on the west side of the gulch. At a board of review in late September 1949, officials asked Cooley and the survivors if they had any concerns about the fire, which appeared to be relatively small and burning lazily near the top of the ridge dividing Mann Gulch and Meriwether Canyon. None recalled any worry.

"I remember thinking it would be an awful fire to mop up because it was rocky and steep, but it never occurred to me that it was dangerous," Rumsey told the review board.

The crew left the plane during several passes over the landing spot. Later, the plane would drop tools and supplies, but from a higher altitude than usual because of the turbulent air over the gulch. The drop left equipment scattered over a sizable area but claimed just one casualty—the crew's radio, which was heavily damaged in the drop and rendered unusable.

The crew gathered the supplies and headed down the gulch toward the fire, with Hellman in charge. Dodge went to find Jim Harrison, the Meriwether recreation guard, who had been fighting the fire for much of the day. Dodge found Harrison, and the two men reunited with the crew. Dodge and others noticed the fire was growing more intense, so instead of attacking it head-on, the foreman changed course and led the crew to the other side of Mann Gulch. They headed down toward the Missouri River, planning to fight the fire more safely from behind. But as the crew descended the gulch, the fire continued to grow. More critically, the fire had moved into the timbered bottom of the gulch and across to its north side, creating a wall of flames between the firefighters and their perceived safe haven at the bottom of the gulch near the river. Adding peril was the fact that the fire was burning uphill, driven in part by winds blowing up the gulch and also by the fire's own increasingly fierce behavior.

Realizing that the fire was blowing up, Wag Dodge again changed course, leading the crew on an angled path up the increasingly steep north ridge of Mann Gulch, away from the approaching fire. As they climbed, the pine trees began to thin out, and the route away from the fire was largely made up of grasses deeply cured by a long, hot summer.

Nearly fifty years later, Richard Rothermel, a Forest Service fire behavior scientist, used mathematical models to re-create how fast the fire could move in such conditions. He overlaid that with how fast the crew could likely move, going in the same direction, up a slope that at points was as steep as 76 degrees. The title of Rothermel's resulting study reveals his conclusion: *Mann Gulch Fire: A Race That Couldn't Be Won.*

Rothermel's calculations put the fire's peak pace, as it raced through the scattered trees and dry grass, at about 660 feet per minute. The temperature of the flames streaking up the hill was likely between 1,500 and 1,800 degrees Fahrenheit.

Not long after reversing course and angling up the gulch, Dodge ordered the crew to drop their heavy tools—saws, water containers, and other items. Prior to this point, the crew had moved at a steady pace, with survivors noting that one member had even stopped to take pictures of the fire.

Rumsey recalled pitching a large crosscut saw into brush and also hearing the roar of the approaching blaze. "The fire was catching up with us," he would write about a dozen years later. "We were all practically exhausted from our climb up the mountainside, but now we increased our pace through fear. I think we all knew the danger we were in."

The details of the next few minutes are obscured by the heavy smoke, falling ash, intense heat, and the deafening roar of the large fire that overran the crew. Fear,

The steep, rugged terrain of Mann Gulch.
PHOTOGRAPH COURTESY OF THE U.S. FOREST SERVICE.

clouded communication, and hazy memories add to the swirl of uncertainty.

The crew was likely scattered over several hundred yards of the steep slope. Shortly after Dodge's order to drop tools, with the fire bearing down on them, Dodge used matches to start a fire that raced straight up toward the top of the ridge. He later explained to investigators that he intended to burn an area the firefighters could take refuge in. But use of what was called an "escape fire" was not then part of firefighting training.

"I was near enough to see his lips moving, but I couldn't hear his voice as he shouted to make us hear above the roar," Rumsey recalled. "His plan was for us to get in this burned-out area ahead of the main fire and so save ourselves. His shouted orders were lost in the roar of the fire, even to those of us who were close by."

Sallee and Rumsey, with Hellman and Diettert nearby, scrambled straight up the ridge, desperately hoping to reach the top, where they believed the fire's movement would slow. Dodge entered the burned area, laid down, and covered his head. None of the crew joined him.

"I looked back and saw three men silhouetted against a sheet of red flame," Rumsey wrote later. "I didn't look back a second time."

Sallee and Rumsey made it over the hill and found safety in a patch of rocks as the fire raced by. They later found Hellman nearby, badly burned but alive. Crew member Joe Sylvia was alive but in similar condition. They soon were joined by Dodge, who emerged unscathed from the area he burned. While Rumsey stayed with Hellman, Dodge and Sallee searched for other survivors. "They soon returned," Rumsey noted, "to tell us that the other men were beyond help."

Dodge and Sallee headed down the steep slope in an area that would become known as Rescue Gulch and were eventually able to signal a boater, who took them upstream to Meriwether, where they reported the fire, injuries, and the grim status of much of the crew to Robert Jansson, the Canyon Ferry district ranger who had submitted the request for smoke-jumpers, and others.

Retrieving the victims' bodies was strenuous, somber work.
PHOTOGRAPH COURTESY OF THE U.S. FOREST SERVICE.

Hellman and Sylvia were carried by stretcher to the river and taken to the hospital in Helena. Both died the next day.

Over the next two days, crews combed the steep slope of Mann Gulch and recovered the bodies of Harrison (the recreation guard) and smokejumpers Diettert, Robert Bennett, Philip McVey, David Navon, Leonard Piper, Stanley Reba, Marvin Sherman, Henry Thol Jr., Newton Thompson, and Silas Thompson.

As word of the tragedy made headlines across the nation, so did outrage and misinformation. Some news accounts erroneously reported that the smokejumpers had been dropped into the fire, while others said at least some of the jumpers had been burned by the fire after their chutes were caught in trees.

A *Life* magazine writer and photographer were among those who joined the crews that recovered the bodies. An article and photos about the smokejumpers and the deadly Mann Gulch fire appeared in the August 22, 1949, issue of *Life*. A few years after the fire, a movie, *Red Skies of Montana*, would loosely portray some events tied to the Mann Gulch tragedy. A poster for the movie portrays a smokejumper coming to the ground against a wall of flame.

A five-member U.S. Forest Service board of review met in Missoula less than two months after the fire and heard from officials involved in the fire and the survivors. The inquiry included extensive discussion of Dodge's escape fire. The crew foreman defended his actions. "It just seemed the logical thing to do. I had been instructed, if possible, to get into a burned area." Dodge said he believed his crew members were nearby and could have heard him ordering them into the burned area. "They didn't seem to pay attention. That is the part I don't understand. They seemed to have something on their minds—all headed in one direction."

Sallee and Rumsey, while admittedly unclear about Dodge's intent with the fire, defended the foreman's actions before the review board. Both men

After the fire, investigators combed the slopes where men and wildfire held a deadly race.
PHOTOGRAPH COURTESY OF THE U.S. FOREST SERVICE.

said they ran along the edge of the area burned by the escape fire. "Well, the ridge looked so close; it looked like we were almost there," said Sallee. Even in the hours after the fire, "we chastised ourselves for being so stupid for not going into his fire," added Rumsey.

Many years later, Sallee offered a more spirited defense of the crew foreman. "Wag Dodge did some real fine things up there," he said in a 1988 article published in the *Missoulian*. "He gave them an opportunity to live. If the guys had followed him, he would have been a hero. But they didn't."

But the words of Henry J. Thol, the father of one of the dead smokejumpers who spoke at the review, cast Dodge's actions differently. Thol, a longtime Forest Service employee on the Flathead National Forest and an experienced firefighter, made several trips to Mann Gulch in the weeks after his son's death. Before the review board, Thol questioned many of the decisions made by Dodge and accused the Forest Service investigators of conspiring to whitewash the actual events in Mann Gulch.

Thol accused Dodge of picking an unsafe landing spot, failing to identify an escape route for the crew, and using poor judgment in leading his crew toward the fire. The Flathead ranger contended the crew foreman should have noticed the more intense fire behavior and led his crew up the ridge much earlier instead of trying to go around the fire toward the river.

The escape fire burned hot with Thol. Noting the lack of training about the possible use of such a fire, he also accused Dodge of not knowing where his crew was when he lit the fire. He claimed the fire burned some of the crew fleeing toward the ridgetop. "As far as he [Dodge] was concerned, the value of human life didn't mean much," the grieving father told the review board. "His own fire prevented those below him from going to the top. The poor boys were caught—they had no escape."

Thol repeated his accusations in letters to several Montana newspapers in the months following the fire. A lawsuit he filed against the Forest Service was later dismissed. The board of review, which also extensively questioned the area ranger, Jansson, ultimately found no wrongdoing on the part of Dodge or any others.

But the tentacles of the tragedy are long. The Associated Press deemed "the man-killing Mann Gulch fire, a national headliner," as Montana's biggest news story in 1949.

Seeking to learn about the extreme fire behavior in Mann Gulch, Forest Service fire expert Harry Gisborne headed to the fire scene in early November 1949. Gisborne, fifty-six, was never able to share his observations or findings. While inspecting the site, he suffered a fatal heart attack in Rescue Gulch, within a few hundred yards of where many of the smokejumpers perished.

Wag Dodge died of cancer in 1955 at the age of thirty-nine. Some suspect the trauma and controversy of the fire contributed to his early death. In a letter to Maclean after her husband's death, Dodge's widow expressed bitterness about the controversy surrounding the fire and the author's research. "Although Wag physically lived through the fire, he died that day," she wrote. "Thank you, Dr. Maclean, for the resurrection of unwanted memories."

Lois Jansson later told John Maclean, the author's son, that her husband, who died in 1965, was haunted by the fire and subsequent investigation and "passed away without feeling understood, supported or his fire actions vindicated. . . . The book came out too late to ease his anxiety."

In his last years, Norman Maclean was consumed by what he described as his "fire report." The author spent the last fifteen years of his life working on *Young Men and Fire*, making trips to Mann Gulch, contacting survivors or relatives, and digging for long-lost records to piece together what happened in this remote slice of Montana. Maclean died at age eighty-seven, in 1990, before the book was completed.

His son and daughter, joined by others, helped bring it to publication. *Young Men and Fire* won literary awards, sold well, and rekindled interest in the four-decades-old fire. The author described his work as a means "of building a small memorial of knowledge to the men who died in Mann Gulch. They were young and did not have much behind them and need someone to remember them." In accepting the National Book Critics Circle

Award on behalf of his father, John Maclean noted that there may be no way to end the grief of those who lost family in the Mann Gulch fire. But his father's book "provided explanation, and that alone is a kind of consolation."

Rumsey and Sallee went to Mann Gulch in 1978 with Norman Maclean and Laird Robinson, a Forest Service public affairs officer, who offered extensive help in the author's quest to reconstruct the key events of the fire. For the two former smokejumpers, it was their first trip back to Mann Gulch since their race to the ridgetop in 1949. The two rarely spoke about the fire or controversy for many years. Rumsey died at age fifty-two in the crash of a commuter plane in 1980 near Omaha, Nebraska.

Sallee, who backed away from working with Maclean over disagreements about some of the theories developed by the author and the Forest Service, died in 2014. He had told his family that *Young Men and Fire* "was a good read, but it wasn't accurate."

In an obituary in *The New York Times*, his son, Eric, noted that his father said little about the fire for many years. "I think there were two reasons for that," Eric said. "First, he was seventeen, and he'd had an absolutely traumatic experience. He helped haul those bodies off that mountain that day." Second, there was the controversy and lawsuits. "They thought the escape fire killed their kids, and my dad had to testify in court proceedings. The whole thing was a nasty experience.

But the elder Sallee, the youngest of the young men, spoke eloquently about the fire at a fiftieth commemoration in 1999, recalling his fellow crew members and the allure of jumping from a plane to fight a wildfire. They were men "who knew what is like to step out the open door of an airplane and the shock of an opening parachute—the glorious feeling that goes with seeing that beautiful white canopy overhead and the exaltation of knowing that you have done it," Sallee said. "They also knew that the parachute was—and still is—the quickest and best way to get to a fire in a remote area.

"While it's fitting to honor these men, I think it's also important that we recognize the pain, the trauma, and yes, the hard feelings that came after this fire—and maybe still persist to this day—and put all that away."

Smokejumpers installed memorial markers for each
of the men who died in the Mann Gulch fire.
PHOTOGRAPH COURTESY OF THE U.S. FOREST SERVICE.

Sallee continued, "It's time to rededicate ourselves to the memory of these fine young men and the lessons their deaths taught us; that wildfires are and will always be dangerous and we must respect its potential to put firefighters in harm's way, and that life is precious and for some, very short."

Physical memorials have taken different forms over the years. The crews that located and retrieved the bodies in the days after the fire built stone cairns where bodies were found. In 1950, white concrete crosses with nameplates were erected at those sites. In 1997, smokejumpers raised money for granite markers to replace the eroding crosses. The markers were brought to Mann Gulch by horseback, while a crew of six smokejumpers parachuted in to install the markers. Mann Gulch is sacred ground to many smokejumpers, noted Jim Beck, one of those who came in 1997 and for whom the trip marked his eighth or ninth visit. "One of the reasons

The thirteen men who died in the Mann Gulch fire.
PHOTOGRAPH COURTESY OF THE U.S. FOREST SERVICE.

I came here was to make sure what happened before isn't forgotten," said Beck, in an interview with the author, who was also there to witness the marker installation. "I think there are a lot of guys who would have liked to make this jump."

Eric Sallee said his father, like many survivors, never seemed to make sense of why he and Rumsey lived and so many of the crew didn't. "If he was sitting here, he'd tell you, 'We were just goddamned lucky.'"

While Sallee was the last of the Mann Gulch crew, the C-47 plane that dropped the crew in 1949 still exists. In June 2019, a crew flew it from Missoula to Normandy, France, to take part in the seventy-fifth anniversary of the D-Day invasion. Refurbished and retooled, the plane dubbed *Miss Montana* flew over Mann Gulch on the first leg of its 16,000-mile round-trip. The plane is on display at the Museum of Mountain Flying in Missoula.

SOURCES

The Fires of 1910

The Anaconda Standard. August 23, 1910.

Bilbrey, Wade. "The Great Fire of 1910." www.1910fire.com.

Bilbrey, Wade. Personal interview. April 2019.

Breysee, Thomas. "Taft: The Wickedest City in America." Spokane Historical Society. www.spokanehistory.org.

Daily Missoulian. August 21–25, 1910.

Egan, Timothy. *The Big Burn: Teddy Roosevelt and the Fire that Saved America.* 2009.

Forest History Society. "The 1910 Fires." www.foresthistory.org.

Los Angeles Herald. August 23, 1910.

Mineral Independent, Superior, Montana. "Taft Mountains Hold 'Secret' of Missing Cemetery." August 22, 2018.

Montana Historical Society. *Montana Place Names: From Alzada to Zortman.* 2009.

Pyne, Stephen J. *The Source.* Lecture, Joint Conference of the American Society of Environmental History and Forest History Society. 2001.

Pyne, Stephen J. *Year of the Fires: The Story of the Great Fires of 1910.* Viking Adult, 2001.

Shontz, John. Personal interview. May 2020.

The Spokesman Review, Spokane, Washington. August 21–26, 1910; March 21, 2010; August 20, 2010; June 21, 2017.

U.S. Forest Service. *When the Mountains Roared: Stories of the 1910 Fire.* 1978.

Woodford, Kathleen. "The Missing Cemetery of Taft, Montana, the 'Wickedest City in America.'" *Montana The Magazine of Western History.* Spring 2020.

Waldron Creek Fire

Choteau Acantha. August 27, 1931; September 3 and 10, 1931; August 20, 2014.

Ecke, Richard. "Spray of the Falls." *Great Falls Tribune.* September 19, 2011.

Great Falls Tribune. August 28–31, 1931.

Palmer, Dr. Charles. Personal interview. March 20, 2019.

Thornton, Nancy. "Fire Comes to the Forest." *Choteau Acantha.* June 11, 2003.

Thornton, Nancy. Personal interview. April 2019.

Lodge Pole Fire

Boston Globe. "Lowell Man Among 3 Dead in Forest Fire." July 28, 1936.

Chicago Tribune. "Student at N. U. And 2 Others Die in a Forest Fire." July 28, 1936.

Great Falls Tribune. July 26 to August 1, 1936.

Independent Record. Helena, Montana. July 30, 1936.

Phillips County News. Malta, Montana. "New Fire Threatens Landusky Community; Flames Menace Mine." July 30, 1936.

Mann Gulch Fire

Daily Inter Lake, Kalispell, Montana. "Forest Fire Probe Called Whitewash." November 8, 1949.

Great Falls Tribune. "The Old Man and The Fire." April 25, 1993.

Great Falls Tribune. "Revisiting Mann Gulch." May 21, 1997.

Independent Record, Helena, Montana. November 10, 1949.

Jenkins, Starr. *Some of the Men of Mann Gulch.* Self-published, 1993.

Maclean, John. Personal interview. April 1993.

Maclean, Norman. *Young Men and Fire: A True Story of the Mann Gulch Fire.* University of Chicago Press, 1992.

"Mann Gulch Remembered; Remarks of Bob Sallee." *Smokejumper Magazine*, 2002.

Montana Standard, Butte, Montana. "Top News Story in 1949." December 22, 1949.

The New York Times. Robert Sallee obituary. May 31, 2014.

Official Record of Board of Review, Mann Gulch Fire, Helena National Forest, August 5, 1949. September 26–28, Missoula, Montana.

Rothermel, Richard. *A Race that Couldn't Be Won.* U.S. Forest Service, 1993.

The Spokesman Review, Spokane, Washington. "Last survivor of Mann Gulch fire Robert Sallee dies." May 29, 2014.

EXPLOSIONS AND FIRES

IT IS UNLIKELY THAT THERE IS A CITY OR TOWN IN MONTANA THAT has not experienced a dramatic fire or explosion. Homes, schools, businesses, or in some cases entire blocks of buildings have been lost. Often, these incidents become "remember-when" events that continue to spark a community's collective memory. Recollections of many older events have been blurred by time.

Before 2009, it's unlikely that more than a handful of people in Bozeman were aware of a fire that consumed a big chunk of the city's business district on December 15, 1922. But a devastating explosion nearly ninety years later prompted local historians to share the story of the earlier fire.

The 1922 fire, dubbed "the most disastrous fire in the history of Bozeman" in newspaper accounts at the time, destroyed the small city's Story and Fechter blocks, left two businesses (A. A. Braten Cloak and Suit and Conaty & Hines Specialty Boot Company) in total ruin, burned the Club Café, and did significant damage to a number of other nearby businesses. An office belonging to Nelson Story Jr., Montana's lieutenant governor at the time and a member of one of Bozeman's prominent early-day families, was also destroyed. The damages were estimated at $250,000 in 1922, about $3.8 million in today's dollars.

The fire started near the coal furnace in the basement of the Club Café at about 8 A.M. Firefighters responded quickly and thought they had a handle on the blaze, only to see it reappear in upper portions of the building that housed the café and other enterprises. From there, "the fire moved with a swiftness that was astonishing," according to news accounts. State leaders mobilized the National Guard to help establish fire lines around the downtown area. Concerned that the blaze might consume the city's entire business section, local officials used dynamite to destroy parts of downtown structures to slow its spread.

The fire burned much of the day and came with a deadly price tag. Ernest Robertson, a thirty-year-old Bozeman firefighter, died while battling the blaze. Fire chief W. G. Alexander found the stricken firefighter in the basement of the Club Café, but he couldn't carry Robertson out of the building alive. Robertson likely died of smoke inhalation. Nearly a century later, he remains the only Bozeman firefighter to die in the line of duty.

Fire and death returned to Bozeman's Main Street on March 5, 2009. Shortly after 8 A.M. on a snowy Thursday morning, a natural-gas explosion ripped apart at least half of the north side of the 200 block of Main, destroying or heavily damaging five historic buildings. The explosion shattered store windows, shoving parked vehicles into the street, and caused bricks and boards to rain from the sky blocks away.

"I don't want to overstate it, but it literally looks like a bomb went off in downtown Bozeman," Chuck Winn, the city's assistant manager, told a reporter a few hours later.

More than a half-dozen businesses were heavily damaged in the blast, including restaurants, bars, a children's store, an architect's office, and an art gallery. In the hours after the explosion, natural gas continued to flow into the site, fueling a persistent fire.

In the ensuing hours, firefighters worked to quell the flames, and crews from NorthWestern Energy worked to shut off the natural gas to the area, their efforts impeded by the explosion's rubble. Local officials were unable to search the site for hours, and the initial list of those feared missing carried nearly a dozen names.

But it wasn't long before just one name remained: Tara Reistad Bowman, thirty-six, who had gotten an early start that morning in her job as director of the Montana Trails Gallery. A Bozeman native, she was known for her smile and love of the city's downtown. "She brought light up and down Main Street," said one business owner. Bowman's body was eventually recovered from the rubble.

The explosion was investigated by local fire officials and the U.S. Bureau of Alcohol, Tobacco and Firearms. The investigation yielded evidence of a damaged gas line running from a gas main in the alley to the art gallery, allowing leaking gas to build up in the building. The line may have been damaged by an underground frost heave, or even by a motor vehicle hitting a gas meter in the alley. Investigators never reached a solid conclusion about what caused the line to rupture.

Other towns have also been rocked by explosions. In February 1989, Kim Sutton was killed and his twelve-year-old son Travis was seriously injured when a propane tank exploded in the basement of their Billings home. Little remained of the home, and several adjacent homes were significantly damaged. In April that same year, a gas explosion woke 124 guests at the Billings Super 8 motel. At least 31 guests were injured, but remarkably no one was killed.

Helena experienced a massive explosion one brutally cold February morning in 1989. A string of rail cars, accidentally separated from locomotives on the Continental Divide, rumbled into the city and collided with a helper set of locomotives. The resulting explosion and power outage set the capital on its heels for several days (see full story beginning on page 97).

In March 2021 a propane explosion ripped apart a mobile home in Ryegate, killing Curtis Ronning and Christine Debuff, owners of the Ryegate Bar and Café. The blast rattled windows throughout town and was heard by a rancher five miles away.

In most cases, those who witness these traumatic events are convinced that they will never be forgotten. Indeed, in Butte, locals predicted that many would "forever mark time" by a devastating 1895 warehouse fire, only to see memories of the event erode over the decades.

KENYON-CONNELL EXPLOSIONS, 1895
BUTTE'S NIGHT OF HORROR

In the 1890s, Butte was a city on a hill bustling with all the activity that came with large-scale underground mining. Its "Uptown" city center featured tall buildings so grand that they were the architectural peers of those found in urban centers far from remote, rural Montana. Hotels, boarding-houses, brothels, bars, eateries, shops, horse-drawn carriages, and street-cars completed the scene in the growing city that sat atop what had been proclaimed "The Richest Hill on Earth."

On the fringes of Uptown were the mines, their stark headframes studding the mostly treeless hill. Near the bottom of the hill was a nondescript area of railroad tracks, depots, warehouses, and other buildings. To many this area was South Butte, a grid of state-name avenues such as Arizona, Wyoming, Utah, and Colorado, crossed by those bearing metallic names, including Gold, Aluminum, Platinum, and Iron.

The Kenyon-Connell Commercial Company maintained a warehouse in South Butte, where it stored mining and milling supplies along with, as newspaper advertisements of the day touted, Hercules Powder, a brand of explosive used to blast ore deep in the Butte Hill. Next door, the Butte Hardware Company had similar inventory. The warehouses and other nearby businesses benefited from proximity to the mines and the railroad tracks, which brought vital supplies to the growing Mining City.

The night of January 15, 1895, was a cold one in Butte, the mercury dipping well below zero. The report of a fire, made by a policeman from a fire box at the intersection of Utah and Iron shortly before 10 P.M., brought firefighters from the Central Fire Station on East Broadway down the hill. Two horse-drawn wagons carrying fire hose and ladders, a crew of nine full-time firemen, and a handful of part-time volunteers made the chilly trip to the fire, which might have started at an overheated woodstove.

The fire seemed routine, and the firemen, led by chief Angus Cameron, used axes and other tools to pry away pieces of the exterior of the Kenyon-Connell warehouse to allow access to the flames inside. A small explosion that sent flames through the roof gave the firemen momentary pause, as did a report from onlookers of the possibility of blasting powder being stored in the warehouse. But as witness George "Chat" Burns told an interviewer later, "the report was quickly denied, and the boys went to work all unconscious of the awful fate that was in store for them."

The first big explosion came at about 10:08 P.M. on what became known as "Butte's Night of Horror."

"From Walkerville to South Butte and from Meaderville to Rocker," *The Anaconda Standard* reported the next day, "a frighted people rushed from their homes, from stores, from saloons, from hotels, to see a volcano of fire extending hundreds of feet in the air."

The blast leveled the Kenyon-Connell warehouse, and other structures nearby were set ablaze. Of the fifteen firemen who first came to the scene, all but two were dead. One of the two survivors was John Flannery, "the plug man," who was at a hydrant some distance away from the warehouse. The other survivor was Dave McGee, who had retreated from the warehouse several hundred feet to a fire wagon to put blankets on the horses during that frigid night.

"I did not see anything," McGee said later, "but only remember the awful roar and being knocked down." Likely unconscious for a time, McGee came to underneath a portion of an overturned fire wagon and a dead horse, which had likely shielded him from much of the force of the blast.

J. R. Dutton, an electrician, was riding a streetcar near the scene and saw the policeman pull the fire alarm. He told an interviewer he was likely the third person at the scene. He stepped some distance away when he heard the unsubstantiated talk of the possible explosives in the warehouse.

Of the explosion, he said, "The sight was simply awful. The firemen were thrown in all directions, and the air was filled with shrieks and screams which could be heard even in the terrible roar."

Residents and others rushed to the scene, some to help and others to watch. Some estimates put the gathered crowd at several hundred people. The second large explosion came within minutes of the first, likely centered in the Butte Hardware Company warehouse. It was followed by a third blast of uncertain origin.

All three blasts occurred within a span of about fifteen minutes, a period the *Standard* called "the most horrible quarter hour in Butte history." At least six buildings in the warehouse district were destroyed and others were damaged. The blasts were strong enough to shatter glass storefronts far up the hill near the intersection of Main and Broadway. One local man reported that the first explosion shook his house and "rattled the dishes on his table." He lived in Telegraph Gulch, fifteen miles west of the city.

The human toll was horrific. Along with the 13 firemen killed in the

Men stand amid the wreckage of the Kenyon-Connell explosion.
PHOTOGRAPH COURTESY OF BUTTE-SILVER BOW PUBLIC ARCHIVES.

first blast, at least 44 others died during or shortly after the second explosion. An estimated 300 others suffered injuries of varying severity. By all accounts, the scene in South Butte was gruesome.

It took several days for searchers to tally the final death toll, as bodies and body parts were found scattered over a wide area. The dead were taken to undertaking parlors and the wounded to hospitals and private homes, many ferried by residents in wagons and carriages. Undertakers assigned numbers to bodies, and newspapers for several days published names of the known victims and descriptions of the unidentified.

The principal explanation for the bloody carnage centered on the contents of the warehouses. Along with blasting powder, the buildings brimmed with other industrial elements, including saw blades, corrugated tin, nails, and pieces of metal known as "rabble heads." Used in the metal smelting process, the rabble heads, of varying thickness and about six inches long, became projectiles that pierced walls and flesh during the explosions. One witness, Otto Fioto, was helping carry away victims after the first blast when he "saw a flying object passing by and upon investigation found it to be a human head," *The Anaconda Standard* reported.

Those closest to the warehouses, the firemen, were in some cases shredded by flying metal. The only identifiable trace of Cameron, the fire chief, was his cap, found filled with blood. He left behind a widow and five young children, with another child having been buried just days before the warehouse explosions. The Sloan family was also decimated by the disaster. Three family members, including two firefighters, Jack and Ed, died in the explosions. Along with Cameron and the two Sloans, the full-time firefighters killed were Dave Mose, George Fifer, Peter Norling, and Sam Ash. The "volunteers," who were paid by the hour when they responded to a fire, included J. F. Bowman, W. A. Brokaw, Thomas Burns, William Copeland, Steve DeLaughery, and W. H. Nolan.

All but one of the horses driven to the fire were killed. The lone survivor, "Jim," was injured but recovered and lived for several years as a celebrity of sorts.

The blast demolished at least six buildings in the warehouse district.
PHOTOGRAPH COURTESY OF BUTTE-SILVER BOW PUBLIC ARCHIVES.

The explosions also consumed many gallons of ink in the Mining City's four newspapers. *The Daily Inter Mountain,* in its January 19, 1895, issue, colorfully summarized the tragedy this way: "The spectre of death hovered o'er Butte last night, and never in the history of Montana has a newspaper been called upon to chronicle a more appalling disaster."

News accounts from the Mining City traveled quickly. Telegrams poured in from across the country and even overseas, the senders inquiring about the well-being of relatives. One telegram, to Butte resident Emil Weinberger from his brother, Joe, in Denver, read, "Are you dead? Let me know at once."

A series of funerals began a couple of days after the explosion. The newspapers estimated that more than 20,000 people gathered along the route of the funeral procession, which began at City Hall and stretched to the cemeteries where the firemen and some of the other victims were buried. The procession itself, estimated at 3,000 people on foot or in carriages, included large delegations of firefighters from across the state and Montana governor John Rickards, who walked the entire route.

The newspapers reported that every store and office in Butte closed, and even the bars locked their doors during the funeral procession on that cold January afternoon. Of the roughly thirty people buried that day, most were placed in graves with tombstones. The coffins of nine victims that authorities were unable to identify were carried on a makeshift hearse to unmarked graves. What were believed to be the remains of four of the Butte firemen: Angus Cameron, thirty-four; Dave Mose, twenty-five; Sam Ash, thirty-seven; and Peter Norling, twenty-one, were buried in a single casket.

"The sun smiled from a clear sky but the bright sunshine seemed a mockery while every heart was filled with gloom and every eye was dimmed with tears," *The Anaconda Standard* reported of the firemen's funeral.

In the days after the explosion, a relief fund for families of the victims soon swelled to more than $40,000. Donations came from all quarters, including from the deep coffers of Marcus Daly and F. Augustus Heinze, and eventually from the third Butte "copper king," William A. Clark, who cabled from Paris a $1,000 donation.

In the time of mourning, questions about the explosion and demands for an explanation of how much explosive material was stored in the warehouses also began to percolate. Local ordinance and state law allowed no more than 150 pounds of explosive material to be stored in the city limits. Speculation among the many residents familiar with explosives put the amount needed to produce explosions at the scale of those of January 15 at many, many tons.

William R. Kenyon, a director and general manager of the Kenyon-Connell Commercial Company, soon publicly claimed that no more than 150 pounds were in the warehouse and when that supply dwindled, it was replenished from a site well outside the city. An official of Butte Hardware made a similar statement.

But within a day, a former Kenyon-Connell employee alleged that significantly more blasting powder was routinely in the warehouse. Another fact brought added scrutiny to the statements of the warehouse owners. While combing the site in the days after the explosion, searchers found many unexploded sticks of blasting powder, enough by itself to exceed what the law allowed. Those familiar with blasting powder's characteristics noted that the cold, snowy weather may have prevented some of the powder from exploding. That speculation led *The Anaconda Standard* to observe, "There can be no doubt that had the explosion occurred in the summer when the powder was dry, most of Butte would have been demolished, and the consequent loss of life would have been something that is horrifying to simply contemplate."

During a ten-day coroner's inquest, the volume of stored explosives was a key question. The jury ultimately found the warehouse owners criminally liable in the explosion deaths. Considerable legal wrangling ensued. Four years later, a lawsuit filed by the family of Cameron, the fire chief, raised the question of whether the corporate directors of Kenyon-Connell were liable for damages. While the Montana Supreme Court ruled in favor of the Cameron family, it is unclear whether they, or the families of any of the victims, received any formal financial compensation from the company.

John Paull, a Butte firefighter for thirty-five years, dove into learning about the 1895 explosions in the late 1980s. "From everything I have read, there were no fines, no jail time," he said. "Pretty much nothing happened to those guys." Along with William Kenyon, the directors included Michael Connell, a businessman who found great success in retailing, the lumber trade, and development in Butte, Missoula, and Deer Lodge. Another Kenyon-Connell director of note was William A. Clark.

News accounts say that Kenyon, who served as mayor of Butte in 1887–1888, left the city for the East not long after the explosions, while Michael Connell, the president of Kenyon-Connell Commercial Company, despite having a grand home in Butte, was rarely seen in the Mining City after 1895.

The community relief fund provided some assistance to families of the dead firemen, but the amount was less than three months of wages. In part due to the Butte explosions, Paull said, in 1899 the Montana Legislature created a death-disability fund for firefighters in the state, funded in part by fire insurance premiums.

One key figure in the explosions, Patrick Largey, the owner of the Butte Hardware Company, remained in Butte. Largey owned logging, mining, and publishing interests and was also president of the State Savings Bank near the corner of Main and Park in Butte.

Just shy of three years after the explosions, William J. Riley hobbled into the bank to talk to Largey, as he had done frequently in the recent weeks. Riley, who lost a leg in the warehouse explosions, spoke with Largey for several minutes at a teller's window before pulling out a pistol. Within moments, with gunshot wounds in his head and chest, the banker lay dying on the floor.

Riley walked out of the bank and was quickly arrested by law officers. Newspaper accounts the next day noted Riley had struggled to find or keep work after the explosions and had received money from Largey, as well as from Kenyon and Connell. (Ellen Crain, director of the Butte-Silver Bow Archives, says that, in the era before workers' compensation laws, worker sickness or death payments in Butte were often informally provided by fraternal or religious societies or organizations.)

The Butte Miner reported that, moments after his arrest, Riley confessed to the shooting, expressed a willingness to hang for his actions, and asked for a quick trial. As for Largey, Riley said the businessman had failed to keep promises to get him a job. "I had told him that I thought someone who was responsible for my condition ought to do something for me and he was responsible."

Riley was found guilty of second-degree murder and served thirty-nine years in prison before being pardoned in 1937 by Governor Roy Ayers. Noting that Riley showed no continuing bitterness, Ayers proclaimed "he is now entitled to mercy."

In the days, weeks, and months after the warehouse explosions and funerals, it seemed the event, described "as the greatest holocaust in the history of Butte or the West," would be deeply etched in the collective memory of the Mining City.

For a time, it was. But the ongoing history of Butte seemed to eclipse the 1895 explosions. Even to Paull, the veteran firefighter, and his co-workers, the story and its significance seemed to have eroded. "As guys retired and left," Paull said, "the story was never passed down."

Elements of the tragedy smoldered, however, and have slowly rekindled interest in recent years. Paull began piecing together the story in advance of a firefighter convention held in Butte in 1989. In 2010, Montana PBS released a well-received documentary film on the explosion, and the event has found its way into the local high school curriculum.

More than 120 years after the second-deadliest event in Butte history, a local resident combing the site of the warehouse explosions found several tarnished badges believed to have belonged to firemen killed in 1895.

In summer 2019, a Butte group started work on a public memorial for the firefighters and other warehouse fire victims, guided by a lament from local historian Jim McCarthy, who said, "We have memorials for miners, memorials for servicemen, and even a memorial for a dog from the Pit." (The dog, named "the Auditor" for his practice of showing up unexpectedly, lived near the Berkeley Pit. He was first spotted in about 1986 and died in 2003. Residents raised money for a 300-pound bronze statue of the shaggy dog.) "But we have no memory," McCarthy added, "of this blast."

EUREKA HOTEL FIRE, 1950
"IF IT HAD NOT BEEN FOR THE BOYS,
I COULD NEVER HAD GOTTEN OUT"

Winter held a paralyzing grip on northern Montana in late January and early February 1950. The state's northern tier was locked in what officials would call a "winter emergency," with prolonged sub-zero temperatures, deep snow, and howling winds.

For at least 500 miles across the state's northern tier, deep drifts had blocked roads and paralyzed entire communities. Browning, just east of Glacier National Park and the center of the Blackfeet Indian Reservation, was in the storm's icy epicenter. U.S. Highway 2 was closed, blocked by snow to the east and west, and conditions were similar on U.S. 89, preventing travel north and south from the town.

County and state officials worked to reach people stranded across the isolated reservation, some for several weeks. State newspapers reported that Air Force cargo planes from the base in Great Falls were preparing "to bomb the Blackfeet reservation with food and clothing," adding that flights over reservations found conditions to be desolate and the plight of rural residents to be "pitiful."

When coach Jess LaBuff and his basketball team boarded a westbound train near the end of the first week of February, the storm had finally waned, leaving behind drifts that reached second-story windows in Browning. The Great Northern rail line, intermittently closed due to heavy snow, had opened, allowing the team to board a train and travel to games in Columbia Falls and, on Saturday night, at Lincoln County High School in Eureka.

The Browning Indians lost to the Columbia Falls Wildcats 50 to 35 on Friday night, but bounced back on Saturday in Eureka, beating the Lions 49 to 48. A night in the Montana Hotel in Eureka awaited the victorious visitors, who would catch the train back to Browning the next day.

The Montana Hotel, on the town's main street, was a wood-framed, two-story structure that offered the best lodging in Eureka. Along with about twenty-five guest rooms, many on the second floor, the hotel included several apartments and the post office, which was reportedly home to the town's sole telephone.

It had also been a tough winter in Eureka, about six miles from the Canadian border. In December 1949, fire had destroyed the American Legion Hall. Then, just a few days before the weekend Eureka-Browning

A truck laden with Christmas trees passes in front of the Montana Hotel
just months before the building burned to the ground.
PHOTOGRAPH COURTESY OF THE DARRIS FLANAGAN COLLECTION.

basketball game, another fire half a block from the Montana Hotel consumed three businesses—Bud's Coffee Shop, Betty's Beauty Shop, and
Hank's Barbershop—on a night that temperatures bottomed out at 30
below zero. An overheated stove was the suspected cause.

That same night, a local woman, Mary Pomeroy, died after being critically burned a day earlier when a hot furnace grate in her home set her
dress on fire.

Early on Sunday, February 5, 1950, as the Browning basketball team
and others in the Montana Hotel slept, a furnace in the hotel exploded.
Flames shot through the building. The hotel operator, L. A. "Larry" Riley,
ran from an apartment he occupied with his wife and pounded on doors,
trying to awaken sleeping guests.

On the second floor, Ronnie Norman, a member of the Browning
team, was stretched across his bed at about 3 A.M., reading a magazine,

when he heard a woman scream "fire." According to an account in the *Browning Chief*, a weekly newspaper, Norman "rushed out of his room into the hall, which was dense with smoke, the atmosphere being suffocating," and pounded on nearby doors to roust his teammates.

Norman, joined by Jimmie Lahr, another player, managed to wake their coach and all their teammates except two, Johnny Powell and Delano Grayson. Attempting to reach the room occupied by the two, Norman reported he was driven back by intense smoke.

"All the others," the *Chief* reported, "succeeded in making their escape, and occupying the second floor of the building, found themselves faced by a high jump out of windows. With the first floor a mass of flames, this was their only alternative."

Possibly cushioned by deep piles of snow, only two team members, Roland Kennerly and Albert Flamand, were injured in the roughly twenty-foot jump to the ground. Local folks, who gathered quickly to fight the fire, witnessed the boys, mostly in their night clothes, leaping to safety.

"Those who did not get out right away, did not get out at all," an unidentified witness told the *Daily Missoulian* in a story published on February 6, 1950. Shortly after the boys jumped, "the upper floors collapsed into the fire below."

Jess LaBuff, the Browning coach, credited his team with saving his life and likely others. The players "roused everyone possible in the few minutes before the whole place was in flames," LaBuff said in the *Daily Missoulian* account. "They literally shoved me through a door and we jumped from the second-story window into the snow. If it had not been for the boys, I could never had gotten out."

Local volunteer firefighters poured water on the blaze and, aided by local U.S. Forest Service employees, pumped water from the nearby Tobacco River. Sparks and debris flew to the roofs of nearby buildings. But witnesses credited deep snow and bitter cold from keeping the fire from spreading to other structures.

Local fire chief George Davis, who owned a nearby restaurant, arrived at the hotel shortly after the fire was reported. He said the hotel was destroyed within a half hour. "I never saw a building burn so fast," Davis told the *Daily Inter Lake* in Kalispell.

The fire consumed not only the hotel but the post office and its telephone. Also lost was the hotel's guest registry, leaving firefighters and would-be rescuers unable to determine how many made it out alive.

A head count on the Browning team yielded a sad answer: two from the team were missing—Powell, a junior guard, and Grayson, the team manager.

News of the fire and the missing boys was relayed to the reservation by a Great Northern Railway operator, who was able to reach the Browning School superintendent at about 4:15 A.M. News of the tragedy spread quickly.

As firefighters probed the smoldering structure, the Browning team moved to cabins elsewhere in town. LaBuff, the coach, stayed at the fire scene much of the day, harboring dim hope that the missing boys survived. On Sunday afternoon, the coach and his team boarded a train to head home. "I couldn't stay here another night," the coach said.

The Montana Hotel was reduced to a pile of ashes and debris.
PHOTOGRAPH COURTESY OF THE DARRIS FLANAGAN COLLECTION.

IN MEMORIAM

JOHN POWELL

DELANO GRAYSON

Johnny Powell and Delano Grayson in the school yearbook.
PHOTOGRAPH COURTESY OF AMY ANDREAS, BROWNING HIGH SCHOOL.

The bodies of Powell and Grayson were found later Sunday, along with those of three others: Ed LaFrance, sixty, a clerk in the hotel; Charles Cameron, eighty-four, a well-known local farmer and rancher; and William Peterson, sixty-four, a railroad employee, possibly from Great Falls.

In the coming days, Eureka residents, including members of the local basketball team, would travel to Browning for the funerals of Powell and Grayson. Eureka didn't have a community newspaper in 1950, but the February 24, 1950, issue of *The Evergreen*, the high school newspaper, published a letter to the Eureka community from Helen Kelly, the aunt of Johnny Powell, who wrote on behalf of the boy's mother and other family members, many of whom lived in Babb, a community northwest of Browning.

"We hope that you all will understand how very much your kindness has meant to all of us," she wrote. "Your town and school representatives at the funeral was only something that a town with a heart would think of. That one gesture gave more than you will ever know. . . . My sister hopes that all the people who cared for our boys all day Sunday will know how very much their mothers want to see them, and in some way, show their appreciation."

Powell was buried near his family home in Babb, with his teammates serving as pallbearers. An obituary in the *Chief* cited the seventeen-year-old's love of football and basketball, noting, "He had looked forward to the coming district tournament with pleasure and with determination to do his part towards winning the championship."

Funeral services for Delano Grayson, sixteen, were also held in Babb. A Boy Scout, he was described as a worthy and capable student who also "showed a high devotion to athletics." An older brother, Gordon, had earlier played basketball for Browning.

The Powell and Grayson families published a note in the *Chief* about two weeks after the fire, thanking people on the reservation and in Eureka. "It seems that everyone in this community has found an individual and kindly means of showing us that our sorrow is shared," they wrote. "If there is any alleviation of sorrow possible in an experience such as we have gone through, it would certainly be found in all this kindness."

The Browning team finished in a second-place tie with Sunburst in regular season play and entered the district tournament, which was held in Browning in early March, with hopes of a championship. After winning games against Brady and Oilmont, the Indians lost to Valier 43 to 27 and finished third in the tournament. The members of the tournament team, according to the Browning newspaper, were Eugene Kipp, Fred Pambrun, Jimmie Lahr, Bobbie Powell, Robert Kennerly, Roland Kennerly, Albert Flamand, Ronnie Norman, Sylvester Arrowtop, and Carl Guardipee. Grayson's family operated a store on the Blackfeet Reservation. Not long after losing Delano, the family left the area.

Members of the Browning basketball team, 1950.
PHOTOGRAPH COURTESY OF AMY ANDREAS, BROWNING HIGH SCHOOL.

LaBuff, the coach, born in Browning in 1919, left the reservation to take a teaching and coaching job in Shelby the next year. He died in 1973, at fifty-three. He was later inducted into the Montana Indian Athletic Hall of Fame and the Montana Coaches Association Hall of Fame.

A young Earl Old Person played basketball for Browning in 1949 with several members of the team that visited Eureka the following year. Nearly seventy years later, Old Person, the chief of the Blackfeet tribe, hasn't forgotten the pall cast by the boys' deaths. "When that took place, it was a sad time for Browning," he said. "There are some that remember, but it's been a long time."

BELT TRAIN EXPLOSION, 1976
HELL ON WHEELS

It was the day after Thanksgiving and Belt, Montana, a little town about twenty miles east of Great Falls, had enough fresh snow to lure Eric, Mike, and Darrell Spragg and their skis to a hill across the road from their home. From the hill, just north of a small rail overpass, they could see Belt's main street and the activity at the nearby Farmers Union Oil Company gas station and bulk-fuel plant. The hill also offered a close-up view of passing Burlington Northern trains.

For Eric Spragg, that chilly Friday often unfolds in his mind more than forty years later. It was just about 3 P.M. and his skiing siblings had paused to watch a freight train rumble by. "All of a sudden, the train cars, they started tipping back and forth."

The Spragg boys watched as rail cars, some loaded with petroleum products, left the tracks and collided with large Farmers Union fuel storage tanks along the tracks. Sensing trouble, the boys began to run down the hill. Eric Spragg remembers falling, taking off his ski boots, and continuing to run in his stocking feet. Somewhere in this blur of events, the first explosion came.

Off the hill, the boys looked back. "We saw our house and it was totally engulfed in flames," Eric Spragg, then twelve, remembered. As the brothers gathered away from hill and tracks, "We said, 'Oh my god, I think Dad's dead.'"

Their father, who managed to get his wife and daughter out of the burning house and into a nearby ravine, worried that the boys might have perished until the family was later reunited on Belt's main thoroughfare, stunned by the horror unfolding around them.

"It was really something," Spragg said. "The streets on fire, the houses on fire." It wasn't long before even Belt Creek was on fire, as emergency crews scrambled to funnel the flaming fuels running down the street away from the town's center and into the creek.

While the Spragg family avoided tragedy, the scene next door at the Farmers Union was grim.

Charlie Pimperton, seventy-two, a retired rancher, was last seen standing next to his car, which was on a hoist in the service station. Tim Ostlie, seventeen, in the station shopping for tires, was last spotted running toward the front door, seconds after the first explosion. The remains of both were found by search dogs, buried in rubble, several weeks later.

Others in or near the Farmers Union were injured, including Ken Brown, an employee, who was apparently blown from the area near the

building by the explosion and was later spotted near the home of Marlin Johnson, across Belt Creek from where the Farmers Union stood. Johnson told a reporter from the *Great Falls Tribune* that he was outside, throwing snow on burning metal that had

Belt homes and businesses sit destroyed while rail cars continue to smolder.
PHOTOGRAPH COURTESY OF THE HISTORY MUSEUM, GREAT FALLS, MONTANA.

struck his home, when he spotted Brown, staggering nearby, moaning "help me, help me" and "get ambulances."

Brown was taken to the hospital in Great Falls by ambulance. He was joined by young Eric Spragg, who had suffered burns near his belt line. Spragg, who was well acquainted with Brown, said he didn't recognize him during the ride due to the extent of the man's burns.

The 121-car Burlington Northern train had departed Great Falls and made its way southeast to Belt on its way to Laurel. Some of the rail cars held propane, while a handful of others were carrying petroleum fuel oil from a refinery in Cut Bank, destined for Akron, Ohio, where it could be used in tire manufacturing. As the train entered Belt and reached the viaduct, a broken piece of rail caused the cars to derail. Some of the cars carrying fuel oil were punctured and they ignited, sparking the initial explosion.

Eventually, twenty-four cars derailed, with some of them smashing into the large Farmers Union storage tanks near the tracks. The tanks, which held gasoline and fuel oil, also ignited. A mix of oil and gas began to

Toppled train cars straddle the Belt viaduct.
PHOTOGRAPH COURTESY OF THE HISTORY MUSEUM, GREAT FALLS, MONTANA.

flow down the street, and the sense of panic in Belt swelled as the flaming stew spread. Making things worse, much of the town lost electricity and the ability to make phone calls.

"At first I thought it was an earthquake," Toots Langan told a reporter who called the Black Diamond Bar. "Now there is something coming down the creek and the creek is on fire."

Resident Ewart Brurud reported, "There are roof fires around town. The Farmers Union building and three houses have been demolished. People were living in those houses. People with children. We don't know if they were home or not. It couldn't be worse."

At Walt's Tavern, owner Marian Manion summarized the situation in three words: "It's a holocaust."

Help came as quickly as possible, and more than 100 firefighters from surrounding communities converged on Belt. A command post was set up in the local bank. At least six separate fires were triggered by the series of explosions. About half of the town's residents were evacuated.

About two hours after the first explosions, an overheated rail car loaded with propane ignited. A *Great Falls Tribune* staffer flying over the community snapping photos estimated the fireball climbed more than 1,000 feet into the sky as dusk settled over Belt. Several firefighters reported being knocked from roofs by the force of the blast.

But Belt got a break late in the day when a plan to divert the fuel running through the center of town was successful, thanks in large part to state highway department trucks and workers who were in the area, planning to sand snowy roads. The sand instead was used to form a dike that guided the flaming fuel into the creek. About a mile of the brush and trees along the creek burned before they could be extinguished, with residents reporting flames fifty feet high along the stream that runs through town. Officials later estimated that at least 40,000 gallons of a mix of petroleum products reached the creek. Crews created fences of chicken wire and hay bales in an attempt to corral the fuel, but the creek still suffered significant damage.

The amount of destruction seemed surreal in the small town of Belt.
PHOTOGRAPH COURTESY OF THE HISTORY MUSEUM, GREAT FALLS, MONTANA.

While some of the smaller fires were quelled on Friday, crews fearing further explosions worked cautiously around the rail cars and were only able to relieve the danger the next day. Some of the fires burned for more than twelve hours.

Montana's lieutenant governor, Bill Christiansen, dispatched National Guard troops to help in Belt, and with good cause. Along with the Farmers Union Oil buildings, other commercial structures lost included Belt Building Supply, the *Belt Valley Times*, the old Miner's Union Hall, and several buildings near the General Mills elevator, itself damaged by flames.

Five homes were destroyed and sixteen others were significantly damaged, with more than half the homes in town reporting windows broken or damaged by the explosions. Pieces of metal debris were found more than a mile away from the Burlington Northern tracks, the epicenter of the conflagration. Nineteen vehicles were destroyed.

Longtime *Tribune* reporter and photographer Wayne Arnst was in Belt the next day and wrote that "hell on wheels" had rumbled through town, leaving a scene similar to "what one might expect after a small battle or aerial bombardment."

Beyond the deaths of Pimperton, a well-known local figure, and Ostlie, a Belt High School junior who had moved with his family to Belt the summer before, twenty-two people had suffered injuries of varying severity. The cost of damage to the town was pegged at $4.54 million.

In its report on the incident, the National Transportation Safety Board (NTSB) noted several issues that contributed to the breadth of the incident. The train, while not exceeding speed limits for the area, was likely too heavy for the rail in place in the Belt area. Investigators concluded that a small "fissure" in a rail near the viaduct caused the rail to break apart under the heavy load of the freight train. The rail line through Belt had been inspected about five months before the derailment. A Burlington Northern track inspector had also passed over the track earlier on the day of the derailment and reported no issues. The NTSB also chided the railroad for being slow in sharing information on the explosive contents of the rail cars with local officials, which increased the risk to emergency workers.

While stunned by the destruction in Belt, Arnst, like many others, was also struck by how many more people could have been injured or killed. "When one views the area the day after and reflects on what could have happened," he wrote, "it may be well to label the situation not as the Belt Disaster but rather the Belt Miracle."

A photo of charred bicycles near what was left of the Spragg home appeared on the front page of the *Great Falls Tribune* two days after the explosion. The family of six, which lost nearly all its possessions, sought clothes at the Salvation Army and lived for a time in a two-room unit at the Shasta Motel in Belt.

Ed Spragg, a teacher in Belt, used a small settlement from the railroad and a bank loan to build a new home for the family in the Armington area on the outskirts of Belt.

His son Eric credits his father's positive attitude with helping the family rebuild its life after the fire and explosions. "It was a real growing opportunity for me, to learn how to appreciate life," Spragg said. "It was a huge event. It was a real defining moment in my life, that's for sure."

Today, Eric Spragg says his most vivid memory is not of the fires, explosions, or lost possessions but of Ken Brown, his fellow ambulance passenger. "He is what I think about to this day. He was burned so bad and he was telling me that I was going to be okay."

HELENA TRAIN EXPLOSION, 1989

This Helena-centered disaster actually started in northcentral Montana when 103 mile-per-hour winds pummeled Cut Bank on the last day of January 1989. A vicious cold front followed, with more wind, snow, and bitter subzero temperatures. In Great Falls, where thermometers reached a record high of 62 F. for the date on January 31, the mercury sat at minus 17 F. less than 24 hours later, a drop of 79 degrees.

For folks in Helena, there was no warning that the punishing Arctic air mass gripping the city would soon be seared into their collective memory. In the early morning of February 2, most Helenans were sound asleep, snug in their warm beds, while temperatures outside hovered around minus 30 F., with a windchill of minus 70 F. Such cold snaps aren't unheard of in Montana, so locals know to weatherize their homes and vehicles and hunker down to wait out the worst of it. But people and machines both tend to not function as well in extreme cold.

That morning, on a mountain grade west of town, a Montana Rail Link (MRL) crew was struggling with the severe cold. Their lead engine lost heat in its crew cab, and a track signal was malfunctioning. The crew parked the train on the Austin siding below Mullan Pass, set the airbrakes (but not the handbrakes on the rail cars), and uncoupled the locomotives to rearrange them. In the extreme cold, the rail cars' airbrakes failed, and the string of forty-eight cars rumbled ten miles downhill and back into Helena.

Immediately east of the Benton Avenue crossing next to Carroll College, a "helper set" of three MRL locomotives sat idling. At about 4:30 A.M., crew member Mike McNellis hopped off to throw a switch by hand so the helper set could connect with a nearby train. With no warning, the runaway cars slammed into the helper set and twenty-one cars derailed. Six of the derailed cars carried hazardous materials, and at least one of them had ruptured, leaking its contents. And then it caught fire.

McNellis, a newly married twenty-three-year-old, had stepped off the lead locomotive just moments before the collision. Seconds after hearing the crash, "a locomotive shot toward me," McNellis told the Helena *Independent Record*. "I just jumped off the track. The [locomotive] handrail brushed my coveralls." McNellis began to run with the cars derailing behind him. "I said to myself, don't stop running or your wife's gonna be a widow."

When everything came to a stop, the engineer of the helper set, Mark VanOrtmann, joined McNellis on the north side of the tracks. A nearby resident, Marc Cramer, had heard the collision and walked up to the two men. The workers radioed dispatch and began walking to meet an MRL van sent to pick them up. But before they reached the vehicle, McNellis noticed flames coming from a tanker car. Just as he warned VanOrtmann, the tanker exploded.

VanOrtmann dove under the crew van, and McNellis was thrown fifteen feet in the air. "It was like some kind of atomic bomb exploding like you see on TV," McNellis said. "First it was white, then it exploded again and it was blue. I was kind of laying on the ground when it exploded again. It was a couple hundred feet high at least." The second blast tossed McNellis into the ditch beside Benton Avenue.

McNellis, VanOrtmann, and Cramer picked themselves up, none of them noticing obvious injuries. McNellis said his ears were ringing, and his nose and eyes were burning from the acrid smoke billowing from the tanker. (Later that day, McNellis went to the hospital as a precaution; the blasts permanently damaged his hearing.) Jeff Meyer, who lived not far from the scene, said, "The explosions shook the whole house. I saw the flash of light between our Venetian blinds. I was thinking World War III or something."

Acrid smoke billows from the derailed train near the Benton Avenue crossing.
PHOTOGRAPH BY GENE FISCHER, COURTESY OF THE HELENA *INDEPENDENT RECORD*.

Soon, all of Helena knew something was amiss. The blasts damaged a nearby electric transmission line, knocking out power—and lighting and heat—across much of the Helena Valley. In the ensuing hours, the local Red Cross set up several evacuation centers where residents huddled for warmth. Electricity was restored for some by late morning, but the loss of power, coupled with a thick plume of smoke, scattered debris, and the bitter cold, created an apocalyptic scenario in the state's capital.

Many homes and buildings within a mile radius suffered cracked or shattered windows and structural damage from the force of the explosions. A few homes were damaged by flying debris. A train axle flew over four-story St. Charles Hall on Carroll's campus and crashed through the roof and ceiling of seventy-nine-year-old Catherine Debree's home. The axle landed in her living room while she slept in an adjacent bedroom. Debree's granddaughter, Chris Everett, told the *Independent Record*, "If it had been one foot over, it would have landed on her as she slept."

Another chunk of debris pierced the roof, ceiling, and floor of Delores Lee's home in the 2200 block of North Benton Avenue. Awakened by what she thought was an earthquake, Lee stumbled from bed into her living room where she tumbled into a hole in the floor. Unable to stop herself, she landed in the home's basement. While traumatized, her only physical injuries were bruises and scratches.

The blast's punch reached the lower portion of Helena's downtown and even to the Cathedral of St. Helena, where it cracked some of the ornate marble pillars inside. But hardest hit was Carroll College—campus was littered with rail-car remnants that Russ Ritter, a Carroll administrator and the city's mayor at the time, said looked "like shrapnel."

The college's Health and Physical Education Center, closest to the explosion, suffered damage to its roof, ceiling, walls, and many windows, and later, water damage from frozen pipes. Nearby, on the north side of one wing of Guadalupe Hall, a women's dormitory, almost every window was shattered as the more than 200 dorm residents slept. Debra Dacar was in her second-floor room and remembered, "All of a sudden the lights start flashing and the windows blew in, and then tiles started falling off the [ceiling.]" The night before, on a whim, she and her roommate had rearranged the room, moving her bed away from the window that shattered just hours later. Other dorm residents had closed heavy curtains against the cold air circulating off the windows, which later helped contain flying shards of glass.

The blast blew out windows at Guadalupe Hall,
a woman's dorm on the Carroll College campus. Amazingly,
none of the student residents were seriously injured.
PHOTOGRAPH BY GENE FISCHER, COURTESY OF THE HELENA *INDEPENDENT RECORD*.

While none of the students in Guadalupe or elsewhere on campus were injured, the pre-dawn scene was hardly calm. "The whole building just shook," Lisa Downs, a Guadalupe resident, told a reporter. "Everybody was pretty much screaming. It was frightening not knowing what it was. I didn't know if it was a bomb. It was the most frightening moment of my life."

All Carroll students were evacuated to shelters elsewhere in town. Some moved back to their dorms within a few days, while others were housed by kind-hearted local families. Carroll suspended classes for ten days while officials sorted through the havoc on campus, where at least ten buildings were damaged. Initial estimates pegged the damage at Carroll at nearly $10 million, but the final NTSB report put it at $2.5 million. Citywide, damage from the explosions totaled $6 million, according to the NTSB.

Across the city, as power was gradually restored, residents watched the plume of black smoke from the persistent fire, digested news reports of the early morning explosions, and wondered what might happen next.

"For the first forty-eight hours, people were on edge," J. R. Feucht recalled in July 2021, more than three decades after the explosions. A Helena firefighter stationed on the city's east side, Feucht and two others were among the first emergency workers to arrive on scene. Along with the subzero temperatures and eerie darkness because of the power outage, a failed backup radio system left responders with little information about what caused the explosion and what was fueling the intense fire. "It was just kind of a crazy, convoluted mess," Feucht said. "We were just feeling our way through it until we figured out what was going on."

After a few hours, firefighters had learned that the burning rail cars contained hydrogen peroxide, isopropyl alcohol, acetone, and liquid coal

Investigators get a closer look at the twisted, ice-coated wreckage.
PHOTOGRAPH BY GENE FISCHER, COURTESY OF THE HELENA *INDEPENDENT RECORD*.

tar pitch, all highly flammable and considered hazardous. Another tanker that didn't explode or catch fire contained drums of paint and solid coal tar pitch, also officially hazardous. Firefighters poured water on the burning wreckage, and the scene was eventually covered in ice.

Given the intensity of the blasts, widespread damage, and extreme conditions, it's remarkable that no one was killed. As Mayor Ritter said, "I think the thing that we have to emphasize was that no one was [seriously] hurt. That, in itself, was a miracle."

Feucht worked for the Helena Fire Department for thirty-two years, retiring as fire chief in 2012. He still marvels at the lack of injuries at Carroll and among his fellow firefighters and early responders. Luckily, the power outage and hampered communications had delayed first responders. "My crew and I could all be dead," Feucht said. "If we had been called right away and had a normal response, we could have been down there. It's just amazing to me that nobody, nobody, died."

Paul Spengler, Lewis & Clark County's disaster and emergency services coordinator, was grateful the blast hit in the early morning when few people were up and about. "[That] is when you want an explosion in your town when you have to have one," he told an interviewer.

While Helenans quickly accepted the "it-could-have-been-worse" view, details about what led to the train collision were slower to emerge. Various federal investigators offered little public comment. Two days after the blast, a story in the *Independent Record* listed some of the unanswered questions: How did a forty-eight-car train break loose and roll into Helena? Could the crew have given advance warning? Why did it take so long to identify the hazardous materials in the rail cars?

On February 7, an *Independent Record* story offered the first hints about what led to the disaster. According to a lead NTSB investigator, the cold's effect on the train's airbrake system may have gone undetected or unreported. Additionally, there was no sign that the crew set hand brakes on the mountain grade, as rules required. More details about confusion and disagreement among the train crew emerged at a NTSB hearing in May. The lead of three locomotives added to the train in Helena, intended to help the train climb Mullan Pass, developed heater problems in the bitter cold. The engineer in this helper set decided to stop the train, disconnect the rail cars to rearrange the locomotives, and put one with better heat at the front. The "road" engineer, who had guided the train to Helena, disagreed with the plan and offered to take control of the cold locomotive himself. As the NTSB later noted, it was unclear which engineer was in charge at the time of the runaway, and it appeared they did not discuss safer alternatives to disconnecting the rail cars.

The full NTSB report, released in December 1989, outlined numerous errors by the train crew in their communications and failure to inspect the airbrake system and set the hand brakes, the latter of which would have required walking the length of the train in the cold. The NTSB noted that several crew members lacked adequate clothing for the cold. The board said failure of the crew to properly secure the train was the probable cause of the crash and explosion.

The NTSB also questioned the crew's decision to pursue, without permission, the runaway train in the locomotives rather than immediately report the situation to MRL and emergency authorities in Helena. An eventual radio call to MRL dispatch warning of the runaway came just moments before the collision. The NTSB also chided Helena officials for failing to have backup power for the emergency radio system. (Helena and Lewis & Clark County soon installed a backup generator.)

Looking back, Feucht, the firefighter, noted the string "of individual decisions" that led to the explosions in the February darkness. "It was a weird series of events that turned it into what it was," he said. "We caught a break and nobody got killed."

The NTSB has no authority to levy fines. None of the train crew were fired, but some faced disciplinary action. Bill Brodsky, then MRL's president, said the railroad and its insurance company would cover the $6 million in damages. Within two months, property owners logged more than 2,400 damage claims along with claims from more than 290 Carroll College students.

On December 31, 1989, the *Independent Record* tabbed the February train explosion as the top local news story in Helena for the year, topping the local celebration of the state's centennial in November, an event which featured a visit from President George H. W. Bush and brought a crowd of 15,000 to a ceremony at the capitol.

SOURCES

Introduction

Billings Gazette. "Bozeman rocked: Blast destroys 4 businesses; 1 person missing." March 6, 2009.

Bozeman Daily Chronicle. "Downtown rocked by explosion." March 5, 2009.

Butte Miner. "Bozeman Fireman Dies of Suffocation in Blaze Subdued After Inflicting Damage of $250,000." December 16, 1922.

The New York Times. "Blast Wounds City to Its Core." March 17, 2009

Kenyon-Connell Explosions

The Anaconda Standard. January 16–21, 1895.

Butte Miner. "Slain In His Office." January 12, 1898.

Crain, Ellen. Personal interview. July 2019.

The Daily Inter Mountain, Butte, Montana. January 16, 1895.

Independent Record, Helena, Montana. August 8, 1937.

Montana Historical Society Research Center, Helena, Montana. "Patrick Largey Family Papers, 1863–1965."

Montana Standard, Butte, Montana. "Blast from the past: Explosion reverberated for years to come." January 14, 2001.

Montana Standard, Butte, Montana. "Butte nonprofit breaks ground on warehouse disaster memorial." June 9, 2019.

Paull, John. Personal interview. July 2019.

Western Mining History. "Total Devastation: The Butte, Montana, Explosion of 1895." www.westernmininghistory.com.

Eureka Hotel Fire

Browning Chief. February 10, 17, 24; March 10, 1950.

Daily Inter Lake, Kalispell, Montana. February 4–6, 1950.

Daily Missoulian. February 6, 1950.

Etaikasi. Browning High School yearbook. 1950.

The Evergreen. Lincoln County High School newspaper. Eureka, Montana. February 24, 1950.

Great Falls Tribune. February 6, 1950.

Montana Indian Athletic Hall of Fame. www.montanaindianathletichof.org.

Old Person, Earl. Personal interview. May 2019.

Belt Train Explosion

Associated Press. "Belt disaster explained." March 21, 1977.

Great Falls Tribune. November 27–29, 1976.

National Transportation Safety Board. "Derailment of a Burlington Northern Freight Train. Belt, Montana. November 26, 1976." NTSB RAR-77-7, September 29, 1977.

Spragg, Eric. Personal interview. June 2019.

MINE DISASTERS

FOLLOWING THE TWISTS AND TURNS AND UPS AND DOWNS OF Montana highways, the distance between Butte, in Silver Bow County, and Bearcreek, to the east in Carbon County, is about 235 miles.

In 1917, during World War I, Butte was cranking out copper to feed the war effort and, more broadly, to supply copper that would be refined into the wire that was rapidly bringing electricity to homes and businesses across America.

In Bearcreek, just a few miles east of Red Lodge, the product was coal and the demand in 1943 was driven by the need to heat homes, power locomotives, and fuel the U.S. effort in World War II.

But a pair of mine accidents, separated by a quarter century and framed by a shared pressure "to put rock in the box," tragically link the two communities in Montana history.

GRANITE MOUNTAIN–SPECULATOR FIRE, 1917
A SLEEP WITHOUT SUFFERING

The headlines in *The Anaconda Standard* on June 8, 1917, paint a telling portrait of a day in the life of the Mining City: In Europe, an offensive to regain Belgium from the Germans was under way. Butte electricians were to vote on a possible strike, with the outcome likely to affect the operations of streetcars, railroads, and the sprawling network of mines underneath Butte. The mines had enjoyed record payrolls the previous month, likely reflecting a war-fueled copper frenzy. The minimum pay for an underground miner had also risen, to $4.75 per day.

The June 9, 1917, below-the-fold headline in the *Standard* read, "Big Fire Rages in Speculator." While smoke poured into the shaft of the mine owned by the North Butte Mining Company, officials said they were not aware of any loss of life but admitted "it is impossible to ascertain what conditions are below the 2,400-foot level."

The scale of the fire and tragedy quickly came into focus. The June 10, 1917, *Standard* headline declared, "Death Exacts Enormous Toll From Miners: Butte Stands Appalled At Great Sacrifice."

In the coming days, the fire that started in the Granite Mountain shaft, sending flames and poisonous gas into the nearby Speculator shaft and the comb of nearby subterranean passages, claimed the lives of at least 163 miners. That's according to the official report. A memorial to the victims on the Butte Hill puts the number at 168. Another tally of the dead says 173. More than 100 years later, the North Butte Mining disaster remains the worst hard-rock mining accident in U.S. history. (The second-deadliest hard-rock mining incident in the United States took place in the Sunshine Mine near Kellogg, Idaho, in 1972, when ninety-one miners died.)

The Granite Mountain fire and deaths were part of a remarkable period in Butte in which a labor leader was lynched, miners launched a lengthy strike, ethnic tensions about the nation's role in the First World War reached a boiling point, and state and federal governments enacted controversial restrictions on free speech.

The North Butte disaster also reflected the hard reality about mining and life in Butte. Just two years earlier, a dynamite explosion in the Granite Mountain mine killed sixteen men. In 1917, despite the hazardous working conditions, the population of the Mining City was about

90,000, possibly its peak. More than thirty languages could be heard on the streets and in the mines, of which there were more than 100. A city directory at the time revealed at least 42 churches and an estimated 240 drinking establishments. There were three daily newspapers.

Another business segment thrived in Butte during the World War I era—funeral parlors. Between 1916 and 1920 in Butte, 410 men died underground. Many others died of mining-related respiratory disease.

Brian Shovers, a Montana historian, delved into the deadly nature of Butte mining and concluded that, while underground mining was inherently dangerous, its conduct in the Mining City exacted a particularly heavy toll. Shovers wrote, "Butte ranked as one of the most dangerous mining districts in the world, with a fatal accident rate three times higher than traditional mining districts in Cornwall, [England]." In his master's thesis, Shovers attributed the death rate between 1880 and 1920 in part to the booming demand for copper due to the increased use of electricity, the telephone, and, later, World War I. Related factors, he wrote, included the corporate ownership of the mines, the mixed attitudes and ethnicity of miners, changing mining technology, and insufficient training.

The means of death included fires, explosions, falling rocks, hoisting accidents, and, over time, the diseases caused by extended exposure to the silica dust created by drilling rock underground. All of these threats played out in Butte, where mining was dominated by the Anaconda Company, which was the world leader in copper production for many decades.

Tiny in comparison to the Anaconda operation, the North Butte Mining Company was the second-largest copper producer in Butte in 1917. It had more than 1,100 employees working in the northeast part of the Butte Hill. The company produced a record amount of copper in 1916 (and a profit of nearly $2.5 million) and was on pace in 1917 to do even better.

The North Butte mines had a reputation for well-ventilated mines, making them somewhat safer than others, thanks to a system of fans and compressors that pushed air in and out of the mines. The two mine shafts, the Granite Mountain and the Speculator, were roughly parallel to each other, about 800 feet apart. They were connected at many levels by passageways and also linked underground with other nearby mines. Some of the connecting passages featured locked doors; others were unblocked. In making their way through this labyrinth, miners often relied on personal knowledge and experience.

On the evening of June 8, 410 miners descended the Granite Mountain shaft on the night shift. Earlier in the day, a crew had worked to run a three-ton electric cable down the shaft. The cable would supply power for a fire sprinkler system in the mine.

That evening, a large section of the freshly installed cable broke away from clamps and fell into a heap at the 2,400-foot level of the Granite Mountain shaft. After learning of the cable break, a group of four, including assistant foreman Ernest Sallau, descended into the shaft to inspect the situation. Deep in the mine, the men found the cable, which in places had its protective sheathing stripped away, exposing highly flammable insulation. During this inspection, the flame from Sallau's carbide headlamp ignited a section of the stripped cable. Fire and smoke began to penetrate the Granite Mountain–Speculator shafts.

One hundred years later, the *Montana Standard* described that moment shortly before midnight on June 8, 1917, as "a split second in Butte" that would change "the course of mining history."

The fire quickly spread to wooden timbers and other flammable material, driven in part by the ventilation system. Mechanical devices pushed air down the Granite Mountain shaft and sucked it up the Speculator shaft. The result was a subterranean hell, already dark, hot, and humid, now laced with flames, smoke, and carbon monoxide and other deadly gases.

Investigators later estimated that gases, often lethal, contaminated about 300 miles of underground workings. Other perils included cave-ins and areas flooded by water poured into the shafts in an attempt to quell the fire. It is likely only a few of the miners were killed by flames, while

Smoke pours from the Granite Mountain–Speculator Mine on June 9, 1917.
PHOTOGRAPH COURTESY OF THE BUTTE-SILVER BOW PUBLIC ARCHIVES.

some were burned by scalding water. About 150 of the dead showed signs of carbon monoxide poisoning.

Of the 410 men who entered the mine, 247 managed to reach safety. Of those, about 180 found escape routes through neighboring mines, such as the Badger, Diamond, and High Ore. Others somehow emerged after spending many hours behind hastily constructed bulkheads that served as makeshift shields against the killer gases.

Rescue and recovery efforts lasted more than a week, and the Mining City endured a roller-coaster ride of tragedy and miraculous survival. On June 10, as the depth of the fire became apparent, *The Anaconda Standard* published on its front page the names of the dead, along with those missing and "probably dead."

"Butte is in deep mourning," one news story began, "near to 200 of her men lie silent in their last sleep, while hundreds of sorrowing relatives are plunged into grief that tears the hearts of men."

The large headline in the June 11, 1917, *Anaconda Standard* read: "Thrill of Joy Sweeps Over City When Twenty-Five Are Found Alive in Mine." With the rescue of miners came stories of bravery deep underground.

One unlikely hero was Sallau, whose lamp sparked the fire. While the others dispatched to inspect the cable fled the mine shaft after the flames broke out, Sallau walked and ran through the maze of passages to warn miners of the fire and help lead them to safety. He was credited with saving at least fifty miners. "In doing so, he lost his own life, though he had ample opportunity of saving himself had he been willing to abandon his men," read the federal Bureau of Mines report on the fire.

Others came to be heroes of the mine disaster through letters they wrote by candlelight while they sought safety. Shift boss James D. Moore led the construction of a bulkhead at the 2,200-foot level, using picks, saws, hammers, board, nails, and any other materials that might help thwart the deadly gas spewed by the fire. Along with seven others, Moore lived for more than two days behind the barrier, where investigators later pegged temperatures at 84 degrees and the humidity at 97 percent.

Moore wrote a note to his wife, whom he called "Pet," about his situation: "This may be the last message you will get from me. The gas broke at about 11:15. I tried to get all the men out, but the smoke was too strong. I got some of the boys with me in a drift and put in a bulkhead. If anything happens to me, you had better sell the house and go to California and live. You will know your Jim died like a man and his last thought was for his wife that I love better than anyone on earth. We will meet again. Tell mother and the boys goodbye. With love to you my Pet, may God take care of you. Your loving Jim."

A second letter from Moore, recorded in a time book he carried, read: "Well, we are all waiting for the end. I guess it won't be long. We take turns rapping on the pipe, so if the rescue crew is around, they will hear us. . . . There is a young fellow here, Clarence Manthey. He has a wife and two kiddies. Tell her we done the best we could, but the cards were against us."

Another letter, later: "Seven o'clock, all alive, but air is getting bad. One small piece of candle left. Nine o'clock, in the dark, all is lost."

Six of the men with Moore were found unconscious but alive after an estimated fifty-five hours trapped underground. Moore and another man didn't survive, with investigators concluding their deaths may have come not long before rescuers arrived.

Another Butte man, Manus Dugan, attained folk-hero status for his efforts underground. Dugan, who sharpened the tools used by the miners, was better acquainted with the workings than most. He is credited with leading the construction of a bulkhead and was one of twenty-nine men who sought safety from gas behind it for roughly thirty-six hours. (Along with the groups led by Dugan and Moore, other miners sought safety behind bulkheads. The Bureau of Mines investigation concluded that thirty-one of the fifty-six men who barricaded themselves behind bulkheads survived.)

Tales of Dugan's actions were told by survivors and shared widely in news accounts of the day. Miner John Wirta, the second man to emerge alive from the mine, according to the *Standard*, relayed what he described as "the super-human vitality of Dugan" and his plan to build the bulkhead "and stay there as long as we could. We all thought we were facing death, so we readily agreed to any plan."

While some in the group played cards, there was also talk from some of suicide during the thirty-six-hour stint behind the bulkhead. Dugan wrote notes to his wife, Madge, outlining the

Manus Dugan, a hero of the Granite Mountain mine disaster.
PHOTOGRAPH COURTESY OF THE BUTTE-SILVER BOW PUBLIC ARCHIVES.

group's predicament and efforts to survive. "I realize the hard work ahead of the rescue men," he wrote. "Have not confided my fears to anyone but welcome death with open arms, as it is the last act we all must pass through, and it is but natural, it is God's will. We shall have no objection."

Another note to his pregnant wife: "It takes my heart to be taken from you so suddenly and unexpectedly but think not of me, for if death comes, it will be in a sleep without suffering. I ask forgiveness for any suffering or pain that I caused. Madge, dear, the place is for you and the child."

The group left the area behind the bulkhead after thirty-six hours of waiting for rescuers. Moving in the dark without lights, a group of four, including Dugan, became separated. The remaining twenty-five made their way to the surface. Investigators believed Dugan and the three others succumbed to the gas in the mine.

The period between the emergence of the twenty-five survivors and the discovery of Dugan's body was chronicled in newspaper accounts. "Dugan Missing; Fear He's Dead," read one headline for a story that speculated about the man's fate. "The question on every lip at the mine and among miners who knew of his heroism was 'Is Dugan safe?'"

Interviewed on June 11, Madge Dugan described her missing thirty-year-old husband as "the finest looking man whoever walked the earth" and noted she had not given up hope for his return. "I have nothing to say until I get either his dead body or his living body. I think he is still alive; anyway I won't give up hope."

On June 15, 1917, after a funeral reportedly attended by thousands, a copper casket carrying Dugan's body was taken to St. Patrick's Cemetery, escorted by a large group of family and friends, and buried beneath a gravestone made of granite.

Madge Dugan gave birth to her daughter, whom she named Manus, on July 7, about three weeks after burying her husband. She received $75 from the North Butte Mining Company for burial costs. Under state law, she received less than $4,000 in workers' compensation for her husband's death, paid in weekly $10 installments. She may have been one of the lucky ones. Due to the weakness of the compensation laws and the many limits and exclusions, the families of some fire victims received no formal compensation at all. (Madge went on to serve as public administrator for Butte, trained to be a bookkeeper, and later owned a dressmaking shop. She died at age sixty-eight in 1965.)

Strikes among miners and related workers began in the days after the bodies were recovered from the North Butte mines. Tensions fanned by the Anaconda Company and union leaders reached a boil, with the federal government paying close attention, in large part due to the need for Butte's copper in the war effort.

The Industrial Workers of the World and its fiery leader Frank Little bore much of the blame for the agitated workers and strikes, at least in the eyes of the Anaconda Company and its newspapers. In the pre-dawn hours on August 1, 1917, a group of masked men broke into Little's boarding-house room and stuffed him, in his underwear, into a waiting car, which roared away. His body, which appeared to have been dragged behind the car, was found a few hours later hanging from a railroad trestle. While many suspected that thugs hired by the Anaconda Company murdered Little, no charges were ever filed.

Frank Little grave marker in Mountain View Cemetery, Butte.
PHOTOGRAPH BY BUTCH LARCOMBE.

Today, a memorial to the men who died stands near
the Granite Mountain and Speculator mines.
PHOTOGRAPH BY BANJODOG, CC BY-SA 3.0.

Labor strife, often violent, continued for several more years in Butte. At the North Butte operations, the damage from the fire, estimated at about $1 million, was repaired and mining resumed. But copper prices tumbled after the end of World War I, and the mine operated only sporadically over a number of years. The Granite Mountain and Speculator mines were eventually purchased by the Anaconda Company in the 1950s.

On June 8, 1996, a memorial dedicated to the mine fire and its human toll was completed near the disaster site. With stark mine headframes to the north and south, the view from the memorial runs to the east, encompassing the Berkeley Pit, the vast open-pit copper mine that over several decades gobbled up the Granite Mountain and Speculator shafts and a sizable chunk of the Butte Hill.

A sign at the memorial notes that more than 2,500 men in Butte died from mine-related causes from 1870 to 1983. It also reminds visitors that they are "standing on hallowed ground."

SMITH MINE EXPLOSION, 1943

"WE DIED AN EASY DEATH"

Gold, silver, and copper all played a large role in the early development of Montana, which still proudly proclaims itself to be the "Treasure State." In south-central Montana, not far from the Wyoming border, for decades the treasure was coal—dark, useful, and, inevitably, dangerous.

The first coal mine in Red Lodge began operation in 1887. Just a few miles to the east, the coulees in the narrow Bear Creek Valley were loaded with long seams of high-grade coal that ran deep into the hills where mining began in the 1890s. But it was the arrival of the short-line Montana, Wyoming & Southern Railroad in 1906 that spurred the full development of mines and fledgling communities, including Belfry, Bearcreek, and Washoe. Within a decade of the arrival of the rail line, which connected the remote mines with the sprawling Northern Pacific Railway network, there were an estimated 1,200 miners working in a half-dozen coal mines in the Bear Creek Valley. (The town name is consistently spelled as one word, unlike the broader valley that encompasses it.)

The town of Bearcreek.
PHOTOGRAPH COURTESY OF THE CARBON COUNTY HISTORICAL SOCIETY AND MUSEUM.

Coal from these mines provided heat for homes, fueled steam-powered locomotives, and fired copper smelting and refining operations in Anaconda and Great Falls. And the coal provided a steady living for miners and their families, many of whom had come from across Europe to work the underground mines.

In their heyday, the towns bustled. During World War I, Bearcreek was home to nearly 2,000 people, a close-knit community with schools, bars, pool halls, grocery and hardware stores, a bank, and two hotels. The development of a water system and concrete sidewalks gave it a feeling of permanence uncommon in many boom-and-bust mining towns. Unlike Washoe, a "company town" developed by the Anaconda Company, the mines that drove work and life in Bearcreek had a variety of owners, as did local businesses.

Bearcreek rode the ups and downs of coal prices and demand over the decades. And life wasn't easy in the cold hills of the Bear Creek Valley. Agnes Waisanen, the wife of a second-generation Bearcreek miner, recalled lean times during World War II in a 1988 interview with the *Carbon County News*, a weekly newspaper in Red Lodge.

"You know, we didn't have anything. Times were tough, but it was a good mining camp. Good dances, good orchestras, too. We were all family over there." Those bonds were formed in part from the risky work. When coal is mined or transported, a fine, highly explosive dust is created, and toxic gases are common in coal mines. For these reasons, underground coal mining is widely considered to be more dangerous than underground hard-rock mining. (The worst coal-mining disaster in the United States claimed 362 lives at Monongah, West Virginia, on December 6, 1907. The deadliest coal mine disaster in the world took place in 1942 in China, where a coal-dust explosion killed 1,549 people. Such numbers eclipse those of hard-rock disasters.)

Waisanen's first husband, Emil Anderson, was one of seventy-seven miners who reported for the morning shift at the Smith Mine No. 3 on February 26, 1943. It was a Saturday and the miners would be paid time and a half for the shift as the Montana Coal and Iron Company pushed to meet the wartime demand for coal.

"All the time, it was 'get the coal out,'" she said. "I don't really blame anyone for it, but it was always 'get the coal out.' Everyone wanted coal, all over the country."

Life for the miner's wife, and many others, took a tragic turn that Saturday morning. Just after 9:30 A.M., an explosion ripped through the Smith Mine, which sat between Bearcreek and Washoe. While few outside the mine heard or felt the blast, smoke pouring from its entrance served as the alarm.

Within an hour, three miners, dazed and suffering from gas poisoning, were helped from the mine. Over the coming days, rescuers would comb the underground workings, battling deadly gases and cave-ins in search of other survivors. They found only bodies, seventy-four of them, scattered throughout the mine.

The deaths represent Montana's worst coal-mine disaster and the second-worst mine accident of any sort in state history, trailing only the Granite Mountain–Speculator Fire in Butte in 1917. In April 1943, would-be rescuer Matt Woodrow was sickened by gas and died while he and others searched the Smith Mine for possible survivors, pushing the toll to seventy-five.

The explosion ripped the heart out of Bearcreek and nearby towns. The miners ranged in age from twenty-one to seventy-two. Some were immigrants who had sought a new life in Montana, others the sons of immigrants. Many had worked shoulder-to-shoulder for years, and their families had gathered together to celebrate birthdays, holidays, and other events in the small communities.

Loren Newman, a foreman and fire boss in the Smith Mine, had finished a night shift a few hours before the explosion and hastily returned after learning of the disaster to help search for the miners, some of whom he had known for forty years.

"I can still name every man and where we found them—even the day we found them," Newman said in 1988, forty-five years later. "The greatest tragedy of my life was that disaster. Never a day passes that I don't think of it."

While the search for the living proved fruitless, the effort was valiant. Miners and others quickly gathered, and some went in, even without gas masks to protect themselves from the dangerous carbon monoxide and other threats they knew awaited them. At the same time, mine officials notified state and federal authorities of the explosion and trained rescuers rushed to the scene. A crew from Butte flew on a military transport plane to Billings and was ferried to the mine by the Montana Highway Patrol. Other miners from Nye, Stockett, and Sand Coulee near Great Falls, Roundup, and Klein came to help.

The first crew of local miners was able to rescue Alex Hawthorne, Eli Houtonen, and Willard Reid, miners who worked apart from the others and were nearest the mine entrance. Although sickened, the three survived. Reid, who worked on the mine's pumps, said the mine lost power moments before the explosion. Making his way to the main shaft, "it sounded like there was a big windstorm coming. When I heard the roar, I threw myself to the ground."

The wind, likely an explosive blast, roared over Reid and Houtonen as they lay on the floor. As they remained face down, another wave passed over them. They stumbled toward the mine entrance where they encountered rescuers. Reid recalled his jacket "looked like someone slit it repeatedly with a knife."

But as would-be rescuers tried to push deeper into the mine, they encountered air laced with carbon monoxide and were rebuffed. Later, rescuers with special breathing devices were able to venture further but only in short stints. At the same time, workers scrambled to reconstruct the mine's ventilation system, which was damaged in the explosion. That work consumed several days and hindered rescue efforts.

A makeshift hospital was set up in Red Lodge, where officials planned to care for sick or injured miners. The day after the explosion, the hospital had treated sixty-two men, none of whom had been in the mine at the time of the explosion; they were rescue workers sickened by gas.

Two days after the explosion, a news account in *The Billings Gazette* noted that some experienced miners at the scene thought there was just "a thousand to one chance" those in the mine would be found alive, but optimism reigned among wives and family members who had been at the mine since the explosion, awaiting word.

"I know they are coming out," said one woman whose husband, father, and brother-in-law were unaccounted for. "Everyone's doing all that can be done. I have all the confidence in the world."

Two teenage girls who had lost their mother twelve years earlier waited for their father, Sam Barovich, to come out of the mine. "I know they must be all right," Martha Barovich, his oldest daughter, told a reporter. "We are all praying for them. God will hear us, I know."

Agnes, the wife of forty-year-old Emil Anderson, expressed similar hope, saying, "Emil knows every inch of that mine—he's an electrician. He'd know what to do. He'd protect himself. We can't stop hoping. We won't."

The next day, the *Gazette* reported that nineteen bodies had been found and that the official view was that no miners would be found alive. Once the ventilation system and rail system in the mine were made functional, bodies wrapped in canvas were ferried from the mine. The last body, that of Elmer Price, the head mine foreman, was removed on Sunday, March 7, nine days after the explosion.

Bill Romek, assistant manager of the mining company, recalled driving from Billings to the mine in unseasonably warm weather on the day of the explosion. That night, as the disaster unfolded, a blizzard struck, bringing snow and deep cold. Once the last body was removed, the rescue crews, officials, and others who had been in Bearcreek for days departed, leaving the little town empty and desolate.

Romek's wife, Janice, a former Bearcreek schoolteacher, played piano at several of the funerals. "You can't imagine what a mournful town it was,"

Bill said. "They had a memorial service and then all the funerals. There were fifty-nine widows and fifty-two children left fatherless."

Agnes Anderson never forgot the chill at the funeral of Emil, her husband of twenty-one years. "Standing at the cemetery, the snow was so deep, you could just see the heads of the people go by."

Officials later estimated that about thirty of the miners died from the explosions and a few others from blast-related injuries, with the remainder succumbing to carbon monoxide and other gases. Most of the deaths came relatively quickly.

Evidence that some of the trapped miners survived for a few hours was found as rescuers combed the shaft and passageways. Near some bodies were rough pieces of wood, likely from boxes that held blasting powder, with messages scrawled in chalk.

From Walter Joki and John Sudar: "Goodbye wives and daughters, we died an easy death. Love from us both, be good." The back of the board read, "We try our best but couldn't get out."

And Agnes Anderson heard from her husband a last time: "It is 5 minutes pass 11 o'clock. Dear Agnes and children. I am sorry we had to go this way—God bless you all, Emil, with kisses."

Miner Emil Anderson's note to his wife, written on a board, was found next to his body.
PHOTOGRAPH COURTESY OF THE CARBON COUNTY HISTORICAL SOCIETY.

Investigation of the Smith Mine explosion began shortly after the miners' funerals. The federal Bureau of Mines weighed in, as did the state coal mine inspector. A third view came from the mine owner, the Montana Coal and Iron Company. The three parties agreed on a few facts centering on the role of methane gas in the explosion. The Smith Mine No. 3 had a reputation for being "gassy," and mine employees would spend time during each shift detecting gas and taking steps to alleviate it, often with added ventilation.

But the agencies and mining company disagreed on where the explosion began and what sparked it. The Bureau of Mines said an open flame from a miner's lamp ignited the methane and, subsequently, coal dust, which magnified the explosion. The state report also noted a miner's lamp as a likely cause, but had it originating in a different area of the mine. The mining company, and at least some of its employees, blamed an electrical issue in an area where cement barricades had been built in an attempt to wall off concentrations of methane. The company said a cave-in allowed large amounts of gas to escape from the sealed-off area, and the electrical malfunction sparked the explosion.

The Smith Mine had been the first in Montana to be inspected by the Bureau of Mines, in November 1942. The agency had issued some preliminary findings but didn't complete a final report until after the late-February explosion. A state safety inspector had visited the mine about a month before the explosion.

Concerns raised included the use of open-flame rather than battery-powered headlamps by some miners, the fact that some miners smoked in the mine, the need for improved ventilation, and a conclusion that "rock-dusting" (the application of non-combustible material, such as pulverized limestone or gypsum) would reduce the amount of dangerous coal dust in the mine.

The company noted that it had worked to address a number of the concerns but pointed out that battery headlamps and rock-dusting equipment were limited in supply due to "war conditions." It noted the mine had just one incident of a miner being injured by methane gas in its decades of operation. Company officials also reminded the government inspectors that they had offered to temporarily shut down the mine to address safety concerns prior to the explosion. The federal agency, worried about the importance of coal in the war effort, found no need for a shutdown.

A coroner's inquest held in Red Lodge less than two months after the explosions and deaths, while noting the role of gas and coal dust, concluded that "no one will ever know for sure what sparked the explosion or exactly where it originated."

The Smith Mine reopened a few months after the explosion, but production tapered off, especially after the end of World War II. Economic realities came to bear: Americans were turning to natural gas to heat their homes, and railroads were increasingly using diesel locomotives. Open-pit coal mining was cheaper and safer than underground mining.

It didn't take long for Bearcreek to fade away. Many families left the community after the explosion. The Lamport Hotel, a local fixture built in 1907, was razed in about 1945. Schools closed and houses were moved or torn down. The Smith Mine closed in 1953, and the little railroad that linked the valley's coal to the rest of the nation ceased operations and its tracks were removed. While one coal mine lingered into the 1970s, the mining industry that had given Carbon County its name was dead. The population of Bearcreek, once measured in the thousands, was seventy-nine in 2010, according to the U.S. Census.

The three survivors of the explosion suffered the effects of gas exposure for a number of years. Alex Hawthorne died in 1962; Eli Houtonen two years later. Willard Reid recalled a conversation with Houtonen years after the explosion in which the latter asked, "Why didn't you leave me there? I would have been better off."

Reid lost his father to a Pennsylvania mine cave-in, and a brother and a cousin died in the Smith Mine disaster. A miner since he turned sixteen, Reid returned to the industry after being treated for gas poisoning.

He was later diagnosed with black lung, a respiratory ailment tied to coal dust exposure. He died at age seventy-nine, one day after the forty-fifth anniversary of the Montana explosion.

Local historian Jeff McNeish attended several Smith Mine memorial events in Bearcreek over the years. Two great-uncles had died in the mine in the 1930s, and his great-grandfather, James McNeish, perished in the 1943 explosion. Several relatives, including his grandfather, had helped search for survivors but rarely spoke of the disaster.

"It clearly wasn't a good time in his life. The family story is that he was part of the crew that found his father's body," McNeish said of his grandfather. After a visit to the history museum in Red Lodge, the Billings-area resident "got sucked in" to the story of the mine, the explosion, and the history of the Clark's Fork valley. He produced a three-volume set of books on the mine disaster, plus another on Bearcreek and surrounding communities, driven by family connection and a desire "to just figure out what I didn't know."

The mine disaster, while dramatic locally, "went largely unnoticed in the United States," McNeish said, largely due to its occurrence during a global war. Efforts to find the actual cause of the explosion and resulting deaths appeared to have gotten deeply tangled in attempts to shift blame and limit liability.

McNeish harbors little hope of fully understanding the cause of the deadly explosion. "The bottom line," he said, "is that a lot of guys died, and a community was wrecked."

SOURCES

Granite Mountain–Speculator Fire

The Anaconda Standard. June 8-12, 1917.

Butte Daily Post. June 9, 1917

Granite Mountain–Speculator Mine Memorial website. www.minememorial.org.

Harrington, Daniel. "Lessons From the Granite Mountain Shaft Fire, Butte."

U.S. Department of the Interior, Bureau of Mines. 1922.

Harrington, James D. "A Reexamination of the Granite Mountain-Speculator Fire."
    Montana The Magazine of Western History. Autumn 1998.
Montana Standard, Butte, Montana. "A split second in Butte changed
    the course of mining history." June 8, 2017.
Punke, Michael. *Fire and Brimstone*. Hyperion, 2006.
Shovers, Brian Lee. "Mines, Managers and Machines: Industrial Accidents
    and Occupational Disease in the Butte Underground, 1880-1920." Thesis, M.A.
    History, Montana State University. April 1987.

Smith Mine Explosion
Billings Gazette. February 28 through March 5, 1943.
Billings Gazette. "75 Years Ago, the Smith Mine Disaster Decimated the Small
    Montana Coal Town of Bearcreek." February 27, 2018.
Carbon County News. Red Lodge, Montana. March 12, 1943.
Carbon County News. Red Lodge, Montana. "Smith Mine Disaster Remembered."
    March 10, 1988.
McNeish, Jeff. Personal interview. August 2019.
"Report on a Mine Explosion That Occurred at the Smith Mine, Washoe, Montana,
    on February 27, 1943." Montana Coal and Iron Company, Billings. June 10, 1943.
U.S. Department of the Interior, Bureau of Mines. "Final Report of Mine
    Explosion, Smith Mine, Montana Coal and Iron Company, Washoe, Carbon
    County, Montana." February 27, 1943.

DAM FAILURES

GOLD, SILVER, AND COPPER HELPED BUILD THE TREASURE STATE, but the most valuable commodity in Montana may be water.

Snowmelt and rain send vast amounts of water down Montana's rivers and streams each year. Since the arrival of the first white settlers, Montanans have worked to corral this flow and use it to sustain livestock, irrigate crops, generate electricity, and provide recreational boating, fishing, and swimming.

More than 13,000 dams dot the Montana landscape. Most are small earthen embankments that capture runoff to create stock ponds. But Montana has about 3,500 "inventoried" dams, of which about 150 are labeled as "high-hazard," which means if they were to fail, human life would be at risk.

The risk of dam failure, while small, is a reality of Montana life. That reality has unfolded in dramatic and sometimes deadly fashion as a result of our attempts to control our watery treasure.

HAUSER DAM FAILURE, 1908
A RUSH FOR THE HILLTOPS

In the first years of the twentieth century, Montana was a land of opportunity, at least in the eyes of men like Samuel T. Hauser. An entrepreneur

The original steel and masonry Hauser Dam.
PHOTOGRAPH FROM *STONE AND WEBSTER PUBLIC SERVICE JOURNAL*, 1908.

and governor of the Montana territory from 1885 to 1887, Hauser ran an array of business ventures ranging from ranching to railroads and banks. Hauser set his sights on another sure-fire deal when he announced the construction of one dam and quietly did groundwork for another, both on the Missouri River north of Helena. The dams would supply electricity to the mines in Butte and speed the conversion of their hoist operations from steam to electricity.

The Helena Power and Transmission Company started work on Hauser Dam in 1906. The dam would be constructed of masonry and steel, one of just a few in the world utilizing this innovative design. Work on the first dam was completed early in 1907, at a cost of $1.2 million.

F. A. Ross, a former Helena resident who managed mining operations for copper king Marcus Daly, offered effusive praise for the completed Hauser Dam and another dam downstream after a March 1908 tour. He told a gathering at Helena's grand Montana Club that the dam work was "one of the greatest engineering feats ever inaugurated," and that Martin

Gerry, the manager of Hauser's hydroelectric endeavors, "is one of the best engineers in the United States."

On a rainy afternoon on April 14, 1908, just a month after Ross's gushing appraisal and about fifteen months after the steel dam began producing electricity, a 300-foot section of its face gave way, sending a sixty- to seventy-foot wave of water down the Missouri River. The dam's powerhouse, just below the face, was flooded, and workers scrambled to safety, as did family members who lived in houses nearby.

"Men, women, and children were rushing for the hilltops and heart-rending screams were heard on all sides from those who believed that we would all be drowned," dam employee M. A. Currie told the *Helena Independent*. An account in the *Great Falls Tribune* described the dam's destruction as a "huge mass," that "writhed and screamed like a live thing" as it gave way.

Investigators later concluded that steel pilings were far too short to solidly anchor the dam. The pilings reached only into gravel, not bedrock, at the base of the dam, which surrendered to the intensity of spring runoff.

Dam workers managed to telephone emergency messages to the downstream communities of Wolf Creek and Craig before fleeing. Along with destroying the dam, the water ripped away houses and barns and other buildings, tore at rail lines in the river canyon, and swallowed livestock.

Hauser Dam in 1908 after the flood; note the powerhouse, far left, still standing.
PHOTOGRAPH FROM *STONE AND WEBSTER PUBLIC SERVICE JOURNAL*, 1908.

In Great Falls, where another dam and industrial operations were located along the river, the dam's failure sparked fear. "Rumors of all kinds were current, and many believed the city would be wiped out within a few hours," the *Great Falls Tribune* reported on April 15, 1908. But the concern was greatly exaggerated—the river rose seven feet but inflicted little damage.

Reconstruction of Hauser Dam, this time with concrete, started in 1910 and was finished the next year. Hauser, his financial position deeply eroded by the dam failure and cost of rebuilding, lost control of his namesake dam to the fledgling Montana Power Company. Montana Power fulfilled the second part of Hauser's hydroelectric vision with the 1918 completion of Holter Dam, named for Anton M. Holter, a Helena-area entrepreneur and one of Hauser's early enthusiastic investors.

Money was lost and ambitions were diminished by the failure of Hauser Dam. But no lives were lost to the waters of the mighty Missouri. About thirty years later and hundreds of miles downstream, the partial failure at another grand dam project took a human toll.

FORT PECK DAM LANDSLIDE, 1938
A MOVING, MUDDY HELL

From its earliest days, northeast Montana's Fort Peck Dam stretched the human imagination. A four-mile-long dam across the Missouri River would take years and thousands of workers to build, creating a reservoir, billed as the "first of the Missouri's Great Lakes," more than 130 miles long and with more shoreline than the Pacific Coast of California.

In October 1932, two executive officers from the U.S. Army Corps of Engineers pulled their car to the crest of a hill overlooking the Missouri River southeast of Glasgow. They were joined by Leo Coleman, the mayor of Glasgow, and Sam Rugg of the local chamber of commerce. The engineers outlined to the wide-eyed local men a federal government plan to build what would be the largest earthen-filled dam in the world across the river below, a spot chosen in part because of its topography and "favorable foundation conditions."

Coleman was incredulous: "My god, man," he told the Corps engineers. "It would cost a million dollars to build a dam across there!"

The project turned out to be much grander than anyone imagined. From the beginning of construction in 1933 to the dam's completion in 1940, the tab for building Fort Peck Dam would reach $160 million. Employment at Fort Peck peaked at more than 10,000 workers in 1936; a common laborer made 50 cents per hour and beer sold for a nickel. It spawned a new community—Fort Peck—and more than a dozen colorful boomtowns that sported names such as Wheeler (named for Burton K. Wheeler, an influential Montana senator), New Deal, Square Deal, Delano Heights, Wilson, and Park Grove. Franklin Delano Roosevelt visited the project in 1934 and 1937. Harry Truman visited in 1950, about a decade after the dam's completion. Fort Peck even landed on the cover of the first issue of *Life* magazine, with an iconic photo of the dam's spillway. That November 23, 1936, issue included seventeen photos from Fort Peck by Margaret Bourke-White and an accompanying story that described Fort Peck as a "Wild West" town, "a place stuffed to the seams with construction men, engineers, welders, quack doctors, barmaids [and] fancy ladies."

The centerpiece of Franklin Delano Roosevelt's New Deal, the dam would bring flood control and more predictable navigation to the lower Missouri, a key congressional selling point

Fort Peck commercial area in 1936.
PHOTOGRAPH COURTESY OF U.S. ARMY CORPS OF ENGINEERS.

for the massive project. Senator Wheeler was a key player in the development of the dam in northeast Montana and a leader in the U.S. Senate. Writer M. R. Montgomery, in a 1989 article in *The New Yorker* magazine, wrote: "The primary function of the Fort Peck Dam, after you scrape away the official cost-benefit analysis, was to keep Franklin Delano Roosevelt on the good side of Senator Burton K. Wheeler."

Communities in the parched region would benefit from a potential water supply and irrigation for crops. But the key benefit would be the most precious commodity—jobs.

As Sam Gilluly, the editor of *The Glasgow Courier* during the construction of Fort Peck Dam would later note, "It was not only two-bit wheat and five-cent beef that plagued the farmers" in northeast Montana during the Great Depression. Like much of the country, the region had been pummeled by drought, bank failures, grasshoppers, and dust.

Gilluly, who later became the director of the Montana Historical Society, wrote a lengthy recollection of the dam construction era for the *Great Falls Tribune* in 1977, noting that Valley County health officials reported numerous cases of malnutrition during the Depression. The American Red Cross in 1933 estimated that more than half of the 1,800 farm families in Valley County were getting weekly food relief from the agency.

"Farm wives were canning gophers to put meat on the table for their families," Gilluly wrote. "And ranchers were feeding thistles to their cattle [described by some as 'Hoover hay']. It was the only feed available. There was no hope for the people in the whole expanse of eastern Montana. Fort Peck Dam was their salvation."

The economic boost stretched far beyond Fort Peck, Glasgow, and Valley County. Gravel and fill for the dam came from excavations in neighboring counties. Rock for the dam's face was hauled by train from Snake Butte south of Harlem, with a new spur line built to Fort Peck by the Great Northern Railway. The Montana Power Company built an electric transmission line from Rainbow Dam near Great Falls to power the dam project. At Wheeler's insistence, Montanans were given hiring preference at Fort Peck.

But salvation came at a price. According to Army Corps of Engineers records, nearly sixty workers died building Fort Peck Dam. The worst year for fatalities was 1938, and the deadliest day was on September 22, 1938, when, in the words of crew foreman James "Monty" Montfort, "machinery and men alike were swallowed up in the moving, muddy hell."

Early on a Thursday afternoon, about two weeks after the completion of the main section of dam, an area known as the core pool, where dredged material was placed as work progressed, began to move. Unlike most dam failures, this collapse went upstream, into the reservoir. The upstream face of the dam split away in a massive landslide. The slide lasted about ten minutes, according to witnesses, who saw trains, track, pipelines, boats, and workers tossed about by the slide.

Gilluly, the *Courier* editor, rushed from Glasgow to Fort Peck and offered a grim assessment of the scene. "No one," he said at the time, "buried under that slide could possibly be alive."

There were about 180 workers in the area of the slide. Of those, 34 were injured when the ground gave way. Eight were killed. The dead were Albert Stoeser, Archie R. Moir, Douglas Moore, Oliver Bucher, John Johnson, Walter Lubbinge, Dolphie Paulson, and Nelson P. Van Stone. Most were young. All were from Montana, many from Fort Peck or the nearby shanty towns. The body of Stoeser was recovered the day of the slide. Moore's body was found days later floating in the reservoir. The bodies of the others were never found, and they are believed to be buried somewhere beneath the estimated 5.2 million cubic yards of rock and dirt that slid away into the river.

Those who did survive had stories to tell.

Jerry Mason, in a news account from the United Press, told how he and others ran for their lives. "It started in the core pool and kept sliding away

An aerial shot taken the day of the dam failure shows
the massive scale of the slumped earth.
PHOTOGRAPH COURTESY OF U.S. ARMY CORPS OF ENGINEERS.

like when you knock over dominoes. I ran with twenty other fellows with
the crack almost catching up with us, and cracks opening up all around."

Art "Bud" Granum, a fifteen-year-old high school student, had just
finished his lunch and was heading back to work when the earth began to
give way. "I ran what I consider my fastest one-quarter to half-mile run
of my career, in steel-toed shoes no less, with the famous Fort Peck Dam
slide right on my heels," he recalled years later. "I was the last of our crew
who made it to safety."

Granum, who later became an engineer and had a decades-long career
with the Corps of Engineers, recalled seeing a co-worker, caught in the
slide, latch onto a chunk of pipeline, "which he rode like a Chinese drag-
on, covered up several times with gravel, rocks, earth, trestle poles, ledgers,

mud, and water." The man was later spotted by rescuers on one of the islands in the reservoir formed by the slide, "crawling out of the mud and all you could see were his teeth, eyes, and a big grin."

It wasn't only the rank-and-file that narrowly escaped. A carload of Corps officials, checking possible construction issues reported by a night crew, was driving on the top of the dam when the ground began to move. The group included Major Clark Kittrell, the Army Corps district engineer overseeing the Fort Peck project. "The fellow who was driving the car (identified later as Gene Tourtlotte) threw it in reverse and backed up as fast as it would go," said Mason, his account supported by statements from the Army Corps.

Helen Tourtlotte later recalled her husband's role at the wheel of the Ford sedan, noting, "by a miracle the engineers and my husband were saved." Gene Tourtlotte received a special citation for his actions, which his wife said he downplayed with this statement: "Well, you know, I was saving my own skin, too." Some survivors reported being carried by waves of dirt and rock. In some cases, the shifting material tore away clothes. Erma Bell Flaherty, who helped provide medical care to slide victims, recalled working a twelve-hour shift "cleaning mud, sand, and water out of the ears and noses of patients who were fortunate enough to have survived."

As news of the disastrous slide spread across Fort Peck, so did rumors about the soundness of the main dam. A number of those who lived nearby and downstream anxiously sought higher ground. Kittrell, despite his near-death escape, issued a statement late the day of the slide that offered assurance about the state of the main section of the dam. "A preliminary survey of the damage would not indicate that any reason for alarm should exist regarding the security of the main dam," the engineer's statement said.

While the landslide tore away a roughly 2,000-foot section of dam abutment and created a chasm 200 feet deep in places, the main dam held, and water was released through massive tunnels to reduce pressure on the dam and also to provide water for downstream navigation.

Work was halted as the Corps began to investigate what became known as the "Big Slide." The probe began with witness statements and later dug deep into the area's geology, focusing on Bear Paw Shale and a substance called bentonite.

The big dam sits on the shale, named for the north-central Montana mountain range, which, as rock goes, is weak and easily penetrable. Interlaced in the area's shale are seams of bentonite, a crystalline volcanic ash. When it gets wet, bentonite becomes very slippery; in fact it has been described as "the slickest dirt in the world."

After two years, investigators concluded that an undetected seam of bentonite below the face of the dam became wet and squeezed through cracks in the shale. As pressure increased from the weight of the rock, sand, and mud dredged from the river bottom to form the dam, its foundation essentially slid away on the shale that had been greased by the wet bentonite.

While some involved in the investigation raised other issues that may have contributed to the slide, including poor engineering and the rapid

Another view of the big slide.
PHOTOGRAPH BY ROBERT A. MIDTHUN, COURTESY U.S. ARMY CORPS OF ENGINEERS.

pace of construction that didn't allow dredged material to properly settle, the official report downplayed those concerns. The report concluded that "the slope of the dam was too steep for the material of which it was made." It placed no human blame for the slide and also concluded that the deaths and injuries were unavoidable.

As the damaged section of the dam was rebuilt, its base was widened, which lessened the steepness of the upstream face, a move intended to reduce pressure on the shale beneath. Among other steps, the Army Corps also installed instruments to measure the pressure against the face of the dam.

Speaking at the dam, prior to the Big Slide, President Roosevelt stated his confidence that the Montana dam project was "going to be carried through to the success and the glory of the nation." In October 1940, less than thirteen months after the deadly slide, the dam was declared complete, and the big upstream reservoir began to rise, fulfilling the grand vision outlined by Roosevelt and other architects of the New Deal.

Writing in the *Tribune* nearly four decades after the Big Slide, Gilluly, the Glasgow newspaper editor, tried to put the massive project into local perspective. Despite its list of watery benefits, "it was a make-work project," he wrote. "The Corps couldn't justify it all on the basis of cold economics. But in the hindsight of history, Fort Peck has proven itself."

Dam building during the Great Depression was tough, hazardous work. More than 350 miles to the west of Fort Peck, on the Flathead River near Polson, the construction of Kerr Dam (today known as Seli'š Ksanka Qlispe' Dam) killed at least fifteen workers, many of them tribal members. The deadliest incident occurred just after midnight on March 3, 1937, when a series of rockslides killed eight workers and injured three others. Investigators concluded that melting snow may have loosened rocks and dirt that slid and buried the workers as they readied the site of the dam's foundation for the placement of concrete.

While the official number of work-related deaths at Fort Peck sits at fifty-nine, writer M. R. Montgomery, in his article in *The New Yorker*,

Building Fort Peck Dam was dangerous, including boring massive tunnels through shale, but during the Depression, men were hungry for jobs.
PHOTOGRAPH COURTESY OF U.S. ARMY CORPS OF ENGINEERS.

noted that number does not include those who died from "tunnel pneumonia," an often deadly respiratory condition caused when workers breathed the abrasive shale dust created during the boring of the dam's massive intake tunnels that allow water to pass through the dam. Montgomery's article, headlined "Impalpable Dust," appeared in the March 27, 1989, issue of *The New Yorker*. Montgomery's father was an engineer who worked on the dam's concrete spillway. Even though he left Fort Peck before the Big Slide, Montgomery's father over the years shared concerns about poor engineering on the project and its possible role in the deaths on that September afternoon in 1938.

The elder Montgomery even spoke of the haunting incident on his deathbed in 1981, forty-three years after the disaster. "It was the last thing he would remember," his son wrote.

SOURCES

Hauser Dam Failure

Great Falls Tribune. April 15–17, 1908.

Helena Independent. March 13, 1908.

Kirk, Cecil H. *A History of the Montana Power Company.* Published by Donn
Kirk, 2008.

Parrett, Aaron. "The Huge Mass Writhed and Screamed Like a Live Thing:
Revisiting the Failure of Hauser Dam." *Montana The Magazine of Western
History.* Winter 2009.

Fort Peck Dam Landslide

Billings Gazette. September 23–24 1938.

Doig, Ivan. *Bucking the Sun.* Simon & Schuster, 1996.

Gilluly, Sam. "Fort Peck Dam-Reservoir Has Proven Itself." *Great Falls Tribune.*
July 24, 1977.

Great Falls Tribune. September 23–25, 1938.

Montgomery, M. R. "Impalpable Dust." *The New Yorker.* March 27, 1989.

Quinn, Kevin R. "A Short Course in a Big Dam's History." U.S. Army Corps
of Engineers, Omaha District. June 23, 2012.

"Then Came the Slide of 1938." www.FortPeckDam.com.

U.S. Army Corp of Engineers, Omaha District. "Historical Vignette: Fort Peck
Dam." January 26, 2015.

U.S. Army Corps of Engineers, Omaha District. "Fort Peck Dam: 75 Years
of Service. 2012.

FLOODS

WHEN HISTORIAN K. ROSS TOOLE DESCRIBED MONTANA AS A STATE of extremes, he was making an observation about politics, history, and geography. Variabilities in the Big Sky state's climate and weather only added to Toole's assertion. Montana holds the record for the coldest temperature ever recorded in the Lower 48 at 70 below zero at Rogers Pass on January 20, 1954, but the mercury has also hit a sweltering 117 degrees, in Glendive on July 20, 1893, and again at Medicine Lake on July 5, 1937.

A look at precipitation averages also reveals Montana's extremes. In the northwest, the high elevations of Glacier National Park average about sixty inches of precipitation each year. In south-central Montana's Carbon County, near the Clark's Fork of the Yellowstone River, the yearly precipitation is just 6.6 inches, the lowest in the state.

Rain and snowmelt, when it happens in rapid, dramatic fashion, has spawned tragedy across Montana. In May and June of 1908, Montana saw some of the worst flooding in its history as snowmelt and steady rains pushed streams and rivers out of their banks across the central and southwestern valleys. Flooding was widespread, damaging property, roads, bridges, and rail lines from Great Falls and Livingston to Butte, Missoula, and points west. At Fort Benton, Missouri River flows measured 140,000 cubic feet per second (cfs). To put that in perspective, that same gauging station has never topped 80,000 cfs in the decades since.

Floodwaters attack the Orr home in Missoula in 1908.
PHOTOGRAPH COURTESY OF ARCHIVES AND SPECIAL COLLECTIONS,
MANSFIELD LIBRARY, THE UNIVERSITY OF MONTANA.

The following stories recount similar spring surpluses that led to catastrophic flooding—in one instance, relatively localized, and in the other, at least as widespread and devastating as those surging waters of 1908.

GRAVELLY COULEE FLOOD, 1938
DOWN INTO THE VALLEY OF DEATH

The Bears Paw Mountains (locally often called the Bear Paws) south of Havre stand tall amid the grazing and grain country that surrounds them. With the tallest of the mountains reaching nearly 7,000 feet, the landmark island range is a magnet for moisture in the mostly arid region of north-central Montana. In the winter, it's snow. In the spring and early summer, it's rain that renders the mountains and nearby hills a dark green.

The water from the mountains drains into a series of coulees, eventually making its way into creeks that deposit water into the Milk River to the north and the Missouri to the south. For many decades, ranchers and others have tried to capture some of the seasonal runoff in reservoirs notched into the coulees.

Because they provided a source of water, the coulees were also logical places for rural families to build homes. In 1938, there were five to seven homes along Gravelly Coulee east of Laredo, a tiny railroad community about a dozen miles southwest of Havre.

In the late afternoon of June 23, 1938, rain began to pound the Bears Paw Mountains and a wide swath of Montana. In what was later described as a cloudburst, water stormed down the draws that fed Gravelly Coulee on the Bears Paw's northwest flank. Margaret Tow was cooking supper when the water began to rush by the family home near the bottom of the coulee. After some discussion with her husband, Wilfrid, dinner was scrapped and the family scrambled up a nearby hill, reaching the crest just in time to see their home washed away by a twenty-foot-high wave of water.

"All the water came down around where our home was and took the house, the barns and everything," recalled daughter Agnes Tow Cook when she was interviewed by historian Joe Manning in 2008. (A portion of the interview is posted on Manning's website, Mornings on Maple Street.)

The Tow family was lucky that day, as were the neighboring families of D. E. Couch and Frank Earl. All told, twenty-two members of the three families were left homeless, even shoeless, by the flash flood. Occupants of three other homes up the coulee likely never had a chance.

Laredo, Montana, near Gravelly Coulee.
FARM SECURITY ADMINISTRATION PHOTOGRAPH,
COURTESY OF THE LIBRARY OF CONGRESS,
LC-USF34- 057986-D [P&P] LOT 503.

Emil and Mildred DeHaan and their four daughters, Donna, seven; Emily, five; Elaine Lois, three; and Flora Catherine, nineteen months; perished in the waters that rampaged down Gravelly Coulee. So did neighbors Herman Wendt, Charles Pratt, and James Brown.

"I think the DeHaans were in the house and did not see it," Margaret Tow told a *Havre Daily News* reporter a few days after the flood. "They had the highest hill near them of any of the families, and they only had to go out their back door to reach it. They probably never saw it until the flood hit them."

Tow also speculated that Pratt and Brown were likely in the basement of a home above the DeHaan place, "and you never hear much in the basement." From the safety of the hill, the Tow family not only saw their home destroyed but watched as the homes of the Earl and Couch families floated by, followed later by the DeHaan house.

"Dad saw it coming right away," Agnes Cook recalled. "He made everybody get out right away." After helping his family to the home of the nearby Cook family on higher ground, Wilfrid Tow sought to help others. "Dad went back and swam the horse across the creek far enough so that he could help members of the other two families, the Earls and Couches, and take them up there also," Agnes said. More than twenty people found refuge at the Cook home. "Some of them slept in cars, some in garages, some in the house."

Parts of some of the homes were found ten miles away. Some of the bodies were found by searchers several miles away, partially buried in mud. All but one of the bodies was found within hours after the floodwaters receded. It was a week later that searchers found three-year-old Elaine DeHaan.

Witnesses reported several surges of water coming down Gravelly Coulee, and Hal Stearns of the *Havre Daily News* wrote that a small dam about six miles above the DeHaan ranch burst during the deluge, possibly creating one of the deadly surges. After visiting the coulee, Stearns noted that none of the families "were able to salvage a single possession of value" after the flash flood.

MONTANA WEATHER
Partly cloudy Friday and Saturday, scattered thundershowers east of divide Friday.

The Billings Gazette

FINAL MORNING EDITION

WYOMING WEATHER
Partly cloudy Friday and Saturday, scattered thundershowers east, extreme south portion Friday.

VOL. L—NO. 232.   ASSOCIATED PRESS   BILLINGS, MONTANA, FRIDAY, JUNE 24, 1938.   UNITED PRESS   PRICE FIVE CENTS.

AT LEAST 9 PERISH IN MONTANA FLOOD

LATIN AMERICA QUITTING WORLD BODY

The Washington Scene . . .
By David Lawrence
(Copyright, 1938.)

GOOD NEIGHBOR POLICY OF U. S. IS ONE REASON

Diminished Prestige of Geneva League, Financial Burden, Distance Are Others.

NICARAGUA IS TO QUIT MONDAY

Honduras Steps Out July 10; Eight Out of 20 Have Quit or Are About to Take Move

WASHINGTON, June 23.—(P)—The republic of Latin America are gradually drifting away from the league of nations.

LAUNCH 'SALES, JOBS' DRIVE

HERE JULY 12

BEET GROWERS TO GET BENEFIT CHECKS FRIDAY

$35,000 to Be Distributed in County as First Payment on Total of $325,000.

HIGHEST SINGLE SUM IS $1,646

Government Paying Producers $1.94 Per Ton Under Program; Cuts Factory Price.

MARION E. MARTIN, who claims the Republican national committee, will address a party dinner gathering here July 16 and speak in five cities of the state.

VICE CHAIRMAN OF REPUBLICANS TO SPEAK HERE

National Committee Officer to Appear in Five Cities of State Next Month

G-MAN QUITS

FORMER G-MAN, GOVERNMENT IN FIGHT ON STORY

L. G. Turrou Seeks to Print Discoveries in His Rounding Up of Spy Ring of Germans

THRONG ATTENDS MASS MEETING IN HIGH SCHOOL

About 300 of Local Businessmen and Others Prepare for Campaign in Area.

FINAL DETAILS ARE IRONED OUT

Tremendous Benefits of Plan Are Given by Remote Control Speeches Thursday.

INFANT IS MISSING IN SECTION SOUTH OF HAVRE THURSDAY

Series of Cloudbursts Inundate Wide Areas; Damage Will Amount to Thousands of Dollars; Harlem Residents Evacuate Homes; Jordan Is Menaced by High Waters.

Havre, June 23.—(AP)—Nine persons were drowned Thursday night in flood-waters that poured down northern Montana coulees in torrents after cloudbursts swept the area.

FLOOD SWEEPS LAUREL

Water Running Foot Deep in Business Area Early Friday.

Laurel, Friday, June 24.—(Special)—Floodwaters at midnight Thursday ran eight to 10 inches down the valley.

P. E. O. MEETING TO OPEN FRIDAY

Red Lodge Is Scene of State Convention of Women's Groups.

W. M. REID, 76, PIONEER STATE STOCKMAN, DIES

Settled in Rosebud County in '86 After Traveling Chisholm Trail From Texas.

I Notice in The Gazette

THE WEATHER.
LOCAL WEATHER REPORT.

STATE WEATHER REPORT.

GAS BURNS KILL CALIFORNIA BOY

Accident Occurs at Casper; Was on Way to Rail Wreck Rites.

200 Are Minus Homes As Result of Blaze

OIL WELL BLAST FATAL TO SEVEN

Five Others Seriously Injured; New Mexico Is Tragedy Scene.

CROP SURPLUSES GET ATTENTION

American Farm Bureau Convenes Annual Meet in Park.

URGE LEGIONNAIRES CARRY ON ITS AMERICAN PROGRAM

HELENA, June 23.—(P)—An appeal to members to carry on the projects and ideals of the American Legion and the auxiliary-Americanism, good citizenship and national defense—was made by national officers of the two organizations at a joint meeting that featured the annual American Legion state convention session here Thursday.

VITAL STATISTICS.

NAME COLLINS DELEGATE TO UNITY CONFERENCE

E. E. COLLINS of Billings was named as delegate of Montana Methodist conference laymen to the Methodist unity conference to be held at St. Louis, Mo., next April at a special meeting of the layman's organization here Thursday afternoon.

The June 24, 1938, edition of *The Billings Gazette* cited floods across much of the state but led with the deaths in Gravelly Coulee.
PHOTOGRAPH COURTESY OF *THE BILLINGS GAZETTE.*

Officials estimated that as much as five inches of rain fell on the Bears Paw Mountains that afternoon, sending torrents of water down coulees and creeks. In Havre, normally dry Bullhook Creek washed into the city, creating rivers in the streets and flooding the basements of about three-quarters of the homes in town, the *Daily News* reported. Thirty miles east of Havre, near Zurich, Fred Tilghman drowned in rampaging Fifteen Mile Creek. The man was sharing a house with another man, Swanson Moore, when the water came, "and both were running for higher ground when Tilghman lost his footing and was swept away in the flood," according to the *Daily News*.

The heavy rain was widespread. Flooding in varying degrees was reported on the Milk River in Harlem; around Great Falls, Lewistown, and Billings; in Townsend, southeast of Helena; and in the Meaderville neighborhood of Butte. In the day after the downpour, the Montana Power Company reported that Missouri River flows near Great Falls climbed from 16,000 cubic feet per second to more than 30,000 cubic feet per second. In the Fort Benton area, officials reported that twenty-seven small bridges were washed out and that the Carter ferry sank after being swamped by high water. Near Laredo, two miles of the Great Northern rail line was washed out by floodwaters.

In the days after their home was swept away, the Tow family moved to a section house owned by the railroad in the little community. The family, with disaster relief assistance, later bought the house and moved it to a small parcel of land nearby.

Wilfrid Tow with his children in 1941, three years after the flood took their home in Gravelly Coulee. Agnes Tow is third from left. PHOTOGRAPH BY MARION POST WOLCOTT, FARM SECURITY ADMINISTRATION, COURTESY OF THE LIBRARY OF CONGRESS, LC-USF34-057988-D.

The Couch family, which averted tragedy at Gravelly Coulee, was not as fortunate. The family found a home about eleven miles southwest of Laredo, and in early July, several of the Couch children went to a nearby reservoir to swim and bathe. Three girls apparently slipped from some rocks into deep water and began to scream. According to news accounts, Drusilla Couch, fourteen, ran into the water to help the girls, despite not being able to swim. While two other girls were pulled from the water by a brother, Drusilla and her sister June, ten, drowned. Their deaths occurred just a little more than three weeks after the Gravelly Coulee flood that took nine lives.

The six members of the DeHaan family—Emil, Mildred, and their four daughters—are buried in Highland Cemetery in Havre. The headstone of their neighbor, Charles Pratt, sits nearby. The unmarked grave of James Brown, who had left his wife in Indiana in search of work and had been hired by Pratt just a few days before the flood, is also in the Havre cemetery; his wife could not afford a headstone or to have his body shipped home. The other victim, Herman Wendt, who had no relatives in Montana, was buried in Green Bay, Wisconsin.

In a front-page commentary on the watery tumult of June 1938, the *Havre Daily News* noted that while financial losses stemming from the area flooding were substantial, "they sink into insignificance beside the havoc wrought in Gravelly Coulee." The article added, "The immortal souls who went down into the valley of death when the relentless flood poured out of the Bears Paw Mountains are not replaceable by humble mortals."

FLATHEAD FLOOD, 1964
A PRIZE-WINNING FLOOD

In 1946, just after the end of World War II, Columbia Falls, like many other parts of the country, was ready for better times. And just a few miles up the South Fork of the Flathead River, the federal government had plans for a big dam that would generate jobs, growth, and opportunity.

Mel Ruder, a North Dakota native and U.S. Navy veteran, came to the Flathead Valley in 1946 with a typewriter, a camera, and a few thousand dollars in savings. Encouraged by the editor of the Whitefish newspaper, he started a weekly newspaper in Columbia Falls in a space shared with a liquor store. With no subscribers or advertisers, it was far from a can't-miss proposition; four other newspapers had failed in the little town between Whitefish and Glacier National Park.

But the *Hungry Horse News,* named for the dam that arose in the steep gorge up the South Fork, took root in the community, nurtured by good timing and Ruder's hard work. By the early 1960s, the newspaper had developed a reputation for its coverage of Glacier National Park, community doings, and its generous use of photographs—sometimes three or four per week—a marvel given the printing capabilities of the time.

In the spring of 1964, buoyed by the dam boom and the construction of the Anaconda Company aluminum smelting plant in the mid-1950s, the population of Columbia Falls was about 2,300, while the little weekly newspaper filled with positive news about "babies, beasts, and beauties" had a paid circulation of more than 3,700.

In its June 5, 1964, issue, the *Hungry Horse News* noted the imminent opening of Glacier's Going-to-the-Sun Road, despite the record amounts of deep, wet snow still lingering in the mountains of the park and across northwest Montana. In the Hellroaring drainage on Big Mountain above Whitefish, there were still fifty-three inches of snow on May 29, the newspaper reported.

The rain started the next day. Within the next few days, officials estimated that up to fifteen inches of rain fell on the snow-laden mountains along the Continental Divide, triggering what the U.S. Geological Survey labeled "the most severe flooding in modern times" in northwest Montana.

For decades, the Dalimata family had lived in Nyack, a tiny community in a tight valley along the Middle Fork of the Flathead River, raising hay and cattle and cutting timber. When the rains came in 1964, the Middle Fork, draining a huge swath of high country, rose furiously. The force of the rampaging river snapped off trees two to three feet in diameter at Nyack, witnesses said.

"The thing I remember is the noise, this great roar," John Dalimata, who was twenty-two years old in 1964, recalled forty years later in the Kalispell *Daily Inter Lake*. "It was terrifying." Dalimata and family members tried to find safe ground for their cattle as water rose rapidly. Much of their herd was washed away. "There were cattle bawling, elk barking," Dalimata said. "Everything was going down river."

Some cattle bearing the family brand were found days later fifty miles downstream, floating in Flathead Lake.

The floodwaters damaged or destroyed about twenty miles of U.S. Highway 2 above and below Nyack. More than six miles of Great Northern rail line was washed out, while the bridge over the Middle Fork at West Glacier—the primary route to Glacier Park's west side—buckled and was rendered unusable. Clobbered by flooding on both sides of the Continental Divide, Glacier National Park was left largely inaccessible.

Eight months pregnant, Ruth Dalimata, John's wife, and a few others were evacuated from Nyack by an airplane that was able to land on a strip of undamaged highway. "As Ruth was flying out, she could see the railroad tunnel just west of here," her husband said. "There was a full stream of water squirting out of it like a garden hose."

The floodwaters surged downstream, with farms, towns, and people squarely in the path. Larry Wilson, a twenty-seven-year-old teacher and the son of the Flathead County sheriff, recalled efforts to help residents find safe ground on the evening of June 7, 1964. "We started pulling trailers out from along the river, but the water kept coming up," the longtime valley resident said in 2014. "It was coming up three or four inches every five minutes. It was mind-boggling. . . . The thing is nobody believed it could be that bad. They just didn't believe it would get any higher than it had in years past."

Columbia Falls resident Leslie Blood, sixty-six, had lived near the Flathead River since 1934 and had seen numerous floods. He wasn't overly

The raging Middle Fork of the Flathead River buckled the main bridge at West Glacier.
PHOTOGRAPH COURTESY OF *HUNGRY HORSE NEWS.*

concerned. "I waited too long, like the rest," he conceded in the June 12, 1964, issue of the *Hungry Horse News.* He was joined in humility by local resident Ralph Robinson, who said, "Sure, we knew there would be heavy runoff, but not getting as high as the house."

As the water reached the broader Flathead Valley, it fanned out over the landscape from Columbia Falls south to Evergreen and west to the edge of Kalispell. On June 9 at Columbia Falls, the Flathead crested at 25.58 feet, nearly 6 feet beyond the previous record high of 19.7 feet in 1894.

The flood left an indelible impression on sixteen-year-old Bruce Young, who boarded a plane in Kalispell with his pilot father. "We flew low over the whole flood," Young recalled. "It was spectacular. . . . We saw many houses in Columbia Falls with just the rooftops showing; we saw the river had widened out of its banks, in some places a mile out.

There were animals standing in fields with just their heads above water."

For Ruder and the crew at the Columbia Falls newspaper, the rising waters were a call to duty. After hearing about the growing danger, Ruder sounded the first media alarm by sharing the news—and a series of well-timed updates—with KGEZ in Kalispell, the only radio station broadcasting in the evening hours on June 8.

In the coming week, Ruder flew over the flooded areas in a plane on numerous occasions. He also boarded a boat and took photographs while navigating the floodwaters. Finding roads washed out, Ruder drove his car on railroad tracks to get a firsthand look at conditions and damage. In addition to two regular weekly editions of the *Hungry Horse News*, Ruder and crew produced two special issues of the newspaper within an eight-day period, a total of more than 12,000 copies, all while sharing updates with the Associated Press and some daily newspapers.

For several issues, Ruder removed paid advertising to make room for more stories and photos, and told readers that the cost of producing the extra issues outstripped advertising revenue. "We like the fact that the *Hungry Horse News* did not seek profit when the Flathead had a catastrophe," Ruder wrote. "It appears this newspaper gained goodwill for attempting to do a decent job covering the flood with a camera and on-the-scene reporting. This, our small staff values."

Decades later, a Ruder friend and editor of the *Hungry Horse News* painted the efforts more glowingly. "He wanted people to know so he kept pumping out the pages," said Tom Lawrence, who eventually wrote a book about the paper and its driven publisher. "It's not an overstatement to say Mel saved people's lives. He was a tremendous journalist."

As the waters subsided, the reality of the scope of the flood settled across much of the valley. Along with damage to Highway 2 and the Great Northern rail line, access to Glacier National Park was cut off for several weeks until an old bridge just upstream from West Glacier could be reinforced and opened to vehicle traffic. Flood damage in the park, the state's leading tourist attraction, totaled in the millions, by National Park Service estimates. Water backing up McDonald Creek from the raging Middle Fork damaged a motel in Apgar. The Lake McDonald Lodge took on water from a nearby creek, while over the divide, the Many Glacier Hotel had more than a foot of water in its lower levels.

Lower McDonald Creek backed up into the lake, swamping the Village Inn in Apgar.
PHOTOGRAPH BY J. MOHLHENRICH, COURTESY OF *HUNGRY HORSE NEWS.*

In Glacier National Park, multiple sections of the Going-to-the-Sun Road were damaged, including this washout at the West Side Tunnel.
PHOTOGRAPH BY WILLIAM S. KELLER, COURTESY OF *HUNGRY HORSE NEWS.*

The Going-to-the-Sun Road was damaged by washouts and rockslides. It didn't open until June 30 and became the only vehicle route linking the park's east and west sides for much of the summer. The Great Northern hired 750 additional workers to repair and reopen its transcontinental rail line that runs along the park's southern border, finishing the job in late June.

Flooding undermined the Great Northern Railway tracks near West Glacier.
PHOTOGRAPH COURTESY OF *HUNGRY HORSE NEWS.*

Flathead Lake's surface level peaked at just above 2,894 feet, which was several feet short of levels reached in 1933 and 1894. But there was little doubt that the presence of Hungry Horse Dam, which corralled waters in the South Fork of the Flathead, played a big role in keeping the lake from reaching a historic high.

Jerry Mahugh, a nineteen-year-old college student driving home to the Flathead from Oregon, recalled his first glimpse of the big lake: "The lake was chocolate brown and there were houses and parts of houses and entire trees with leaves and root systems just floating around. I was in a state of shock because nobody had told me anything and I had no idea what had happened. I thought the dam had broke or someone had bombed it."

When the rains ended, residents began to take measure of the disaster. Officials estimated that nearly 400 homes were damaged by floodwaters and 1,200 head of cattle and pigs were lost. Three barge loads of dead livestock were pulled from Flathead Lake in the weeks after the flood. The total damage estimate on the west side of the divide was pegged at more than $24 million.

In the pages of the *Hungry Horse News*, talk turned to dams. Hungry Horse, locals noted, had kept the historic flood from being even more devastating. The thinking went, wouldn't dams on the other two forks of the Flathead River safeguard the region from flooding? One letter writer noted that a proposed Spruce Park dam in the Middle Fork drainage, rather than being "a crack-pot scheme," was a viable way to stop floodwaters. "Only then," the writer said, "will people in the valley be secure."

Ruder, ever the local economic booster, editorially supported the idea of more dams. But the dam talk receded as the valley dried out. Ruder and the crew at the newspaper returned to the less dramatic diet of local news.

In the wake of the historic flood, Ruder asked Dorothy Johnson to write a letter nominating his little newspaper for the highest honor in U.S. journalism, the Pulitzer Prize. Johnson had grown up in Whitefish and found fame as an author and storyteller—two of her most acclaimed stories,

"The Hanging Tree" and "The Man Who Shot Liberty Valance," became movies. She took on the task with gusto, recalling the history of the *Hungry Horse News*, its remarkable flood coverage, and the efforts of Ruder himself. "I have known Mel Ruder for 15 years," she wrote. "He is a man of integrity, of high ideals, of resolution and dedication. His coverage of the flood is proof of these qualities."

Ruder received news of becoming the first Montanan to win a Pulitzer in May 1965, about eleven months after the big flood, while he was taking photos of local children at a farm. A few weeks later, people in Columbia Falls organized a banquet in his honor. A big box at the newspaper held the many letters and telegrams of congratulations. Ruder and his wife, Ruth, used the $1,000 prize as seed money for a scholarship fund in Columbia Falls. (Ruder won the 1965 Pulitzer Prize for Local Reporting for coverage of the 1964 flood. *The Wall Street Journal* won the award the previous year for coverage of an oil swindle. The following year, *The Los Angeles Times* won the local reporting honor for its coverage of the Watts riots. The only other Montana journalism Pulitzer was awarded to Eric Newhouse of the *Great Falls Tribune* in 2000, when his stories about the impact of alcohol abuse on the local community were honored in the explanatory reporting category.)

While proud of the work that he and his crew accomplished at the newspaper in covering the biggest flood in at least a century, he later deflected credit for the Pulitzer, saying, "I got the thing by the grace of God and Dorothy Johnson."

FLOOD OF '64, BLACKFEET RESERVATION
ONE BY ONE, CHILDREN FLOATED AWAY

In the shadow of the jagged peaks of Glacier National Park and the Rocky Mountain Front, the Two Medicine River and Birch Creek carry water from the high country out to the prairie, feeding farms, ranches, and communities before blending quietly into the Marias River. The Marias, in turn, winds its way to the Missouri, the great river that drains much of Montana.

For many residents of the southern Blackfeet Indian Reservation, the creek bottomland is an oasis. The valleys offer shelter from the punishing wind, trees along the banks provide summer shade and wood for winter heat, and the creeks yield water for humans and livestock. Dams, built to store water for downstream users, brought predictable flows and a semblance of control to those who lived along Birch and Two Medicine.

The spring of 1964 was a cold one. Mountain snowpack at many northwest Montana gauges was as much as 75 percent above normal in May. Early in the month, a National Weather Service climatologist issued a statement about the cold and snow and inevitable arrival of warmth, writing, "We aren't in trouble unless we get a sudden warming and snowpack melts all at once. However, we don't look for that to happen—very rarely does snowmelt by itself cause flooding. But if we get rain on top of it . . . then we're in trouble."

The trouble, first a trickle and quickly a torrent, came in the second week of June. At first, the rain was welcomed. The Blackfeet Reservation had been parched by drought for several years. But the downpour clawed at the snow, rivers and streams rose, and the skies didn't lighten for days. "It came down as one pours from a cup, without stopping, all at once," a Blackfeet elder named Fish Wolf Robe told interviewer Helen West years later.

In a roughly thirty-six-hour period, seven inches of rain was reported at Babb, in the northern part of the reservation, while St. Mary saw nine inches. Some accounts said higher elevations along the Rocky Mountain Front received as much as fifteen inches over several days. The rain, combined with rapidly melting snow, produced water of unfathomable quantity, all of it headed downhill.

For officials at the Blackfeet Indian Agency in Browning, the fierce rain was quick to produce concern. Hundreds of families lived along the creeks that tumbled from the mountains to the plains and bisected the reservation. To the north of Browning is Cut Bank Creek. The Two Medicine River, with a dam up near the mountains, is about a dozen miles south of town. Birch Creek, which marks the southern boundary of the reservation, is closer to the farm town of Valier. In Birch Creek's upper reaches, a reservoir is held by Swift Dam. Other creeks, including Badger Creek, are between the Two Medicine and Birch.

The first hint of tragedy came early on June 8 with a report of a man high in a tree surrounded by the surging waters of the Two Medicine River. Rescuers were dispatched, along with school buses intended to bring residents of imperiled drainages to Browning and Heart Butte. The buses transported some but were often stymied by deep water and washed-out bridges along reservation roads and U.S. Highway 89. The telephone system on much of the reservation had failed hours earlier, and officials used two-way radios to communicate. Some people were able to get news updates and emergency dispatches via KSEN, a Shelby-based radio station. Others faced the disaster quickly unfolding around them with no word from the outside world.

Reservation road superintendent Elmer Morigeau encountered a dramatic scene on the morning of June 8. Driving on a gravel road that ran along the Two Medicine, he spotted a flat-bed truck loaded with people making its way across the river's bottomland, carving a path through water. Morigeau continued down the river to gauge conditions and possibly warn others of the rising water. Retracing his route later, he spotted the truck stalled in a low spot, water climbing toward the cab, people clinging to the vehicle in swirling waters. Via two-way radio, he summoned help and asked for a boat.

Rescuers at one point tossed a tire secured by barbed wire into the raging current, trying to reach the truck and the stranded. Two people were eventually pulled to safety by the tire, while others were later reached by boat. Nine others, members of a large, extended family, succumbed to the vicious, frigid current. Many were young children—the youngest was two-month-old Terry Lee Guardipee; the oldest victim was eighty-four-year-old Rose Grant.

One of the survivors told interviewers that she and other adult occupants of the truck faced a horrible dilemma when the tire came close enough to grab. "The children were too little to send in alone [on the tire] and we couldn't go ourselves and leave them behind on the truck," said Fay Grant.

The horror of Grant and fellow survivor Lucille Guardipee, the mothers of some of the youngest victims, was later recounted by Nellie Buel in the pages of the *Great Falls Tribune.* "One by one, Lucille's children floated away," Buel wrote. "The baby first, two months old, who had been clinging to Lucille's neck, and then the others. Then Fay's little five-year-old floated away."

Another unimaginable tragedy unfolded that June morning to the south on Birch Creek. The Hall home sat not far below Swift Dam, and Tom Hall Jr., the family patriarch, worked for the canal company that parceled out the irrigation water from the reservoir. After several days of rain and cold, Hall left his home and sleeping family early that morning to buy groceries in Dupuyer. He returned to see the home and his family members being shoved down the creek by a wall of water. He never again saw his wife, Dorothy, thirty-three; and his children, Thomas, twelve; Marjorie, ten; Kathy, six; Martin, four; Edward, two; and Judy, one.

Swift Dam was the first to be breached, likely during the late-morning hours. The dam on the Two Medicine apparently failed later in the day—no witness accounts are available. Water cascading down from higher elevations put great pressure on the dams and later came over the top, washing away rock and other fill before breaching the face of the structures, sending waves of water downstream. Many believe that the nineteen victims along Birch Creek likely perished within minutes of the dam's collapse.

Flooding washed away a large portion of Lower Two Medicine Dam.
PHOTOGRAPH BY JOHN J. PALMER, COURTESY OF *HUNGRY HORSE NEWS.*

Evidence of the dam breach on Birch Creek was observed within minutes by those downstream. Abe Rutherford, who lived with his family near the creek, shared the events of June 8 in a story published in *Newsweek* magazine a few weeks after the disaster. Noting the rapidly rising water near his home, Rutherford said he was preparing to move family members up a nearby hill when a boy on the hill screamed, "The dam is busted." Rutherford wrote, "We started to run. We got a little more than halfway up the hill when it came—a wall of water 40 feet high. It took out our house. We got away with nothing but what we were wearing."

Flying over the valley, possibly minutes after the dam burst, pilot Jim Farrer of Shelby told of seeing buildings and livestock being swept downstream. "The most amazing sight," he recalled, "was the crest taking away ranches and snapping telephone and power lines like matches. It was unbelievable." The pilot estimated the wall of water moved downstream at about twenty-two miles per hour.

Reservation resident Woody Kipp recalls listening to a remarkable account of the Birch Creek flooding on KSEN, which had hired the plane to survey the situation. The airborne broadcaster told of a herd of horses running down the creek bed, directly away from the fast-moving water, only to be overtaken and disappear from sight. (KSEN broadcast what was likely life-saving coverage around the clock for five days without any advertising and garnered a national broadcasting award for the radio station.)

Patrick Wyse, the coroner in Pondera County, which was home to the dam and much of Birch Creek, said those who escaped the raging water reported it making "tremendous noise" as it roared eastward. "There was so very little warning that it was amazing how many people got out," he said a few days after the peak flooding. "The rubble is fantastic. The whole Birch Creek valley was swept clean of timber." The coroner also noted that the plan to search for the bodies of the missing would cover an area forty miles long and five to fifteen miles wide.

The U.S. Geological Survey measured the flow of water down Birch Creek after the dam break at 881,000 cubic feet per second (cfs), far greater than the average 400,000 to 700,000 cfs flow of the Mississippi River at St. Louis. Many still marvel at that number, noting the measurement was made seventeen miles below the dam and may have, in reality, understated the peak flow.

While the greatest human tragedy was undeniably on Birch Creek and the Two Medicine River, the tentacles of the flood stretched well beyond the southern portion of the reservation.

Floodwaters surround the Holy Family Mission on the Blackfeet Reservation.
PHOTOGRAPH COURTESY OF THE MONTANA HISTORICAL SOCIETY RESEARCH CENTER.

Woody Kipp, then eighteen and headed to the U.S. Marine Corps, was living on the family ranch along Cut Bank Creek, northeast of Browning. There was no dam upstream, but the creek was a conduit for water gushing from the nooks and crannies of Glacier National Park.

"We had a big wall of water come down, probably from some of the big beaver dams up near Starr School," Kipp recalled nearly fifty years after the flood. "They held back the water, for a while." Kipp, along with his brother John and sister-in-law Mildred, filled sandbags for much of the day on June 8. During a brief meal break, the creek rose to the doorstep of the family's home. The trio fled for higher ground, an escape aided by a four-wheel-drive truck, which at the time, like a telephone, was a rarity in the rural reaches of the reservation. "Within a few minutes, the water was waist deep in the house," Kipp said. "We spent the entire night on about a half-acre of land that didn't get inundated," accompanied by chickens, pigs, and other farm animals. A radio in the truck snagged the KSEN

Water overtopped Gibson Dam during the 1964 flood.
PHOTOGRAPH COURTESY OF THE U.S. GEOLOGICAL SURVEY.

signal, sharing with the stranded family the news of the dam failures and the gloom of tragedy elsewhere on the reservation. The Kipps lost some livestock, but the family home survived.

Similar run-for-your-life accounts unfolded in the days after the crisis. Many families spent hours on hilltops and were later ferried to safety by helicopters from Malmstrom Air Force Base in Great Falls. Near Valier, a group of nearly 100 people found refuge from Birch Creek's rage in a rural schoolhouse. In Choteau, south of the reservation, the water of the Teton River and local creeks corralled much of the community and forced 2,000 residents to evacuate. West of Augusta near where the Sun River leaves the mountains, water overtopped Gibson Dam. The concrete structure somehow held.

But below the dam, the Sun was forging a path of destruction as it made its way to the Missouri at Great Falls. West of Simms, the normally docile river carried dead livestock and debris and, according to one news account, a large barn that somehow remained whole. In Great Falls, the armada of flotsam included bathtubs.

All told, fifteen Montana counties were hit by the flooding; eight of those were declared disaster areas by President Lyndon Johnson. Thirty-one people were dead—all but one on the Blackfeet Reservation—and 337 injured. The other known death was that of Joseph Westfield, seventy, who was last seen on the evening of June 8, 1964, as he left to move cattle away from the Sun River on a ranch east of Augusta. His skeletal remains were found in October 1966 by three teenage hunters about two miles from his ranch home. Bits of clothing helped identify Westfield, who was the subject of an intense search in June 1964.

On the Blackfeet Reservation alone, 256 homes were destroyed. "It was the worst natural disaster ever to hit this state," Montana governor Tim Babcock said at the time. Government estimates in 1964 put the tab at $62 million.

While the disaster made the front pages of *The New York Times* and the *Chicago Tribune* in the days after the flooding and subsequent deaths, in the ensuing months, the story was largely left to the *Glacier Reporter*, the weekly newspaper in Browning. The paper shared news of the search for bodies, typhoid inoculations, boil-water orders, and of families living first in tents and later in hastily constructed "flood homes." (The initial batch of flood homes was constructed in Browning, with the first home placed near tribal headquarters. The homes were modeled after those used in Alaska after a large earthquake earlier in 1964, according to Earl Old Person. "They were supposed to be temporary," he said in a 2019 interview. "But some people are still living in these homes." The flood homes lured some residents from rural areas and remain a reminder of how the flood altered life for reservation residents.)

The newspaper also reflected people's grief and the post-flood rumor mill. Lucille Guardipee responded to gossip in a letter published in the *Reporter* on July 23. "I've been hearing rumors yet—people wondering why all my children drowned and I didn't. I wish some of those people had been in my place at that time—they'd know the reason," she wrote, in part. "People are saying we were warned and why didn't we leave then. We were not warned. I sure wish people would quit talking because I feel bad enough and to hear these remarks and rumors makes me feel I am to blame for the death of my children. I tried my best to save them but God took them. No one will ever know how lonely I feel."

The Blackfeet Tribal Council declared June 8 a permanent day of mourning on the reservation. Each year, ceremonies marking the flood and its human toll are held at the Museum of the Plains Indian in Browning. In the wake of the flood, the Blackfeet Tribal Council hired an archivist at the museum, Helen West, to interview reservation residents about the tragedy. Some of those interviews, published in 1970 in *Flood—The Story of the 1964 Disaster*, provide an intimate look at the tragedy.

In the weeks after the flood, a stunned pall descended over the reservation. "This was something that hurt people a lot, especially those that lost people," recalled Earl Old Person, who was chairman of the Blackfeet

Tribal Council in 1964 and later became chief of the tribe. "Everything just came to a halt. Things just didn't happen for a long time. But then people came back and tried to encourage people who lost their homes or family members. It was sad, but people came back, came back strong."

Out on the Two Medicine River and Birch Creek, fifty-five years after the flood, there are no interpretive sites or even highway signs sharing the story of the tragic "500-year flood." Within a few years, the dams were rebuilt. While the creek beds still show signs of the flood's intense scouring, some trees have grown back.

For many, the memories of 1964 haven't been diminished by the decades. Phillip Rattler was at the Two Medicine River and took part in the attempt to rescue those in the stalled truck. "I watched them drown," he said in a 2014 interview published in the *Great Falls Tribune*. "I used to see them screaming and hollering in my sleep."

Tom Hall Jr. lived just sixteen years after floodwaters took his entire family. "I think it was something he thought about a lot," Mary Barkoske, a Swift Dam tender acquainted with Hall, told an interviewer. According to acquaintances, Hall turned to alcohol to quell the memories. "I'm not sure it's stretching it to say Tommy Hall was another fatality from the dam collapse. It just took him awhile."

SOURCES

Gravelly Coulee Flood

Bernhardt, Dave. National Weather Service, Great Falls, Montana. Personal interview. June 2019.

Billings Gazette. "At Least 9 Perish in Montana Flood." June 24, 1938.

Great Falls Tribune. June 24–29, 1938.

Havre Daily News. June 24–30, 1938.

Manning, Joe. Mornings on Maple Street, www.morningsonmaplestreet.com. Interview with Agnes Tow Cook, 2008.

Montana Standard, Butte, Montana. "Girls Drown in Reservoir." July 12, 1938.

Flathead Flood

Boner, F. C. and Frank Stermitz. "Floods of 1964 in Northwestern Montana."
  U.S. Geological Survey. 1967.

Daily Inter Lake, Kalispell, Montana. "Torrents of Rain, Miles of Misery: 1964." 2004.

Flathead Beacon, Kalispell, Montana. "When All Hell Came Down the Mountains."
  March 28, 2014.

Great Falls Tribune. "It Was a Nightmare Along the Flathead in 1964 Flood."
  May 31, 2014.

Hungry Horse News, Columbia Falls, Montana. June 5–26, 1964.

Johnson, Dorothy M. "No Scrapbook Needed: Ruder's Pulitzer Nomination."
  Montana Journalism Review. Spring 1966. Dorothy Johnson Collection,
  Archives and Special Collections, Mansfield Library, University of Montana.

The New York Times. "Glacier National Park After Montana Floods." June 21, 1964.

Blackfeet Flood

Glacier Reporter, Browning, Montana. June and July 1964.

Great Falls Tribune. June 1964

Great Falls Tribune. "Augusta's 1964 Flood Victim Found." October 31, 1966.

Great Falls Tribune. "Drama at the Head Gates." May 27, 2014.

Kipp, Woody. Personal interview. Spring 2014.

Montana Historical Society, Helena, Montana. General file on Flood of 1964.

Old Person, Earl. Personal interview. May 2019.

Parrett, Aaron. "Natural Disaster—The 1964 Flood on the Blackfeet Indian
  Reservation." *Montana The Magazine of Western History.* Summer 2004.

Puckett, Karl. "I Watched Them Drown: Worst Flood in State's History Left Death,
  Destruction in Wake." *Great Falls Tribune.* May 25, 2014.

West, Helen B. *Flood—The Story of the 1964 Disaster.* Blackfeet Tribal Council, 1970.

AVALANCHES

ON A BRIGHT AUGUST DAY MORE THAN A CENTURY AGO, FIFTY-FOUR-year-old Calvin Fletcher was high in the mountains of Glacier National Park with a group of other climbers. As they climbed on Blackfoot Glacier, one of the largest in the park, Fletcher stopped to take in the wondrous view, a moment captured by the camera of William C. Alden, a geologist with the U.S. Geological Survey.

Then, as Fletcher, a doctor from Indiana with a penchant for traveling the world, was making his way across the glacier, a mass of ice and snow swept down from above and carried him away. When reached by Alden and others, the physician's serious injuries were apparent, and rescuers scrambled to get him off the mountain. Alden recalled the rescue effort and Fletcher's final words in a note to Glacier's superintendent, writing, "He kept saying he was dying, spoke affectionately of his wife and called on Jesus to forgive his sins. He asked for brandy."

Fletcher's demise in 1913 became the first recorded death of a park visitor in the then-brief history of the mountainous national park that had been established just three years earlier in 1910. (The park's first death occurred that same year, in January, when a ranger collapsed on a snowshoe trek in bad weather.)

Many of Montana's steep mountains are streaked with avalanche chutes, where masses of snow have roared down and buried everything in their path. As more of us venture deep into the mountains to hike, ski, or snowmobile, the tally of people killed in avalanches has grown.

In the United States, an average of 27 people die each year in avalanches.

Colorado leads the nation in avalanche deaths, with a total of 275 from 1950 to 2017. Montana contributes to the annual average. Between 1950 and 2017, Montana saw a total of 111 avalanche deaths (an average of 1.7 fatalities a year), and the pace has quickened in the last twenty years. On New Year's Eve in 1993, Montana logged one of its deadliest avalanche events when five snowmobilers were killed in a slide high in the Swan Range east of Kalispell. Four of the victims—three adult men and a seven-year-old boy—were from Alberta. Also killed was forty-six-year-old Patrick Buls, a firefighter from Kalispell.

In Glacier National Park, with its steep peaks and heavy snow, avalanches have been responsible for ten deaths since 1910, the same number attributed to grizzly bears. (The leading causes of death in Glacier are falls, drownings, heart attacks, and vehicle accidents; see *Death and Survival in Glacier National Park*, by Carol Guthrie and Ann and Dan Fagre, Farcountry Press, 2017.)

This chapter tells the stories of two fatal avalanches in Montana that could not be more different from one another except that they both showcase the fearsome power of sliding snow. The first, in the winter of 1969–1970, intersected with the lives of five young Montana men on a steep slope of Glacier Park's highest mountain. In the second incident, forty-five years later, what seemed like an improbable avalanche forever left its mark on a neighborhood within Missoula city limits.

MOUNT CLEVELAND, 1969

The tallest peak in Glacier National Park stands tall above the southern end of Waterton Lake. Known originally as Kaiser Peak, it was renamed in 1898 by conservationist George Bird Grinnell in honor of U.S. president Grover Cleveland.

The north face of Mount Cleveland, seen here on January 7, 1970.
PHOTOGRAPH COURTESY OF GLACIER NATIONAL PARK ARCHIVES.

The north face of Mount Cleveland has a 4,000-foot almost sheer cliff. El Capitan, in California's Yosemite National Park and one of the most famous rock walls in the world, has a face of about 3,000 feet. At 10,448 feet, the massive Cleveland is remote and mysterious, slow to share its secrets. In the winter of 1969–1970, those secrets turned tragic.

On the day after Christmas in 1969, a band of intrepid college students and mountain climbers from Butte, Helena, Bozeman, and Bigfork left their families and the holidays behind and drove north to Glacier with a lofty goal—to scale Mount Cleveland, preferably ascending its imposing 4,000-foot north face. If conditions precluded going up the north face, the men's Plan B was to climb the mountain's more accessible west slope. Either feat would be a first: no climbers had yet reached Cleveland's summit via the north face, and the steep, avalanche-prone mountain had likely never been climbed in the depth of winter.

It was a bold plan, one that had been in the making for several years among several members of the climbing team. Jerry Kanzler, eighteen, had grown up in Columbia Falls and had climbed extensively in Glacier and elsewhere with his father and older brother before enrolling at Montana State University in Bozeman. Jim Anderson, an eighteen-year-old MSU student from Bigfork, loved climbing and had twice climbed Cleveland in warmer months. Mark Levitan, a twenty-year-old MSU student from Helena, had reached the summit of Wyoming's Grand Teton. The remaining two, Clare Pogreba and Ray Martin, were the eldest of the group, both twenty-two-year-old students at Montana Tech in Butte; they were regarded as experienced and skilled climbers.

But Cleveland, in the winter, was deemed too dangerous by some, including Bob Frauson, the St. Mary district ranger, whom the five met with the day before they started the climb. An expert winter mountaineer who had served in the U.S. Army's 10th Mountain Division in World War II, Frauson had extensive knowledge of Glacier's peaks, including Cleveland.

The ranger checked the men's gear and issued warnings about Glacier's unpredictable weather, the slim odds of rescue if they got in trouble, and Cleveland's reputation for avalanches. While there had been relatively little snow in Glacier's high country, Frauson told the climbers of a recent storm that had left the mountain coated with ice. "I talked to them a long time about the danger," the ranger said years later.

Unable to dissuade the five from attempting the climb, Frauson said the men had agreed to not attempt the north face but to undertake their climb on the mountain's west slope. They also told Frauson that they expected to complete the Cleveland climb by January 2.

The five drove to Waterton Townsite and hired a man with a boat to ferry them and their gear up the lake to the valley bottom near the base of Mount Cleveland. After a chilly ride that spanned an international border, the men landed at Glacier's remote Goat Haunt ranger station. On December 27, 1969, the boat driver, Alf Baker, dropped the five men off.

The first hint that the climbers might have found trouble came just two days later when Bud Anderson, an older brother of the Bigfork climber, flew a private plane around Cleveland to check their progress. He didn't spot his brother or any of the others. He did see tracks, maybe human, maybe a mountain goat, on the mountain's west slope. The twenty-five-year-old pilot also saw signs of a fresh avalanche near the tracks.

Two days later, Anderson, joined by a Waterton park warden, took a boat up the lake to search the area near the base of the mountain. They found only skis and snowshoes apparently cached by the climbers. A flurry of phone calls between Glacier and Waterton officials prompted another fruitless aerial search of the area.

The official search began on January 3, and over the ensuing six days would-be rescuers from Glacier and Waterton and expert alpine rescuers from nearby Canadian national parks and Grand Teton National Park traveled to the slopes of the remote Montana peak. They were joined by volunteer searchers, some of them friends or relatives of the missing climbers. But even reaching the search area was difficult as cold temperatures brought increasing ice to Waterton Lake. Snow and low clouds limited the use of aircraft, and at one point officials grounded helicopters for fear they could trigger more avalanches.

The day after the discovery of the skis and snowshoes, searchers found an assortment of climbing and camping gear, possibly a base camp, below the mountain's north face. They also found two snow caves, although they didn't appear to have been used. Tracks believed to belong to the climbers led to the west.

After three more cold, dangerous, fruitless days, on January 6 searchers made a somber discovery. Near the base of a large avalanche area on Cleveland's west slope was a pack belonging to one of the climbers. Nearby was a parka, a camera, and film in a pocket. A Glacier spokesman, Dan Nelson, said it was clear the pack and parka had tumbled from some distance up the mountain. "They were probably swept away in the avalanche from above," he said.

For the next two days, searchers carefully combed the avalanche area, using long probes and a magnetometer, a device that could detect metal

At times, helicopters ferried search supplies to the south end of Waterton Lake.
PHOTOGRAPH COURTESY OF GLACIER NATIONAL PARK ARCHIVES.

buried deep in snow. They found no further traces of the climbers. On January 9, with a snowstorm closing in, officials from both sides of the border told family members standing vigil in Waterton that, fourteen days after their sons and brothers had disappeared, they were suspending the search. They would try again in the summer.

Most family members left quickly, but a few lingered, not fully ready to give up hope. One of those who stayed was Morton Levitan, a Helena physician and, like Frauson and others in the search, a former member of the 10th Mountain Division who had spent time during World War II in a German prisoner-of-war camp.

Matthew Levitan, the second oldest of the five Levitan children and about eighteen months younger than his missing brother, had driven his father to Waterton. He returned home without his father to tell his mother, Audrey, a former World War II U.S. Army nurse, the news.

"I just said to my mom, based on everything that I knew at the time,

A probe team searches the avalanche area on Mount Cleveland's west slope.
PHOTOGRAPH COURTESY OF GLACIER NATIONAL PARK ARCHIVES.

that I didn't think he was alive," Levitan recalled nearly fifty years later. "The conclusion seemed pretty obvious."

Giving up the search was frustrating, even for those who spent days on the flanks of the mountain. Willy Pfeister, a climber from Canada's Jasper National Park, told reporters that he was surprised that the search didn't yield more items belonging to the missing men. Avalanches typically scatter such gear over a wide area. "It is almost as if they were swallowed up," he said.

Another Canadian searcher, park naturalist Kurt Seel, shared a mix of frustration and awe the day officials called off the search. "That mountain," he said, "doesn't give a damn about anyone. It's not inconquerable. It is treacherous. In the summertime, rocks fall constantly. In the wintertime, it's the wind and snow. The mountain is alive all the time."

Jean Kanzler, who lived in Bozeman, seemed to accept that her youngest son was gone forever. In an interview with the *Daily Inter Lake* newspaper in Kalispell published as the winter search ended, she offered a stout defense of her son and the other climbers pursuing what appeared to some as an overly risky endeavor:

> This was Jerry's thing. This was their way. This was something Ray, Clare, and Jerry have been talking about for more than two years. Always, they kept coming back to one all-consuming question: "When are we going to do Cleveland?" They wanted to do a first. They knew Cleveland in the winter would be a first. They wanted to be first, this was the uppermost thought in their lives.

The young climbers had plotted routes, discussed equipment, done practice climbs "as a prelude to what they really wanted to do," she said. "Some people may have thought they were rinky-dinking around, but these boys were dead serious. They studied Mount Cleveland from every angle."

The loss of her son was the second recent personal tragedy in Jean Kanzler's family life. Her hard-charging husband, Hal, who introduced his sons to climbing and outdoor adventure at an early age, had committed suicide just two years earlier. Her oldest son, Jim, was a highly regarded climber who had hoped to join the Cleveland trip but stayed in Bozeman due to work and family obligations. (Jim Kanzler worked as a ski patroller, in ski resort operations, as a climbing guide, and later as an avalanche forecaster. Four days shy of his sixty-third birthday, he was found dead outside his home near Jackson Hole, Wyoming, in 2011. Friends said he committed suicide.)

The mother said the uncertainly of the search for her son and others on a cold, remote mountain was difficult. The suspension brought a small measure of closure. "There are regrets, deep ones of course, but no real ones," she said. "I couldn't live Jerry's life." The mother also predicted that her son's body would be the last to be found on the remote, unforgiving mountain.

It was May 23, 1970, when a couple of rangers made it to the slide area and discovered a camera belonging to Jim Anderson. Photographs developed from the film proved to be a significant find in that they showed all five climbers together on the west slope. The camera find was the first in a series as the snow slowly melted off the mountain. The next was an ice axe, at the mountain's 8,300-foot level, followed by a wool cap, a rucksack, flashlight batteries, a dented canteen, and, in late June, a shirt belonging to one of the missing.

Six days later, on May 29, searchers decided to climb to Cleveland's summit on a route possibly taken by the missing men. In a bowl area just above a waterfall, they spotted a body, with a red climbing rope still attached. It was Ray Martin. That same day, the searchers reached the body of Jim Anderson, attached to a gold rope.

Using photos from Anderson's camera, the searchers suspected they would find Mark Levitan along the path of the gold rope, followed by Clare Pogreba. They believed Jerry Kanzler was linked by the red rope to Martin.

With shovels, pulaskis, and ice chippers, and later using a system that tapped water in a nearby natural pool, the recovery team used a high-pressure stream to speed the removal of snow and debris. On July 3, the searchers reached the remaining bodies and removed them, with the remains of Kanzler the last of the five to be ferried down the mountain. A helicopter took the bodies to a spot near Chief Mountain, where some family members, friends, and the Glacier County coroner had gathered.

The drama of the initial search and eventual recovery of the bodies of the climbers captured headlines across Montana and the nation. *The New York Times* reported the conclusion of the search in a July 5, 1970, article headlined "Bodies of Five Found in Ice in Montana."

The same day, in the *Inter Lake*, the Kalispell newspaper, Glacier superintendent William Briggle, who flew in the helicopter that brought the last body off the mountain, noted the sadness of the deaths but defended the right of the young men to climb.

"If they insist, there is nothing we can do about it. They have the right to make that attempt," he said. As for future adventurers, "we will try to guide them in making their decisions. And we'll tell them the story of five young men and 188 days . . . perhaps Mount Cleveland can speak louder than we can."

Glacier officials pieced together a detailed outline of the Mount Cleveland search operation in an official report on the accident, but conclusions about the deadliest event in Glacier's history are based on discoveries in the snow and some speculation. The report, obtained by the author via a Freedom of Information Act request, concluded the men may have begun the climb on the west face of Cleveland on December 29 or 30 and reached the 8,350-foot level when they were hit by a large avalanche, which pushed them down to the 6,800-foot level, where their bodies were found.

In the coming days and weeks, Jerry Kanzler was buried next to his father in Columbia Falls. Mark Levitan was buried in Helena, while Clare Pogreba and Ray Martin came to their final rest in side-by-side graves in Butte's Mountain View cemetery. The ashes of Jim Anderson were spread over Mount Cleveland, fulfilling an "if anything happens" request that he had made to his family. Shirley Anderson Harrison said her brother embraced the outdoor life, as did his siblings, all encouraged by their father, Edwin Anderson. Jim, she said, "grasped the mountains" and was "a magnanimous personality, full of life and happiness."

The Anderson family, with support of the survivors of the other climbers, built a bridge and a wall-like monument memorializing the five young lives lost on that tall, remote mountain in 1969. The monument, in Yellow Bay State Park, is next to a small creek that trickles peacefully into Flathead Lake.

In September 1976, Jim Kanzler, Terry Kennedy, and Steve Jackson became the first climbers to complete a full ascent of Mount Cleveland's north face, motivated in large part by the 1969–1970 tragedy. Terry Kennedy, who grew up in Columbia Falls near the Kanzler family, said the lure of the looming mountain was strong for the avid young climbers.

He speculates that climbing the north face was the initial goal, while the winter ascent up the west face was the back-up plan.

"They were good climbers for their age," Kennedy said in 2019. "It was the highest, most precipitous face in the lower forty-eight states that hadn't been climbed yet. It was a really big plum to be plucked." Kennedy, a Bozeman physical therapist, is the author of *In Search of the Mount Cleveland*

A memorial at Yellow Bay State Park on Flathead Lake carries the names of the five climbers and a quote from the Bhagavad-Gita. PHOTOGRAPH BY BUTCH LARCOMBE.

Five, which addresses the 1969 climb and technical climbing on many other mountains. (Another book on the incident, *White Death: Tragedy and Heroism in an Avalanche Zone*, was written by McKay Jenkins in 2001.)

In the eyes of Matthew Levitan, the story of the five climbers has a joyful beginning. His older brother had a passion for climbing and found his niche at Montana State, where he met some of the others who would join him on Mount Cleveland. "He was excited to do it. He liked them and they were his friends. It was a great adventure."

He has found a path for remembering his older brother. "When I'm in Yellow Bay, I go visit the wall. When I'm in Helena, I go see his tombstone. When I get to Glacier, I sometimes go over to Waterton and look up at Cleveland. But there are no good memories."

MOUNT JUMBO, 2014

Late February 2014 in the Missoula area had been unseasonably warm, but weather forecasters saw a big change coming for Friday, February 28—heavy snow and winds up to forty or fifty miles per hour provided the recipe for the city's first blizzard in more than fifteen years.

The staff at the West Central Montana Avalanche Center, who monitor snow conditions and issue regular safety advisories typically aimed at backcountry users, were concerned. "The warm weather we had left a sun crust on the snow," Steve Karkanen, the center's director, told a reporter for the *Missoulian* newspaper. "What we are concerned about is how the new snow will bond to the surface. If we get this big storm, especially the high winds, it's definitely going to increase avalanche danger."

The storm materialized as predicted, bringing snow driven by an east wind to the Missoula valley and the mountains around it. School was canceled and the city hunkered down as snow piled up. At midafternoon, four young men toting sleds and a snowboard made their way up the open west slope of Mount Jumbo, the steep boundary of the city's lower Rattlesnake neighborhood. Even though the area was closed to provide refuge to wintering elk, the four were lured to the mountain by the fresh snow, which had piled deep on certain spots on Jumbo, named for its resemblance to the rounded hindquarters of the famous circus elephant.

At one point, the young man who carried the snowboard became separated from the other three. At about 4 P.M., he strapped into his snowboard and began down the slope, only to quickly fall and be carried along by a wave of moving snow. The snowboarder was able to dig into the slope with the board and his hands and stop his slide.

But the wave of snow continued down the mountain, gaining mass and momentum. The sledders, at a different point on Jumbo, reported seeing a cloud of powder snow and watched as the avalanche roared down the slope and into a neighborhood at the base of the mountain.

The next day, the *Missoulian* ran the headline, "Avalanche Buries 3; All Found Alive. Rattlesnake Valley Home Demolished."

The avalanche, which reached an estimated top speed of 120 miles per hour, plowed down Holly Street and out into its intersection with Van Buren Street. In the process, it ripped one home from its foundation and damaged others, trapped two adults and two children, and set in motion a wave of neighbors who scrambled to find survivors.

Neighbors and EMTs rushed to the scene to dig and probe in the avalanche debris.
PHOTOGRAPH BY TOM BAUER.

Cheryl and Archie McMillan had lived in the neighborhood for more than three decades. How often did they think about the possibility of an avalanche? "Never ever ever ever," Cheryl told a reporter. Inside their home, "we heard this huge whump. At first, we thought it was just snow falling off the roof. But it was more like a roar. It didn't last very long." A home visible outside their window was heavily damaged and there was snow and debris scattered over a wide area.

The damaged house belonged to Fred Allendorf, a retired University of Montana professor, and his spouse, artist Michel Colville. The two were trapped in the wreckage of the home, and it took rescuers several hours to extricate them. Allendorf, sixty-six, had serious injuries and Colville, sixty-eight, was in critical condition when she arrived at a local hospital.

Within minutes, rescuers—many of them neighbors—poked at piles of snow in search of eight-year-old Phoenix Scoles-Coburn. The boy had been playing in his backyard with his sister, Coral, ten years old, when they spotted the avalanche coming down the mountain and began running toward their home. Their mother saw the children from a window. Coral

At the base of Mount Jumbo, the slide plowed into
the home of Fred Allendorf and Michel Colville.
PHOTOGRAPH COURTESY OF STEVE KARKANEN.

was buried in snow up to her shoulders and was eventually able to free
herself. Her brother was under several feet of snow, and it took rescuers
nearly an hour of frantic searching to find and free him.

Later, the boy recalled being trapped in the dark, unable to move his
arms or legs and chewing at the snow near his mouth, an act that experts
said may have allowed him to get enough oxygen to avoid suffocation. He
was released from the hospital after a few days.

In roughly the same period, the avalanche turned from a novel occurrence to a tragedy. Michel Colville, severely injured, never regained con-
sciousness after being removed from her home and hospitalized. She died
from her injuries three days after the slide.

Allendorf was hospitalized for about three weeks. On the one-year anniversary of the avalanche, he gave an interview with the *Montana Kaimin*,
the university student newspaper. Allendorf recalled being in the living
room of the couple's wood-frame home, with Colville just a few feet away,
when the snow hit. "The chimney pinned me down," he said. "It broke

seventeen ribs, cracked my sternum, broke three vertebrae and my left foot. But it also saved me."

Being underneath the chimney gave him a pocket of air, enough to allow searchers to pull him alive and breathing from the wrecked home about two hours after the slide. "I remember thinking either I am going to freeze to death, I'm going to suffocate, or they are going to find me. I didn't really care which one happened. I just knew one of those three would."

His wife was found under several feet of snow and debris, about an hour after searchers freed Allendorf. She was about twenty-five feet from where she was sitting when the slide hit.

In 1969, Colville had been the first woman to graduate from the University of Montana's wildlife biology program. Later in life, she was known for her singing, and for her artwork, which included painting, textiles, and glass mosaics. She often created pieces as fundraisers for local charities.

Several days after the slide, two avalanche specialists climbed Jumbo, looking for clues about the mysterious slide, even though the avalanche danger was still high and some residents near the base of the mountain chose to leave until the danger subsided.

Debris from the Allendorf-Colville home. Note the deep, hard-packed snow from the slide. PHOTOGRAPH BY STEVE KARKANEN.

"I did not like being anywhere along that face for about five days after the accident," said Karkanen, more than five years later. "It was spooky."

High on the mountain, the investigators found evidence that snow may have built up in a small basin and that a large slab broke away, triggered by the snowboarder. The names of the snowboarder and sledders were never publicly released. Authorities decided against filing charges against any of the group. All four came down the mountain as quickly as possible and joined the search for those trapped in snow and later voluntarily talked with police.

Looking down the path of the slide from the crown.
PHOTOGRAPH BY STEVE KARKANEN.

Steve Karkanen marked this image to show the 658-foot-long
fracture line at the top or "crown" of the slab.
PHOTOGRAPH BY STEVE KARKANEN.

The point where the slab fractured and slid, the avalanche's crown, was nearly 660 feet long, on a 38-degree slope. The mass of snow, 2.5 to 3 feet thick on average, slid about 2,200 feet, gaining momentum as it entered an even steeper gully that ends where Holly Street begins. Along with destroying the Allendorf-Colville home, it totaled several cars and damaged several other structures.

For many in the neighborhood and the broader Missoula area, the avalanche appeared to be a freakish, unpredictable event. But there was evidence to the contrary. Some residents reported smaller avalanches coming down Jumbo in winters with heavy snowpack; in fact, Allendorf told Karkanen and others that a slide had piled snow against his home's back door several decades earlier. And Steve Karkanen documented a small slide on the same slope that occurred exactly on the fifth anniversary of the 2014 avalanche, this one triggered by elk. It did not reach the neighborhood below.

Looking up the gully on Mount Jumbo from the debris path.
PHOTOGRAPH BY KURT WILSON.

The 2014 avalanche and resulting death was not the first on Mount Jumbo. In January 1993, a thirteen-year-old East Missoula boy died after an avalanche hit him on the mountain's east flank, where he had been hiking with friends in snowy, gusty conditions.

In an article in a professional journal, *The Avalanche Review*, late in 2014, Karkanen acknowledged the shock of a large avalanche reaching the valley floor but noted that the area's short written history might obscure reality. "There is no denying that Mount Jumbo is avalanche terrain when the snow is deep enough and weather factors create instability," he wrote. "There's just no record of a similar event in the past 150 years."

SOURCES

Introduction

The Colorado Avalanche Information Center. avalanche.state.co.us.

Guthrie, C. W., Dan Fagre, and Ann Fagre. *Death and Survival in Glacier National Park*. Farcountry Press. 2017.

Mount Cleveland, 1969

Daily Inter Lake. Kalispell, Montana. December 29, 1969–January 11, 1970; June 29, 1970–July 5, 1970.

Jenkins, McKay. "And None Came Back." Outsideonline.com. February 1, 2000.

Kennedy, Terry G. Personal interview. September 2019.

Levitan, Matthew. Personal interview. September 2019.

Montana Standard. Butte, Montana. January 3, 1970–January 9, 1970.

The New York Times. "Bodies of 5 Found In Ice In Montana." July 5, 1970.

U.S. Department of the Interior, National Park Service. "Report of the Mt. Cleveland Tragedy Involving Five Young Mountain Climbers, December 26, 1969–July 3, 1970." 1970.

Mount Jumbo, 2014

Karkanen, Steve. "Mount Jumbo Accident Report." West Central Montana Avalanche Information Center. Missoula, Montana. February 28, 2014.

Karkanen, Steve. "Mt. Jumbo: Missoula's Urban Avalanche Problem." *The Avalanche Review*. December 2014.

Karkanen, Steve. Personal interview. September 2019.

Missoulian. February 28–March 7, 2014.

Wyllie, Taylor and Erin Loranger. "A Year Later, Mount Jumbo Avalanche Survivor Faces Difficulty Moving On." *Montana Kaimin*. University of Montana, Missoula, Montana. February 27, 2015.

EARTHQUAKES

ON ITS SURFACE, MONTANA IS LACED WITH MOUNTAINS AND PLAINS, rivers and creeks, hills and coulees, all pieces of a gorgeous quilt spread beneath a sprawling sky.

But in Montana's western third, a patchwork of fault lines—cracks in the earth's crust where rocks slip and slide against one another—lurks underground. Known as the northernmost portion of the Intermountain Seismic Belt, this subterranean maze stretches from Yellowstone National Park northwest to the Flathead Valley. Linked with this larger belt is another smaller band, called the Centennial Tectonic Belt, that reaches west from Yellowstone into central Idaho.

Seismologists, including Mike Stickney, director of the Earthquake Studies Office run by the Montana Bureau of Mines and Geology in Butte, keep a close watch on this subterranean network, which is given to shifting. Relying on a network of thirty-five seismic stations, the scientists accept a fact that might startle many: on a typical day, there are between five and ten earthquakes along the Montana portion of the Intermountain Seismic Belt, many of them so small they are noticed only by sensitive instruments and the scientists who monitor and analyze them.

The first official, verified report of an earthquake in Montana came in 1869, from Helena, but earlier accounts hint at activity. Scholars of the Lewis and Clark Expedition note that the explorers reported hearing "unaccountable rumblings" emanating from the west as they neared the Great Falls area in 1805, prompting speculation that the sounds could have come from a seismic event. While the large majority of earthquake activity in Montana takes place in the western part of the state, a magnitude 5.3 to 5.5 quake in May 1909 was centered on the Montana-Saskatchewan border near Scobey, along what is known as the Hinsdale Fault.

Southwest Montana remains the most active seismic region in the state, with the Hebgen Lake area seeing a good share of the activity. Earthquakes in 1959, 1964, 1974, 1977, and 1985 have shaken the area. Montana saw twelve earthquakes of magnitude 6.0 or greater between 1925 and 1960. Since then, powerful quakes have subsided. In July 2005, a magnitude 5.6 quake centered just north of Dillon rattled windows, cracked chimneys, and did other minor damage. In 2017, a 5.8 magnitude quake near Lincoln, north of Helena, did similar damage and earned the distinction of being the strongest Montana quake registered to date west of the Continental Divide.

Stickney says Montana's relatively short span of recorded history doesn't offer any significant clues about future major seismic events. "We have gone sixty years since the last earthquake of magnitude 6.0. Are we in an earthquake drought? We just don't know."

But occasionally, this shaky underworld makes its presence known in dramatic fashion, with most of the notable seismic performances to date staged in southwest Montana.

CLARKSTON VALLEY EARTHQUAKE, 1925
EMOTIONS OF ALARM

On June 27, 1925, a clock in a drugstore in Three Forks, Montana, where three rivers join to form the mighty Missouri, came to a sudden stop at 6:21 P.M. Many miles to the north in Helena, a clock in the state's weather bureau also stopped ticking at precisely the same time that summer evening.

In the ensuing seconds, the earth shook violently enough that U.S. Geological Survey researcher J. T. Pardee reported later that brick buildings were damaged, rocks fell from cliffs, cracks opened in roads, and the area's two-legged "inhabitants experienced the usual symptoms of illness and emotions of alarm."

What eventually became known as the Clarkston Valley earthquake, named for the location of its epicenter about nine miles northeast of Three Forks, was the first destructive quake officially recorded in Montana. At magnitude 6.6, the quake was felt over a wide area.

This quake occurred before the existence of seismic stations, but anecdotal evidence and news accounts reveal that the tremor was felt in Seattle, Calgary, Alberta, and along Montana's border with South Dakota. A clock in the Western Union office in Glasgow, 300 miles northeast of the Three Forks area, stopped at 6:23 P.M., apparently due to the quake. Pardee later estimated the area in which the quake was "sensible" at 310,000 square miles.

Physical damage, although confined to a smaller area, was substantial. Many buildings, especially those made of brick, were damaged in Three Forks, Logan, and Manhattan by the main tremor and aftershocks. Building fronts fell onto the main street of Three Forks, and the Methodist church in town was heavily damaged, as were school buildings there and in Logan and Manhattan. To the northeast, in White Sulphur Springs, bricks fell, and the walls of the county courthouse and jail were cracked during the quake.

A newspaper account from the day after the quake noted that "seismic disturbances" had "disarranged" the schedule of two transcontinental railroads, specifically the Northern Pacific Railway and the Chicago, Milwaukee, St. Paul and Pacific Railroad. Pardee noted that several trains came to a stop, "while huge rocks were falling on the tracks in front of them and behind them and their escape without a scratch seems little short of miraculous."

At a point on the Milwaukee line known as Deer Park, the quake shoved an estimated 40,000 cubic yards of rocks and dirt across tracks and into Sixteenmile Creek, leading to the temporary formation of a lake.

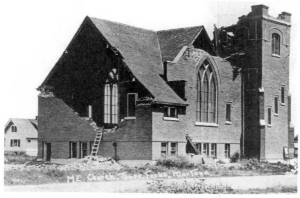

The Methodist church in Three Forks sustained heavy damage.
PHOTOGRAPH COURTESY OF THE U.S. GEOLOGICAL SURVEY.

The county jail in White Sulphur Springs lost parts of its stone façade.
PHOTOGRAPH COURTESY OF THE U.S. GEOLOGICAL SURVEY.

The Manhattan High School suffered extensive damage.
PHOTOGRAPH BY JOSEPH T. PARDEE, COURTESY OF THE U.S. GEOLOGICAL SURVEY.

While there were no fires directly attributed to the 1925 quake, about a month later, a blaze heavily damaged the main business block of Toston, north of Three Forks. Investigators concluded that the fire started in a chimney that had been damaged in the earthquake, which had also damaged a water system, hindering efforts to fight the fire.

On the human ledger, the quake left no marks in the fatality column. News reports recount just two injuries. A woman in Three Forks, possibly

Near Lombard, the quake damaged railroad tracks
and tumbled boulders onto the rail line.
PHOTOGRAPHS BY JOSEPH T. PARDEE AND J. P. SWARTS,
COURTESY OF THE U.S. GEOLOGICAL SURVEY.

fleeing a building, suffered a leg injury, while a male motorist reported that the quake caused him to leave a roadway near Ennis and incur minor injuries.

But there was a clear psychological toll. During the quake and aftershocks, "many persons became wildly excited or hysterical," Pardee reported, which led to moments of odd behavior. In Butte, he noted, a woman disturbed by the tremors "is said to have laid down her baby and picked up a cat."

News of the quake made headlines across the state and region. Accounts of the event dominated the front page of *The Helena Independent* on Sunday, June 28, 1925, under the blaring headline, "Montana Sways in Series of Earthquakes, Many Towns Report Damage."

The quake gave Helena a good shake, prompting a reporter to pen an article that opened with both animistic and biblical references: "Mother Nature picked the 'City of Golden Glow' up in her arms last evening and rocked her around for several seconds, and then deposited her where she belonged, as children rolled out of her homes, office buildings and apartments, wondering whether or not Gabriel would take advantage of the situation and play that long-awaited cornet solo."

HELENA EARTHQUAKES, 1935
"I WASN'T SCARED, I WAS TERRIFIED"

Just over a decade later, there was little colorful waxing in the Helena newspaper, and any horns that blew were likely attached to automobiles loaded with terrified residents scurrying to leave the capital. A remarkable series of earthquakes began in October 1935 and persisted for months.

The first came on October 12 and brought the impact of a 5.9 magnitude quake to the *Independent* newsroom. "The first of the shocks was hair-raising and breathtaking," one account read. "Brick walls in the *Independent* building weaved noticeably and bulged until it seemed they would burst out." The newspaper also noted that the intense shaking began at about 12:51 A.M. and left damage throughout the city.

On October 13, the newspaper noted that the weather bureau had reported thirty-one tremors and vibrations in an eighteen-hour period the previous day. But just a few days later, concern about "shocks that drove thousands into the streets in their night clothes" seemed to have subsided, even in the eyes of experts. A headline in the *Independent* in the October 15 edition read: "Another Bad Earth Shock Extremely Unlikely, Say Leading State Geologists."

Earthquake experts today often label the components of earthquakes as foreshocks, the main shock, and aftershocks. As it turns out, the October 12 quake was a foreshock, part of what Mike Stickney, the seismologist, describes as a persistent earthquake series that began in the first days of October and stretched for many months. In a period of roughly two and a half years, Helena experienced nearly 2,500 earthquakes.

It was a period that brought great physical damage, compounded the challenges of the Great Depression, and cast a pall of uncertainty over Helena.

On the evening of October 18, just a couple of days after experts had assured residents that the seismic worst was behind them, the main shock in the earthquake series occurred. Just before 10 P.M., a magnitude 6.25 quake, centered north of the city, knocked out electric and telephone service and brought walls across the city tumbling down.

Remarkably, only two people were killed by the October 18 quake. Panicked by the shaking, Dave Harris ran out of a building on South Main Street and was crushed when the brick front wall of the Headquarters Building collapsed on him. The next to die, Charles Siggelink, was sleeping in a shelter at the fairgrounds. The quake woke him, and he ran out the door only to be hit by falling debris. He died at St. Peter's Hospital the next morning.

Fred Buck, an engineer who worked for the fledgling State Water

Conservation Board, an agency created to build small dams and irrigation projects, wrote a detailed narrative of work and family life in Helena amid the uncertainty created by the tremors large and small. (Buck started working as an engineer in Helena in 1919. He was appointed state engineer in 1941.)

In the October 12 quake, the first severe shock lasted about twelve seconds, Buck noted, "and shook the house [at 531 5th Avenue] until all the walls seemed to be weaving in all directions. There was no doubt about what happened; nobody stopped to ask, 'Was that an earthquake.' In a few minutes, the populace of the whole town was in the streets. No one could sleep through it. Many people spent the rest of the night in their cars."

While the city suffered minor damage, most people returned to their daily lives and work, despite continuing tremors. Buck wrote, "I asked the state engineer the next morning if he was scared, to which he answered: 'No, I wasn't scared, I was terrified.' This is the best description of one's feelings and just fits the way everyone felt."

After the first severe quake, Buck's spouse, Juanita, packed up bedrolls, suitcases, and clothes, and insisted that her husband put them in the car. But the tremors seemed to lessen, and Buck removed them from the car at noon on October 18, "much against my wife's wishes."

Working late on a Friday night, Buck and other engineers were in their second-story office "when the crash came. We jumped out of our chairs but could stand up only by holding on to something solid. The noise alone of the grinding brick and groaning timbers, the rattling windows, and the roar of the quake itself, were enough to terrify one, to say nothing of being jostled around like a lone marble in a tomato can. . . . [E]very second I expected to be shot out of the window to the pavement below, or have the walls crash around me. This terrible shaking kept up severely and constantly for a period of 32 seconds—it seemed like 32 minutes."

Using matches to light a path, Buck found his way out of the building and to his car. "The pavement was strewn with brick and lumber," he wrote. "[P]eople were running as if they were insane; women were screaming as though in death; the streets were alive with cars; and the weird yellow cast of headlights piercing the thick blanket of dust was uncanny."

Buck arrived as his home, which was heavily damaged, to find his wife, Juanita, his young daughter, and his mother-in-law sitting across the street with the assembled bedding, suitcases, and clothes.

"They knew I must have been killed or I would have been home by now. By this time, there was not a soul in Helena, it was safe to say, that was inside any building. They were out on streets, in cars, and clustered in groups on vacant lots. Fortunately, there was no snow and the night was not very cold."

Buck and his family spent the next several weeks living in a small house with a co-worker, his wife, and three children. Many in Helena slept in tents or their cars, while others moved to neighboring towns. Later, some found temporary homes in Pullman cars brought to Helena by the Great Northern Railway.

The October 18 quake and related tremors left extensive damage. Roughly 460 homes were destroyed or damaged to the point of being

During the October 18 quake, the Nabisco factory at 1308 Boulder Avenue suffered damage typical of brick buildings in Helena.
PHOTOGRAPH COURTESY OF THE SEAN LOGAN COLLECTION.

uninhabitable. The new $500,000 Helena High School was heavily damaged, as was Bryant School, the Lewis and Clark County Courthouse, St. John's Hospital, the National Biscuit Company factory, the Montana Deaconess Home, an orphanage, the poor farm, Intermountain Union College, the county jail, and numerous stores and office buildings. The city's business district was cordoned off to prevent auto travel, while few pedestrians ventured among the damaged taller buildings. Also damaged but repairable were the landmark Shrine Temple, the Cathedral of St. Helena, and two rail depots.

The lead headline in the *Independent* on October 20, 1935, hinted at a city that had been brought to its knees: "Helena Is Almost Deserted After Series of Quakes Rock The City. Business at Standstill And Gathering Forbidden." Along with the two men killed, thirty to forty people had been injured in the quake. The destruction extended to Fort Harrison to the west and to East Helena, where many buildings were weakened and the tall stack of the American Smelting and Refining Company was damaged by the quake.

A day later, the *Independent* tabbed the damage at a total of $3 million. And a page-one headline looked eerily familiar: "Major Quakes in Helena Area Are Over, Say Leading Scientists."

The October 18 quake severely damaged Bryant School,
which was later razed and replaced with an art deco design.
PHOTOGRAPH COURTESY OF THE SEAN LOGAN COLLECTION.

The new high school, dedicated only a month earlier, was 75 percent
destroyed by the quake. It reopened two years later.
PHOTOGRAPH COURTESY OF THE SEAN LOGAN COLLECTION.

Looking east from South Benton over Last Chance Gulch
after the 1935 quakes. Some building sustained major damage, others
lost brick façades, and some were unharmed and are still standing today.
PHOTOGRAPH COURTESY OF THE SEAN LOGAN COLLECTION.

Then, at about 11:37 A.M. on a cold, snowy October 31, another quake
shook the city. The 6.0 magnitude quake did extensive damage, with
much of it inflicted on structures already weakened in the October 18

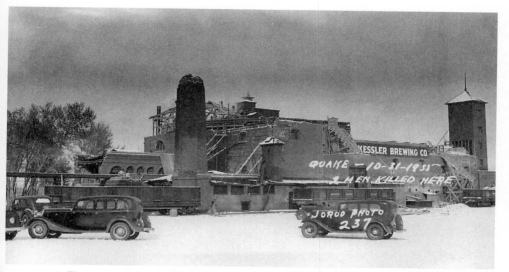

The broken chimney at Kessler Brewery that collapsed on Kennedy and O'Brien.
Workers can be seen cleaning up debris, and bricks still lay scattered.
PHOTOGRAPH BY JORUD PHOTOGRAPHY, COURTESY OF THE DAVID POOR COLLECTION.

quake. The north wall of the new high school came to the ground. West
of town, two brick masons from Salt Lake City—twenty-seven-year-old
Ed O'Brien and twenty-four-year-old Vincent Kennedy—were working
on scaffolding to repair a brick tower at the Kessler Brewery when the
quake hit. Both the scaffolding and tower collapsed, tossing the men to
the ground in a shower of bricks and mortar. Rescuers dug them out, but
one was dead at the scene and the other died soon after.

The *Independent* noted that the latest quake "caught off guard a city
lulled into the belief that the worst had passed and that the disturbing
tremblings of the earth were gradually dying out."

The damage was again severe. Fred Buck wrote of witnessing the collapse of a prominent building and noted the quake during daylight hours
was somewhat less terrifying than the nighttime quakes. Nevertheless, the
Buck family had experienced enough. The engineer made his way home,
gathered his family, a pet collie, and a few belongings. They drove north
to Great Falls where they rented an apartment.

A Helena home destroyed by the quake.
PHOTOGRAPH COURTESY OF THE SEAN LOGAN COLLECTION.

Unreinforced brick and masonry fared poorly in the intense shaking.
PHOTOGRAPH COURTESY OF THE SEAN LOGAN COLLECTION.

On November 28, 1935, a headline in the *Independent* predicted "the Thanksgiving Spirit Will Prevail in Helena Today," noting that the experiences of the past six weeks had brought a "new appreciation and meaning of the purpose of the holiday."

That same day, some people were likely reading the paper when yet another strong earthquake hit the city about 8:40 A.M. While the quake brought even more pieces of the previously damaged buildings crashing down, there was little new damage, officials reported. A seismograph at Montana State College in Bozeman put the intensity of the Thanksgiving quake at magnitude 5.5, on par with the temblor of October 12.

The Helena newspaper reported that the latest earthquake was felt in a number of Montana cities, including Great Falls. Within a few weeks, the Buck family abandoned their perceived safe haven in the Electric City and returned to Helena, settling into a rented house sixty days after the first big quake drove them from their home on Fifth Avenue.

In his account dated December 17, as the earth still occasionally rattled and rumbled, Fred Buck reflected on the quakes and their impact on his family. "The nervous shock far exceeds the physical shock," he wrote. "[A]nd the anxious waiting in anticipation of something more to come is indescribable. It brings one to a sense of realization of how helpless and frail humanity is to battle with natural forces."

MADISON EARTHQUAKE, 1959
TREES FLYING THROUGH THE AIR

The moon was bright and the light danced on the ripples of the Madison River, and most of the people at the Rock Creek Campground were likely asleep, lulled into slumber with fresh memories of the day's fishing or the wonders of nearby Yellowstone National Park.

But the shaking started just twenty-three minutes before midnight on that otherwise peaceful night of August 17, 1959. "I thought someone had coupled on to our trailer and was trying to pull it away," said Hal Weston, who was at the campground with his wife, Polly, and two nephews.

"And then the screaming started," said Polly, in an account published in the *Bozeman Daily Chronicle*. "We saw the mountains falling with the most awful roar. We could see trees flying through the air like toothpicks."

In less than a minute on that August night, the Madison River canyon and the lives of many were transformed by what remains the most significant seismic event in Montana's recorded history—an earthquake felt in nine western states and three Canadian provinces that claimed at least twenty-eight lives and caused $11 million in damage.

The magnitude 7.3 quake, which involved movement along at least two fault lines, sparked a massive landslide, rock falls, and a series of large waves on Hebgen Lake that washed over and threatened to wash away a large dam, which, if it failed, would have sent a tsunami-like wall of water roaring down the Madison River.

The landslide roared down the south flank of the Madison Canyon at 100 miles per hour, carrying an estimated 85 million tons of mountain into the river canyon, partially burying a crowded campground and its occupants, and damming the river, forming what became known as Quake

On August 17, 1959, an entire mountainside collapsed into the valley
of the Madison River, damming the river and burying a campground.
PHOTOGRAPH BY WILLIAM B. HALL, COURTESY OF THE U.S. GEOLOGICAL SURVEY.

Lake. The quake also dropped long sections of U.S. Highway 287 into Hebgen Lake, stranding campers and residents along its edge.

A day after word of the quake rumbled around the nation, Dr. Charles Richter, the nation's best-known seismologist, said the Montana quake "was the largest so far as we know in the present century outside Nevada and California." (The deadliest earthquake in U.S. history hit San Francisco in 1906. The 7.9 magnitude quake left about 3,000 people dead, many of them victims of quake-related fires. The strongest earthquake in U.S. history took place in 1964 near Anchorage, Alaska. The 9.2 magnitude quake left 131 people dead, all but nine the victim of tsunamis.)

The shaking from the Madison quake was felt by many, and concerned callers jammed switchboards across the state, newspapers reported. *The Billings Gazette* called the event a "moderate quake," although it quoted one resident saying "my house shook like a leaf," and Kathryn Wright, the paper's society editor, reported that the quake produced waves "four

The quake startled people staying at a local cabin, and in the dark
they drove their Cadillac over the edge of the fault on
U.S. Highway 191 just south of Duck Creek. No one was injured.
PHOTOGRAPH BY S. W. NILE, COURTESY OF THE U.S. GEOLOGICAL SURVEY.

to six inches high, not sharp, short waves but great undulating rolls" in the swimming pool at her home about 10 miles west of the city (and 120 miles from the epicenter).

The aerial view of the Madison River canyon below Hebgen Lake was unforgettable to Bob Nicol, one of about eight smokejumpers from Missoula summoned to the quake scene to help those stranded or injured. The jumpers dropped into the fractured canyon the morning after the late-night quake.

"When we flew into the Madison canyon from the west, it looked like half the mountain on the south side of the canyon had been cut in half and dumped into the river," Nicol wrote forty years later. "We could see that a portion of the highway was under the slide and there were a lot of vehicles and people trapped between there and Hebgen Lake, a few miles upstream."

The jumpers, likely the first from outside the canyon to reach people in the quake area, worked to get survivors to higher ground, and, as Nicol reported, they "found a lot of hurt people and a few fatalities." Adding urgency to their work was the uncertain condition of Hebgen Dam, which held back millions of gallons of water in a fifteen-mile-long reservoir. Witnesses had watched as large waves of water, one reported at twenty feet high, rolled up and down the lake, sending water over the top of the dam several times.

Quake Lake, formed by the quake-induced landslide,
swallowed homes, trees, and chunks of highways.
PHOTOGRAPH BY J. B. HADLEY, COURTESY OF THE U.S. GEOLOGICAL SURVEY.

"The water in Hebgen Lake had been sloshed about like water in a bathtub," wrote Irving Witkind, a U.S. Geological Survey researcher, "and it continued to oscillate, though less violently, for at least 12 hours after the quake."

The waves, known as a seiche, coupled with the fact that the concrete core of the earthen dam, completed in 1915, had cracked during the quake, spawned fears that the dam could fail, leading to further loss of life and damage downstream. Along with those trapped below the dam, officials also worried about the safety of many others and ordered the evacuation of Ennis, about forty miles down the Madison.

In the canyon, where a portion of the crowded Rock Creek Campground was buried in the landslide, survivors told of a horrific night. Purley and Irene Bennett had loaded their four children into their Ford station wagon early in the day and left their home in northern Idaho, bound for Yellowstone. "We did all the fun things and pulled into camp late," Irene recalled decades later. Asleep, they heard a loud crack and "my husband got up. . . . I saw him grab a tree . . . and that's all I remember."

Bennett, her leg broken, spent the night shivering under tree branches with devastation all around her, yelling for family members. Hours later, she finally heard an answer from Phillip, her sixteen-year-old son. She learned that her husband's body had been found just before she and Phillip, who also was injured, were taken for medical care by rescuers.

"I prayed that the children would be alive, but they would slowly find a body," she said, in an account in *The Spokesman Review* newspaper in 1995. "First Carole, then Tom. It was a long time before they found Susan. I prayed for her to be alive, yet I worried about her being out there by her little self." Carole was seventeen, Tom, eleven, and Susan, just six.

Grover and Lillian Mault, from Temple City, California, had been at the campground for several days. The night of the quake they were awoken by the rocking of their trailer. Grover, recalling earlier warnings, suspected bears. "I thought they were trying to get in our trailer," he told a *Bozeman Daily Chronicle* reporter. "The missus said, 'No, it's an earthquake.' Within seconds, everything was going upside down."

The quake's main fault ran through Cabin Creek Campground,
displacing the ground both vertically and horizontally.
PHOTOGRAPH BY R. W. BAYLEY, COURTESY OF THE U.S. GEOLOGICAL SURVEY.

The couple's trailer fell into the river and became lodged against a tree, the water rising around it. The two managed to get to the trailer roof and later to a tree, which they climbed to avoid rising water.

"We hollered and hollered," Mault told a reporter. People nearby came to help but couldn't reach the tree, which was surrounded by twenty-five to thirty feet of water. "We clung to the tree, our bodies in the water almost up to our necks. My wife went under three or four times. The last time, she was gasping for breath, but I managed to pull her out. She wanted me to let her go. But I told her if she went, I would go too.

"While we clung there, I could see the mountains sliding and falling every few minutes. There'd be a terrific roar followed by more slides. It was pitiful. I thought the world had come to an end." Rescuers in a boat reached the couple at about 8:30 A.M., about nine hours after the earthquake hit. "You don't know what we went through," Mault concluded. "Nobody will ever know."

Despite strong aftershocks that continued in the hours after the 7.3 shock, rescuers were able to eventually remove as many as 300 people trapped in the canyon. The bodies of nine victims were eventually found in the Rock Creek and Cliff Lake Campgrounds. The other nineteen remain buried by tons of rock.

The 1959 Hebgen earthquake is permanently memorialized at the Earthquake Lake Visitor Center, which opened in 1967. The center draws about 50,000 visitors annually who are greeted by a stark, somber scene above Quake Lake.

Some sixty years after the 1959 quake, NorthWestern Corporation completed a nearly $40-million project to update key components at Hebgen Dam to comply with upgraded seismic safety standards.

SOURCES

Clarkston Valley Earthquake

The Helena Independent. "Montana Sways in Series of Earthquakes, Many Towns Report Damage." June 28, 1925.

Montana Bureau of Mines and Geology. mbmg.mtech.edu.

Pardee, J. T. "The Montana Earthquake of June 27, 1925." U.S. Geological Survey. 1926.

Stickney, Michael. Personal interview. August 2019.

University of Utah. Intermountain Seismic Belt Historical Earthquake Project. quake.utah.edu.

Helena Earthquakes

Buck, Fred. "Experiences of the Fred Buck Family in the Helena Earthquakes of 1935." Narrative in collection of Montana Historical Society.

The Helena Independent. October 3–November 1, November 28–29, 1935.

Madison Earthquake

Bozeman Daily Chronicle. August 18–20, 1959.

Holz, Molly K. "Madison River Canyon Earthquake Area." *Montana The Magazine of Western History.* Spring 2003.

Missoulian. "Earthquake Left Dillon Residents Shaking." July 27, 2005.

Nicol, Bob. "Jumper Recalls Yellowstone Quake Rescue." National Museum of Forest Service History. forestservicemuseum.org.

The Spokesman Review, Spokane, Washington. "Quake Survivor Revisits Tragic Scene." September 29, 1995.

DISEASES

LONG BEFORE EURO-AMERICAN EXPLORERS MADE THEIR WAY TO what would become Montana, the region already had a tragic history with disease among native inhabitants.

While there were several forms of disease that traveled over the Great Plains, most of the documented events involved smallpox, the highly contagious affliction with symptoms of fever and pustules that sickened thousands, killed about one in three, and left survivors scarred or blind. The first documented wave of smallpox to hit tribes in what would become Montana arrived about 1780. Another wave that came in about 1800 ravaged the Crow, dropping the population of the tribe from an estimated 16,000 to about 4,000. Another round of smallpox hit the Crow in the 1830s.

Other tribes also fell victim to the disease, including the Assiniboine and Blackfeet. In 1837, a large wave of smallpox sickened up to two-thirds of the Blackfeet and other native inhabitants living along the Missouri River. That outbreak was believed to have been spread, inadvertently, by an American Fur Company boat as it made its way up the river. Other rounds of smallpox spread across the region in ensuing decades, but historians generally believe the worst infections came well before the Lewis and Clark Expedition in the early 1800s. (In 1870, the U.S. Army reported finding evidence of smallpox among survivors of its attack on the Blackfeet on the Marias River. About 200 Blackfeet were killed in the attack, known as the Marias or Baker Massacre.)

English physician Edward Jenner developed a vaccine for smallpox in 1796, but the virus continued to threaten Montana communities into the early 1900s and wasn't completely eliminated in North America until the mid-twentieth century.

Other diseases, mysterious and deadly, are also part of Montana's past.

ROCKY MOUNTAIN SPOTTED FEVER
THE BLACK MEASLES

The threat of smallpox was largely eliminated with the development of vaccines. But other diseases surfaced in the Montana territory, including the "black measles, black fever, or blue disease" that mysteriously plagued the Bitterroot Valley for several decades. The first reported case was in 1873, and the disease, which was characterized by a high fever, body aches, and a dark rash, sickened hundreds. Many who contracted the disease died, including five scientists who did early research into its cause.

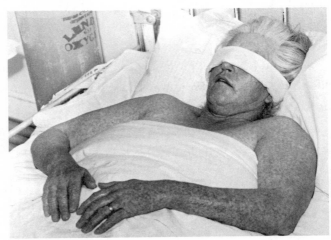

A woman being treated for Rocky Mountain spotted fever exhibits the characteristic rash.
PHOTOGRAPH COURTESY OF ROCKY MOUNTAIN LABORATORIES.

Some residents initially believed the illness, which was largely confined to the area west of the Bitterroot River, was the result of drinking melted snow water. Other folk theories that circulated before formal scientific investigation of the disease began in the early 1900s pinned the source on decaying pine needles or even piles of sawdust at lumber camps.

Working at first from makeshift laboratories in tents, cabins, wood-sheds, and abandoned buildings, early researchers probed numerous potential sources of the mysterious ailment. A pathologist from the University of Chicago, Dr. Howard Ricketts, spent several summers in the Bitterroot studying the disease and based his lab operation in tents set up outside the Northern Pacific Hospital in Missoula. Other researchers theorized that ticks might carry what became known as Rocky Mountain spotted fever, but Ricketts identified the causative bacteria, which is spread by wood ticks common to the valley's western slopes. Dr. Ricketts never completed his study of tick fever in the Bitterroot—he died in 1910 at the age of thirty-nine while investigating a typhus outbreak in Mexico. The bacteria that cause Rocky Mountain spotted fever and several forms of typhus are in the same genus, *Rickettsia*, which was named in his honor.

Field research on "tick fever" was often conducted on horseback.
PHOTOGRAPH COURTESY OF ROCKY MOUNTAIN LABORATORIES.

Interest and funding for spotted fever research spiked and waned in the first decades of the twentieth century. But the 1921 tick fever deaths of two prominent residents, state senator Tyler Worden and his wife, Carrie, reinvigorated the research. Worden was the brother-in-law of Joseph Dixon, Montana's governor and former U.S. senator.

Research into the wood ticks, methods of avoiding tick bites, and possible vaccines continued for decades at a formal laboratory established in

People came out in droves for this spotted fever vaccination clinic in Darby in 1931.
PHOTOGRAPH COURTESY OF ROCKY MOUNTAIN LABORATORIES.

Researchers test the efficacy of tick repellents in 1947 at the lab in Hamilton.
PHOTOGRAPH COURTESY OF ROCKY MOUNTAIN LABORATORIES.

the late 1920s by the State of Montana near Hamilton. While cases of Rocky Mountain spotted fever were eventually reported across the country, antibiotics developed during World War II proved effective in preventing serious illness and deaths from the disease.

Today, the Rocky Mountain Laboratories (under the National Institute of Allergy and Infectious Diseases) is a highly secure, state-of-the-art biomedical research facility where scientists investigate twenty-first-century concerns such as antibiotic-resistant bacteria and the possible weaponized use of infectious diseases. Another area of study is influenza, which sickens and kills many people every year and also left a large, deadly mark on Montana a century ago.

Early in 2020, as a novel coronavirus (SARS-CoV-2) gripped the world, including Montana, Rocky Mountain Laboratories joined in the all-hands-on-deck battle to learn more about the highly contagious, sometimes deadly virus. Five research teams—a total of up to seventy-five people—probed the mysteries of the disease, known as COVID-19, caused by this virus. Their work focused, in part, on possible therapeutic drugs, methods of disinfecting medical masks, and determining how long the virus lives on surfaces. But the most high-profile work involved testing two medicines—a vaccine developed at the Jenner Institute at Oxford University in England, and remdesivir, a broad-spectrum antiviral drug developed by Gilead Sciences, Inc. Early tests of both medicines in rhesus macaque monkeys showed promising results in the late spring of 2020.

The remote laboratories, with their roots in spotted-fever research, also played critical roles in developing a yellow-fever vaccine during World War II, identifying the bacterium that causes Lyme disease (which is also tick-borne), and helping develop an Ebola vaccine.

Regarding the Montana-based COVID-19 research, Charlie Warzel wrote in *The New York Times*, "This is far from the first time that Rocky Mountain Labs has changed the way the world understands diseases."

"SPANISH FLU" EPIDEMIC OF 1918–1919
THE MOST PECULIAR DISEASE

In the spring of 1917, the United States entered World War I, and Montanans were quick to join up, first reporting to military installations across the country before shipping out for Europe. Some eventually died at the hands of the enemy, but by 1919, many more had died from what would become known as the "Spanish flu," a highly contagious viral disease that first infected American soldiers on ships that carried them across the Atlantic on their way to Europe.

The "Great War" and this flu pandemic were deeply interwoven. No one knows for certain where or exactly when the outbreak began. While commonly referred to as the Spanish flu, the pandemic did not start in Spain. Current research places the origin of the flu strain in Kansas, possibly at Camp Funston (aka Fort Riley), and it was then carried to Europe by American soldiers. But Spain played a role—the first full, uncensored accounts of the flu's impact in Europe appeared in Spanish newspapers. Such news was censored among the Allied Powers, including the United States, but Spain remained neutral during the war, and newspapers there freely reported on the flu outbreak. Soon the pandemic was widely labeled as "Spanish."

Regardless of the disease's origin, the movement of soldiers from one continent to another spread the virus around the world. While an exact number of deaths from the Spanish flu and its complications is very difficult to determine, the estimates are staggering. In just three years, worldwide deaths ranged from 25 to 50 million; in the United States, experts believe 675,000 people died of the flu or related complications.

In rural Montana, far from the war and urban population centers, health experts and historians put the flu death toll, conservatively, at more than 5,000, a figure that amounted to about 1 percent of the state's population. Every county in the state saw flu deaths, with Mineral County in western Montana having the fewest with 11, while Silver Bow, home to Butte, the state's largest city at the time, saw at least 780. (These estimates are based on the work of three Montana researchers: Todd Harwell, Greg Holzman, and Steven Helgerson. An account of their findings appears in "No More War, No More Plague: The Spanish Influenza Pandemic Toll in Montana" in the Summer 2018 issue of *Montana The Magazine of Western History*. The researchers included only deaths directly attributed to the flu or related pneumonia.)

The flu deaths swept across the state in waves, the first coming early in mid-January 1918 and starting in Red Lodge, where Silva Whitmore, a 103-year-old resident at the county poor farm, succumbed to the virus or related complications. In the first wave, fifty-three Montanans died from the flu; more than half were in or near Butte.

The second wave, in the late summer and fall of 1918, was much deadlier. The first victim was three-year-old Woodrow Lazyboy of Browning, and a fifteen-year-old girl in Scobey died a few days later. The northeast corner of the state was a hotbed for flu activity, with 157 deaths in about a fifteen-month period in Sheridan County alone.

While the state's population centers—Butte, Great Falls, Billings, Missoula, and Helena—recorded the most flu deaths, rural areas were hardly immune, as the state's smallest communities had few doctors or nurses and, often, no hospital.

In Glasgow, in northeast Montana, the superintendent of the local hospital sounded the alarm on conditions in neighboring communities in a letter published in the *Helena Independent* on October 25, 1918. "I will try to tell you something of the situation, for it is dreadful to say the least," wrote Pamelia A. Clark. A call from neighboring Malta reported twenty flu deaths in the previous ten days. Clark hurried the seventy miles west to the small community, which had no hospital, and set up a makeshift clinic in a hotel. She noted her dismay that large numbers of people continued to gather in the cow town's saloons and pool halls, likely aiding the spread of the disease.

"Do you know," she wrote, "that this is the most peculiar disease I have ever seen? Some people hardly know they are sick until they are dying.

INFLUENZA

Camouflaged by the Word "Spanish"---Not a New Disease
Just the Old Fashioned Grippe

How to Avoid It--How to Care For Those Who Have It

Read and Heed the Following Suggestions of the Billings Health Department

Influenza Symptons---What to Do Until the Doctor Comes

If you feel a sudden chill, followed by muscular pain, headache, backache, unusual tiredness and fever, go to bed at once.

See that there is enough bed clothing to keep you warm.

Open all windows in your bedroom and keep them open at all times, except in rainy weather.

Take medicine to open the bowels freely.

Take some nourishing food, such as milk, egg and milk, or broth every four hours.

Stay in bed until a physician tells you that it is safe to get up.

Allow no one else to sleep in the same room.

Protect others by sneezing and coughing into handkerchiefs or cloths, which should be boiled or burned.

Insist that whoever gives you water or food or enters the sick room for any purpose shall wear a gauze mask. of which may be made at home of four to six folds of gauze and which should cover the nose and mouth and be tied behind the head.

Remember that these masks must be kept clean, must be put on outside the sick room, must not be handled after they are tied on and must be boiled 30 minutes and thoroughly dried every time they are taken off.

To Householders

Keep out of the sick room unless attendance is necessary.

Do not handle articles coming from the sick room until they are boiled.

Allow no visitors, and do not go visiting.

Call a doctor for all inmates who show signs of beginning sickness.

The usual symptoms are: Inflamed and watery eyes, discharging nose, backache, headache, muscular pain, fever.

Keep away from crowded places.

See to it that your children are kept warm and dry, both night and day.

Open your windows at night. If cool weather prevails, add extra bed clothing.

To Nurses

Keep clean. Isolate your patients.

When in attendance upon patients, wear a mask which will cover both the nose and the mouth. When the mask is once in place, do not handle it.

Change the mask every two hours. Owing to the scarcity of gauze, boil half and hour and rinse, then use the gauze again.

Wash your hands each time you come in contact with the patient. Use bichloride of mercury, 1-1,000, or Liquid Cresol compound, 1-100, for hand disinfection.

Obtain at least seven hours' sleep in each twenty-four hours. Eat plenty of good, clean food.

Walk in the fresh air daily.

Sleep with your windows open.

Insist that the patient cough, sneeze or expectorate into cloths that may be disinfected or burned.

Boil all dishes.

To Workers

Walk to work if possible.

Avoid the person who coughs or sneezes.

Wash your hands before eating.

Make full use of all available sunshine.

Do not use a common towel. It spreads disease.

Should you cough or sneeze, cover nose and mouth with a handkerchief.

Sleep is necessary for well being---avoid over-exertion. Eat good, clean food.

Keep away from houses where there are cases of influenza.

If sick, no matter how slightly, see a physician.

If you have had influenza, stay in bed until your doctor says you can safely get up.

The Germs of This Disease Are Spread Through the Secretions of the Mouth and Nose of Sick People and Carriers, and Not by Books, Clothing, Etc.

Don't Be Alarmed--Be Careful!

Neglect Is the Cause of Practically All Fatalities

Any one who can assist at nursing or caring for the sick kindly register at Red Cross Headquarters. More nurses are needed, both professional and practical. We need your help. Call at

Red Cross Headquarters

Rooms: Second Floor Hart-Albin Building

The October 24, 1918, edition of the *Billings Gazette* ran this full-page notice advising "Don't Be Alarmed—Be Careful!"
IMAGE COURTESY OF *THE BILLINGS GAZETTE.*

We have had only three fatalities in Glasgow, but Malta and Wolf Point are suffering dreadfully."

Malta was hardly the only place to see the swift creation of medical facilities to handle the swarm of flu cases. In Billings, Lincoln High School on Fourth Avenue North was converted to a Red Cross hospital. In Polson, the East Side Hotel became an impromptu hospital. James Finlen offered his landmark Butte hotel for use as a hospital, although local officials didn't accept the offer. In Forsyth, which didn't get a hospital until 1920, an emergency hospital was set up in an elementary school. But when officials decided, prematurely as it turned out, that it was safe for classes to resume, the fledgling hospital was in search of another home, a need eventually filled by the local Elks Club building.

The lack of hospital beds wasn't the only issue. Shortages of doctors and nurses, in part due to the war, complicated flu treatment in many areas. At one point, doctors from Washington, Oregon, and California came to Montana to help at the request of state health officials and the U.S. Public Health Service. Some doctors in more populous parts of the state agreed to travel to rural areas to help fill gaps in available care.

The state board of health enacted a slew of regulations aimed at slowing the spread of the flu, and local officials often took additional measures. Schools and movie theaters were closed, and churches and other public gatherings, including political rallies ahead of the early November election, were barred.

The *Great Falls Tribune* reported that when a local pastor in Hingham, a farm town on the Hi-Line between Havre and Chester, was unable to assemble his congregation, he conducted church services via telephone, reaching about forty homes with music and a brief sermon.

In the state's northwest corner, the *Libby Times* reminded residents that "children must stay in their own yards and all should avoid public gatherings. Do not go into stores for longer than necessary."

The University of Montana suspended classes, and later, some courses

During the outbreak in Montana, some classes,
such as this physics lecture, were held outdoors.
PHOTOGRAPH COURTESY OF THE NATIONAL ARCHIVES.

were held outdoors to avoid the perceived risk of indoor gatherings. Members of the Student Army Training Corps lived in tents after a young student soldier died from the flu in early October 1918. In Bozeman, college officials canceled classes until after Christmas.

In Butte, where flu deaths came by the dozens in the fall of 1918, funerals were limited to family and close friends to avoid large gatherings. Flu victims were to be buried within twenty-four hours. The local board of health met almost daily in that long October and got grim updates on the number of new flu cases reported and the daily death count.

The board ordered the local streetcar company to use only open cars, and those cars were to be fumigated daily. Fumigation orders were later extended to public buildings, hotels, and rooming houses. Signs reading "Influenza Here" were posted on the homes of those who reported illness.

These Seattle police officers wore masks to reduce influenza transmission.
PHOTOGRAPH BY HERMAN SCHNITZMEYER, COURTESY OF THE NATIONAL ARCHIVES.

The closure of dance halls and cabarets and the prohibition of parades and bargain sales in stores were met with reluctant acceptance.

While pool halls were ordered closed because they were "places of amusement," the health board stopped short of shuttering saloons in the rough-and-tumble Mining City. But the board did limit sales of alcohol to that which would be consumed elsewhere. Not surprisingly, enforcement of that provision and other perceived limits on commerce sparked vigorous debate and controversy.

W. H. Maloney, Butte's mayor, defended the decision to not close drinking establishments, telling the *Butte Miner* on October 14, 1918, that "reasonable consumption of liquor was better than too much medicine." (Butte was not alone in not closing bars or taverns. In Harlem, in Blaine County, rather than close such drinking establishments, local officials ordered the removal of all stools, tables, and chairs to encourage shorter stays.)

Coughs and Sneezes Spread Diseases

As Dangerous as Poison Gas Shell:

SPREAD OF SPANISH INFLUENZA MENACES OUR WAR PRODUCTION

Public health posters emphasized limiting the spread of the airborne disease.
ORIGINAL IMAGE FROM U.S. PUBLIC HEALTH SERVICE.

In a six-week period during the fall of 1918, more than 3,000 people in Montana died from the flu and related pneumonia. This viral menace, unlike other flu strains that preyed on the very young and the elderly, found a large target among healthy young adults. A demographic breakdown of Montana flu deaths in 1918–1919, based on death records, shows that about 75 percent of the victims were between ages fifteen and forty-four.

Investigators later concluded that, unlike older people who had previous exposure to the flu and had developed some levels of resistance, many young adults lacked such exposure and were left more vulnerable. In some cases, such as in Butte, crowded living conditions and the large numbers of miners, some likely already suffering respiratory issues triggered by mine dust, may partially explain the local severity of the epidemic.

"It seemed like a perfect place for people to become infected," said Todd Harwell, one of the authors of the 2018 report on the Montana influenza epidemic. The administrator of the state health department's Public Health and Safety Division, Harwell also theorizes that the uneven spread of the flu across the nation was tied to the movement of people, who carried the virus in their travels. Butte, at or near its peak population, attracted people from across the country and around the world.

Entombed in the numbers of flu cases, deaths, and rates of infection are many stories of family tragedy.

Near Glasgow, the Ebersold family lost a twelve-year-old girl and a weeks-old infant to the flu in December 1918. Both parents had been too ill to attend the funeral services, *The Glasgow Courier* reported. A month and half later, the mother of the two children died while traveling to get medical treatment. In the central Montana community of Roy, brothers Albert and George Oline, twenty-nine and thirty-two, respectively, were found dead on Christmas Eve in the home they shared.

In southwest Montana's Madison County, three sisters, Winnie, twenty-six, Ruth, twenty-seven, and Jennie Stalcup, thirty-two, all teachers, "answered the final summons" within days of one another, all victims of the flu, according to the *Twin Bridges Independent*.

The Billings Gazette relayed the story from Ismay, a small community east of Miles City. A local man decided to check on neighbors who had not been seen for days. Entering the home, he found a man, his wife, and two children dead in their beds, another child barely alive on the floor. Officials speculated that no one in the family had been well enough to care for the others. Along with the flu, officials suspected an additional factor in their deaths—starvation.

With many doctors away helping with the war effort, "it was the worst possible time for a pandemic to come through rural areas," said Dr. Steven Helgerson, another author of the 2018 flu report that looked at death records across Montana to gauge the impact of the epidemic. Montana's Indian reservations, already short on medical care, were particularly vulnerable to the flu, he noted.

Harwell and Helgerson agree that many communities in Montana were caught off-guard by the epidemic, even though there were news reports of many flu cases in other parts of the country and around the world. Other issues also seemed to outweigh concern about the flu. People were anxious about the war, possible German sympathizers in their communities, and growing enough grain to help meet a war-fueled spike in demand. Helgerson noted that even a 1918 flood on the Yellowstone River seemed to divert attention from the public health risk posed by the flu.

"There was just one small disaster after another, and then boom, it was influenza and people started dying," said Helgerson, who served as Montana's state medical officer from 2005 to 2015. (Based on his flu research, Helgerson wrote a novella, *A Country Doctor and the Epidemics: Montana 1917–1918*, that captures events in southeast Montana during the epidemic.)

The flu's third wave in Montana was far less significant than the horrific second round. The number of deaths from the flu began to taper off as 1918 ended. While flu cases and deaths jumped a bit in March 1919, the numbers of cases and deaths generally continued to ebb as summer approached.

When the "Great War" ended, many Montanans felt shell-shocked by the deadly multi-front battle they had endured. As Pierce Mullen, a Montana State University history professor, mused decades later, they likely "wondered if they would enjoy the benefits of peace."

Like much of the rest of the country, Montanans were ready for a respite from war and disease. "It is just possible," Mullen and co-author Michael L. Nelson wrote in 1987, "that the influenza experience reinforced Montana's desire after the war to isolate itself, to look inward, to find a sense of balance, to seek a place from which to survey a broken world."

SOURCES

Rocky Mountain Spotted Fever

Kalisch, Phillip A. "Rocky Mountain Spotted Fever: The Sickness and the Triumph." *Montana The Magazine of Western History*. Spring 1973.

National Institute of Allergy and Infectious Diseases. "History of Rocky Mountain Labs." Niaid.nih.gov/about/rocky-mountain-history.

Warzel, Charlie. "Is the Cure for Covid in the Rocky Mountains?" *The New York Times*. May 7, 2020.

"Spanish Flu" Epidemic of 1918–1919

Butte Miner. October 14, 1918; December 6, 1918.

Great Falls Daily Tribune. October 20, 1918.

Harwell, Todd, Greg S. Holzman, and Steven D. Helgerson. "No More War, No More Plague: The Spanish Influenza Pandemic Toll on Montana." *Montana The Magazine of Western History*. Summer 2018.

Harwell, Todd. Personal interview. September 2019.

Helgerson, Steven. Personal interview. September 2019.

Mullen, Pierce C. and Michael L. Nelson. "Montanans and 'The Most Peculiar Disease': The Influenza Epidemic and Public Health, 1918-1919."

Montana The Magazine of Western History. Spring 1987.

Thackeray, Lorna. "A Century Ago, Spanish flu ravaged Billings in community's deadliest epidemic." *Billings Gazette.* December 3, 2018.

Thornton, Tracy. "100 years ago: Spanish flu epidemic in Butte and drastic measures must be taken." *Montana Standard*, Butte, Montana. November 4, 2018.

Twin Bridges Independent. "Stalcup Sisters Are Flu Victims." December 13, 1918.

AIRPLANE CRASHES

AIRPLANES CRASH IN MONTANA EVERY YEAR. IN SOME YEARS, YOU can count the crashes on one hand. In others, the count climbs to several dozen or beyond. Sometimes the plane's occupants survive. In most cases, they do not.

On October 28, 1960, a Northwest Airlines plane flying from Spokane to Missoula encountered snow showers as it approached the Missoula airport. The pilot made a sharp left turn and the plane smashed into a mountain in the Ninemile area. All twelve aboard—four crew and eight passengers—were killed.

Decades later, in the final hours of the last day of November 1992, two large U.S. Air Force cargo planes from Washington State collided in the dark not far from the Canadian border in northern Blaine County. A witness reported seeing a fireball in the sky and, moments later, another fiery explosion as the planes fell roughly 25,000 feet to the ground. Thirteen Air Force flyers were killed in what was expected to be a routine training mission.

In Billings on December 8, 1945, witnesses heard a plane overhead, and an air traffic controller saw a C-47 carrying military personnel dip from sight as it approached the airport in a snowstorm. The plane hit a tree and came to a fiery rest between Poly Drive and Rimrock Road, about a half mile from the airport. Of the twenty-three occupants, nineteen were killed. It was Montana's deadliest plane crash at the time.

Several crashes had multiple witnesses. An estimated crowd of 10,000 gathered for a 1979 Labor Day parade in Dillon when a Montana Air National Guard jet smashed into a grain elevator during a flyover. One afternoon in 2009, numerous witnesses along Harrison Avenue in Butte saw a plane carrying several young families on a ski vacation nosedive into Holy Cross Cemetery, killing all fourteen aboard, not far from the main runway of the city's airport.

While Montana has seen hundreds of military, commercial, and private plane crashes, flying in the state is no more dangerous than other places. But flying in Big Sky country does require attention to detail and different skills than in some areas of the United States. "This region is more demanding due to the mountains and the limitations of some of the small planes," said Matt Lundberg, the chief of safety and education for the state's aviation division. "And the weather can be a challenge."

GREAT FALLS AIR SHOW CRASH, 1946
A CHAIN OF ADVERSE CIRCUMSTANCES

In August 1946, it was fair time, and people in Great Falls and across north-central Montana were in the mood for fun. World War II had ended the year before, and the pall that had loomed over many public celebrations had dissipated. More than 53,000 people attended the first two days of the North Montana State Fair, and organizers were proclaiming attendance would top 200,000 by the end of the fair's run.

The pages of the *Great Falls Tribune* were loaded with fair news on August 8, 1946. "Fair Lady," an Ayrshire dairy cow owned by Fergus Mitchell, landed on page one. On tap in coming days were the pet and doll parade and numerous performances by Jimmy Lynch and his "Death Dodgers," a precision driving act. But the biggest attractions were still to come. The North Montana State Fair Derby, the feature horse race, was offering a purse of $2,500, which boosters claimed was the largest in Montana fair history. The derby was set for Saturday afternoon, just after the fair's air show, featuring a variety of military aircraft, a sure-fire hit in the city that was home to the state's largest military installation, the Great Falls Army Air Base, known to locals as East Base. (East Base became Great Falls Air Force Base in 1947, when the Air Force became its own military branch. The facility was renamed Malmstrom Air Force Base in 1955.)

The *Tribune*'s banner headline on August 9, 1946, read, "Army to 'Shoot the Works' at Fair Air Show Today." In a preview of the show two days earlier, photo captions in the newspaper marveled at "how closely the ships zoomed past grandstand crowds."

The opening act of the air show featured a trio of Douglas A-26 Invaders, the light bombers used in World War II (and later in Korea and Vietnam). Each fifty-foot-long Invader had a seventy-foot wingspan and two 2,000-horsepower engines that could push the plane at speeds approaching 400 miles per hour. On a summery Friday afternoon, the three planes, part of an experienced Army demonstration team that had performed dozens of times in recent weeks, roared from the south into view of the grandstand crowd estimated at 20,000, flying in tight formation.

Racehorse owner R. B. Covington, having just left the racetrack, was walking with a mare named Lorraine toward the nearby horse barn. "Suddenly, the horse jumped and

A Douglas A-26 Invader, like the ones flying at the Great Falls Air Show in 1946.
PHOTOGRAPH COURTESY OF RAGNHILD AND NEIL CRAWFORD, CC BY-SA 2.0.

pulled me back," he recalled a few days later in a newspaper interview. Looking to see what spooked the mare, he saw a plane coming in low, at "terrific speed," over the racetrack. "Before I knew it, part of the plane crashed within three rods [about fifteen yards] in front of me, the other part hit the racetrack and then glanced up and hit the top of the barn where the horses where. The [plane's] tank exploded and the place burst into flames."

The fire engulfed the horse barn. Covington, from Rexburg, Idaho, lost six horses, his truck, and all his racing equipment, plus his clothes and bedding. "If my horse, which evidently heard the collision of the planes in the air, had not pulled me back, I would have been in the path of the part of the plane which fell," he said. "I have only one horse left, but I owe my life to that horse."

As the fair disaster unfolded, it was immediately clear that six people had been killed and twenty-five injured, and nineteen racehorses had perished. The bombers had collided in mid-air, and the lead plane, its tail severed from the fuselage, had careened into the horse barn. A second plane, its wing damaged, flew "dizzily" out of view, according to

A ball of flames erupts from the horse barn at the 1946 Great Falls Air Show.
PHOTOGRAPH COURTESY OF THE HISTORY MUSEUM, GREAT FALLS, MONTANA.

witnesses, and crashed into a field a few miles to the north, its path visible to much of the crowd at the fairgrounds. The third bomber, although damaged, managed to make its way back to East Base and landed safely.

The account in the *Tribune* the next day noted that the collision had "brought flaming death" to the fair within a minute of the start of the show. Killed were the four Army flyers in the two planes that crashed and two people in the horse barn. News accounts from the day are inconsistent regarding the number of deaths stemming from the collision. While initial reports noted two civilian deaths in the barn, a later newspaper story noted the possible discovery of another body in the barn the day after the collision. But there's no further mention of that body, and a local official later acknowledged that searchers may have found charred remnants of a body found previously.

The two civilians killed were Dorothy Mae Szabo, a nineteen-year-old who had recently completed her first year at what was then Montana State University in Missoula, and Andrew "Andy" Seman, thirty-six, a Great Falls man who worked at the Anaconda Company zinc plant in Black Eagle. Seman was survived by a wife, Gladys, and three children. Covington, the Idaho horse owner, described Seman as a close friend who "often came to the barns to help me. That's where he was when the plane hit the barn."

Three of the Army flyers who died were stationed in Lake Charles, Louisiana, including twenty-eight-year-old Captain Howard C. McElroy, twenty-seven-year-old Lieutenant George F. Osgood, and twenty-five-year-old Lieutenant George B. Cowell Jr. One flyer who died was stationed at East Base in Great Falls—Lieutenant Arthur Pelletier. The two flyers who landed safely were Lieutenant Branston R. Redmon and Lieutenant Ralston Bennett, both stationed in Lake Charles.

Along with those killed, dozens of others near the horse barn were treated for burns and shock, some at a first-aid station at the fairgrounds. The *Tribune* the next day shared several accounts of close calls among the fair crowd. One man, Frank Seifert of Great Falls, was credited with saving the lives of a man who used a crutch and a small boy sitting in a car near the horse barn when the plane hit. "When the area was engulfed with flames and smoke, the injured man attempted to run with the boy and fell," the *Tribune* reported, adding that Seifert spotted the two and helped them to safety.

Another man, Romeo Ranieri of Black Eagle, was driving near the barn with his son and daughter and a woman, Pia Rose Matteucci. All suffered burns after Ranieri reported driving through flames "with his car afire and parts of the disintegrated bomber on the car."

Also burned was Eddie Meagher, who told investigators that he was in the barn and walking toward a stall to put a bridle on a horse. "The next thing I remember I was out on the ground and everything was on fire," said Meagher, a Great Falls resident who had watched the first race of the day with Andy Seman before returning to the barn. "I never saw Andy after I ran ahead of him. A big sheet of fire came out—that is all I know."

Larry Krattiger, along with two brothers and a couple of cousins, had crawled through a hole in a fence to get in. The boys found their way to the grandstand bleachers to watch the show and horse races. For a nine-year-old from Valier, the fair and hoopla was "quite an occasion."

"We watched the planes go over and when they collided, I guess it just mesmerized us," Krattiger recalled. The boys saw pieces of the planes hit the ground, and they watched the wild scramble to get horses out of the

Spectators stand in shock as smoke and flames billow from the horse barn. Note the airplane tail resting on the track and the impact mark crossing the track toward the barn.
PHOTOGRAPH COURTESY OF THE HISTORY MUSEUM, GREAT FALLS, MONTANA.

flaming barn. "To this day, I can remember those horses screaming. That really bothered us."

The investigation began almost immediately after the barn fire was extinguished. General Carl Spaatz, the commanding general of the Army Air Forces, ordered an inquiry and sent Major General Junius W. Jones, an inspector general from Washington, D.C., to Great Falls to oversee the work. The Army investigators spent several days in Great Falls gathering information and talking to witnesses, but they returned to D.C. without sharing any conclusions or any hints as to why the planes might have collided. Newspaper accounts say the investigators were able to see movie footage of the collision shot by a Great Falls photographer, identified as Art Moon.

A statement from the Army late on the day of the crash said the planes were flying at about 500 feet, which was described as a "safe altitude," and were traveling at about 390 miles per hour when the lead plane's tail section was damaged by a mid-air collision and the plane crashed into the horse barn. A second plane, which observers said had a damaged left wing, continued to fly but eventually crashed about 3.5 miles from East Base. The third plane, slightly damaged, flew the six miles to the base and landed safely.

A local coroner's jury, empaneled to look into the civilian deaths, showed little reluctance to conclude that the planes were flying at "needlessly low altitude" and were also "flying in too close of formation in the presence of large crowds." The jury ruled that the deaths of Szabo and Seman were caused by the fire that occurred after a portion of the plane hit the horse barn, sparking the fire.

The *Tribune*, on the day after the crash, reported that "fuel from the stricken bomber sprayed the barn, turning it into a raging inferno," adding that the two deaths in the barn came in a resulting "holocaust." The newspaper also noted that as the planes neared the center of the grandstand, "a shower of particles" descended to the ground. At first, there was no sign that the particles were not an intended part of the show, but when a portion of the plane hit the barn, about 500 feet north of the grandstand bleacher, reality set in. "Shocked into a stunned silence momentarily by the tragedy," the *Tribune* reported, "men and women in the grandstand cried with a horrified, 'no, no.'"

The Army completed a detailed accident report about a month after the crash, including statements from several witnesses. One witness, Lieutenant Colonel Frank Thornquest, an executive officer at East Base who sat in the grandstand to watch the air show, said he saw the three planes approach the fairgrounds in a very tight V formation and in a shallow dive. The lead plane appeared to pull up slightly but abruptly as it reached the southeast end of the fairgrounds.

"I thought they were dropping confetti or small pieces of paper," Thornquest told investigators who asked about the material that fell over the fairgrounds. Using a flagpole as a guide, he estimated the planes were only 150 feet off the ground when they passed in front of the grandstand and moving at about 300 miles per hour.

William Paluka was at a shop building across the racetrack from the grandstand when the planes approached. "I could see the planes coming . . . just about the time they got over the shop there was a crunch; you could hear the motors were roaring real loud, but you could still detect that crunch, but nothing fell from the plane right then."

As the planes moved ahead, Paluka told investigators, "It looked like the propellers were chewing the back end of the [lead] plane." Seconds later, he heard a crash and saw "a flurry of fire" as pieces of a plane fell around the shop. "It looked like somebody had thrown a bunch of pamphlets out when they hit; it happened so quick you could not tell what the pieces were that were flying about."

In its report, the Army concluded that the plane on the left side of the formation slid to the right and its right propeller hit the tail assembly of the lead plane, essentially severing it from the rest of the plane and sending the lead plane tumbling to the ground. The second plane continued to move to the right and came into contact with the third plane, damaging its rudder and other parts of its tail.

After the lead plane crashed into the north curve of the racetrack and careened into the horse barn, the plane that had collided with it continued to fly to the north. Due to damage it suffered, it was unable to gain altitude. As the damaged plane neared Bootlegger Hill, the pilot apparently tried to lower his landing gear. That move put the plane into a roll, and it hit the ground and burst into flames. The third bomber, although damaged, managed to make an emergency landing at East Base. Its crew told investigators they didn't see the initial collision and couldn't provide any explanation for its cause.

The Army report didn't include a firm explanation as to why the planes collided. While there was some speculation about the possible failure of an engine that might have caused the initial collision with the lead plane, the report said that "prop wash"—the turbulence caused by the lead plane's propellers—was a more likely issue. The sudden climb could have raised the level of prop wash and caused the plane on the left to temporarily lose control and collide with the lead plane. That theory also suggests that the plane, damaged at this point, might have continued to slide into the third plane.

More certainty was attached to other factors. The report concluded the planes were too close together and flew too low, both violations of procedure. The rules stated that planes were to stay at least a distance of half the wingspan apart, about thirty-five feet. Investigators never precisely determined how low the planes flew that day, but they noted that standard rules called for an air show flight no lower than 1,000 feet over populated or congested areas. Most accounts put the planes' altitude over the fairgrounds at 200 feet or less. Investigators noted a lack of clear direction to the pilots about the proper altitude for the Great Falls show. The 1,000-foot rule was frequently violated at air shows, often at the request of civilian show organizers who told the military that flying lower would lead to "a good, hot show" that would please the audience.

Several photographs published in the *Tribune* on August 10, 1946, captured the scene. One shows members of the crowd, some standing, other clutching their heads, as the planes appeared to collide. Another image shows dark smoke billowing from the barn as many in the grandstand watched, with the tail section of a plane sitting on the racetrack.

An Associated Press news account from August 10 reported that some spectators "surged toward the burning barn and plane" and others rushed toward the grandstand exits. But local law enforcement and military personnel formed lines around the burning barn and plane, shielding them as firefighters battled the fire. At least three people were injured by pieces that fell from the planes, according to news reports.

Ken Robison, a seven-year-old who lived on a farm near Square Butte, southeast of Fort Benton, was at the fair grandstand watching the air show that day, along with his mother and older sister. Now an eighty-one-year-old historian living in Great Falls, Robison has not forgotten the huge crowd and atmosphere as the A-26s neared the racetrack.

"We thought it was staged," Robison said. "These pieces came floating down and it was like it was all planned." The three Robisons didn't see the plane hit the horse barn. "We were quickly ushered out of grandstand. It was remarkably orderly."

Writer Cyra McFadden described the scene many years later in *Rain or Shine*, a memoir of her life and family, and notably her father, James Cyrus "Cy" Taillon, "the molasses-voiced king of rodeo announcers," by sharing an account written by Pete Logan, a friend of her father. (In a review of *Rain or Shine* in *The New York Times* in 1986, writer Tom McGuane described McFadden's father as "a wound-up, hard-drinking, hard-gambling, lady-killer rodeo figure.")

In the moments after the collision, the Air Force announcer "froze, unable to say a word," Logan wrote. "Cy immediately took over and calmly explained that there was no danger now. And as the heat from the burning plane, and the awful smell of death permeated the air, the people remained pretty much as they were, transfixed at the horror they had seen. The slightest suggestion of uncertainty or panic would have resulted in deaths of scores of humanity." He added that a seventeen-year-old girl who witnessed the collision "remembers bits of metal falling by her, with tiny sparks falling in her hair, the heat from the burning gasoline, and through it all, hears Cy talking to them."

Rodeo announcer Cy Taillon kept the crowd calm despite the chaos around them.
PHOTOGRAPH COURTESY OF THE STEPHEN C. SHADEGG PAPERS,
GREATER ARIZONA COLLECTION, ARIZONA STATE UNIVERSITY LIBRARY.

Another woman who witnessed the fair collision later told McFadden that she clearly recalled Taillon's voice that day, saying, "I don't know what God looks like, but I know what He sounds like."

For many years after the crash, Taillon worked as the rodeo announcer at the state fair in Great Falls, and at many larger, prestigious rodeos across the country in a nomadic career that led to his enshrinement in the Pro Rodeo Hall of Fame. He described the 1946 fair collision as the saddest moment in his work life. He died in Great Falls in 1980, and his page-one obituary in the *Tribune* recalled his role in the fair tragedy—"Fairgoers who were there say they will never forget how Taillon's calm voice pervaded the grounds, helping all to keep their heads."

In the wake of the crash, officials called off many of the fair events set for the remainder of August 9. The $2,500 North Montana State Fair Derby was rescheduled for the next day, as was a full lineup of rodeo events.

More than 36,000 people came to the fair that Saturday, one day after the crash. The crowd helped the fair set a record attendance total of 201,177, a fact shared boldly on the front page of the *Tribune*. An accompanying story noted the record attendance came in spite of a "chain of adverse circumstances" during the fair week.

MONTANA'S DEADLIEST PLANE CRASH, 1950

The East Ridge that looms over Butte is a steep, rocky spine of trees and massive boulders, stretching from the Elk Park area in the north to Homestake Pass and Interstate 90 in the south. *Our Lady of the Rockies*, the fourth-tallest statue in the United States, is a luminous, vigilant presence on the ridge on clear evenings.

A landmark to locals, the East Ridge is viewed differently by aviators. The steep ridge and other mountainous terrain surrounding Butte, coupled with the altitude, uncertain weather, and the lack of a control tower, landed Butte on a 2017 list of the "most challenging" airports in the United States, according to an aviation consulting firm.

Known today as Bert Mooney Airport, the airfield a few miles southeast of the city's historic mining hill was Butte Municipal Airport in 1950. Northwest Airlines pilot Lloyd Lampman knew it well. The thirty-seven-year-old had been flying Northwest's Billings-to-Seattle route, which included stops in Great Falls, Helena, and Butte, for several years. In the thirty days prior to November 7, 1950, he had made eighteen landings in Butte.

At about 8:15 A.M., Lampman radioed the airport to report that Northwest Flight 115, a twin-engine Martin 202, was at 10,500 feet over Whitehall and beginning its descent into Butte. A forecast in Helena had projected a storm front with snow showers moving through the area. Lampman reported clouds beneath the plane but good vertical visibility and shared no concerns during that radio call.

About twenty-five hours later, a search plane spotted the airliner's wreckage above Homestake Pass. Flight 115 ended about thirty feet from the crest of one of the mountains that forms the East Ridge, leaving no survivors among the twenty-two passengers and crew members. It remains the deadliest plane crash in Montana history.

Flight 115 began in Chicago and continued to Minneapolis and Billings,

A Martin 202, flying under Northwest's livery, similar to Flight 115.
PHOTOGRAPH COURTESY OF THE JAMES BORDEN PHOTOGRAPHY COLLECTION
AT THE NORTHWEST AIRLINES HISTORY CENTER.

where Lampman, co-pilot James Huff, twenty-nine, and stewardesses Laurie Nohr, twenty-three, and Marnie White, twenty-two, took charge of the plane. The flights to Great Falls and Helena were uneventful. In the capital, the plane took on fuel, and Lampman got a fresh weather report and filed a flight plan that would take the plane south to Whitehall and then west into Butte. Rather than rely on visual observations, the flight would follow Instrument Flight Rules (IFR), relying on navigational beacons near Whitehall and on Homestake Pass. Such IFR flights were, and still are, mandated procedure for flights into Butte.

Flight 115 left Helena at 7:53 A.M. and was on course as it passed near Whitehall at 8:14 A.M. Lampman began his descent. What happened next is unclear.

Two witnesses provided investigators with some observations. John Roffler, a rancher, had just finished milking his cows and spotted the airliner through his bathroom window. He estimated it was about a halfmile north of his home, which was about thirteen miles from the East Ridge. The plane disappeared from view as it traveled northwest, obscured by clouds over the mountains. It was not unusual to see planes on a similar course, Roffler noted, although this one appeared to be lower than normal.

While Roffler reported that it was not snowing near his home, another witness, Mrs. Martin Setzer, who lived about four miles north of Homestake Pass, reported she heard but never saw the plane as it came near her home, due to low clouds and falling snow.

In the *Montana Standard* the day following the crash, searcher Charles Judd recalled statements made by Setzer. "She said she was sure she heard the plane crash," Judd said. "The explosion, she told us, shook the house and rattled the windows." Setzer reported the explosion to the home of a Northern Pacific Railway section foreman at Homestake, and the news was relayed to Butte. The report added to the fears of airport personnel, some of whom were on the tarmac hoping to spot the overdue plane.

Several light planes left Butte to fly over the area near the Setzer home, only to be forced back by snow and low visibility. During that long day, another Northwest airliner would circle the area for nearly an hour seeking signs of the missing aircraft. Planes from Belgrade and Whitehall again flew futilely over the area later in the day.

News of the missing plane quickly circulated in Butte, where residents were out and about on election day. Along with a number of contested Silver Bow County races, local residents were likely determined to do their part to re-elect Mike Mansfield, once a Butte miner, to his fifth term in the U.S. House of Representatives. Local authorities, via radio broadcasts, asked residents to report anything that might aid the search, a move that produced a bevy of dubious accounts of the plane being spotted near the Mining City. One person reported possibly seeing the missing plane over Sheridan, about thirty miles south of Whitehall, and noted it appeared to be having engine trouble. Further investigation revealed that this plane was a Western Airlines craft that diverted from Butte to Idaho Falls, Idaho, not long after the Northwest plane was reported missing. The Western Airlines plane reported no mechanical issues.

Working from a base at the Setzer home, a corps of ground searchers that swelled by the hour worked to comb the steep, rocky, snow-covered east slope of the ridge that helps divide the continent. Hikers and hunters were frequently reported lost in this area, one where finding a missing plane among the giant boulders and trees would have been difficult under the best of conditions, the *Standard* noted.

As searchers battled snow, wind, and poor visibility, the airline released the names of the passengers and crew, deepening the unfolding tragedy. Among the eighteen passengers were:

Mrs. Waldemar (Fannie Katharine) Backa, thirty-two, and her two daughters, Karen Kay, four, and Marcia Jo, five months, who lived in Geyser, Montana. They were en route to Spokane, Washington, to visit one of her sisters.

George Killorn, fifty-eight, of Havre, a vice president and general stores manager for the F.A. Buttrey Co., who left a wife, Mercy, and two adult children.

Harold Rhein of Great Falls, who was en route to Missoula for a one-day course on typewriters as part of his work in the office-machines division of the *Great Falls Tribune*. He and his wife, Ann, were expecting their second child.

Mrs. Charles N. (Berniece) Gray of Glasgow, who had traveled to Baltimore with her dentist husband for a convention. She traveled separately from her husband on the return after learning of the death of one her brothers in Whitefish. Her family later held a double funeral for her and her brother.

Mrs. Arnold R. (Mary Lou) Menzel, twenty, of Great Falls, who was married to a U.S. Air Force captain who traveled from his station in Okinawa to Butte to claim her body.

Gerard "Jerry" Verhelst, forty, of Helena, who had three daughters with his wife, Evelyn. Verhelst had recently taken a job as assistant state director of aeronautics.

Walter and Luceile Lundby of San Francisco, who were on their way home to celebrate their four-year-old son's birthday. The couple also had a nine-month-old daughter.

The other passengers were Vincent J. Walsh, Billings, a Butte native; Charles Miller, Eureka, Montana; Louis Phillips, Wayne, Pennsylvania; Arthur Sogaard, Clemens, Minnesota; Mrs. T. Morris, Fedora, South Dakota; Robert Shull, Claire, Michigan;

Lewis Wren, Indianapolis, Indiana; and Mr. S. R. (Margaret) Fairweather, Seattle.

The search for the airliner on the day of the crash was fruitless. But the next morning, a Civil Air Patrol pilot, George Stanich, and Lieutenant Robert Johnstone of Seattle, who had traveled to Butte to help search for stewardess Marnie White, a close friend, spotted the red tail section of the airliner, the only large piece of the plane still intact. A *Standard* reporter would later note that the tail section "resembled a tombstone nestled in the house-sized rocks."

The plane, which carried a heavy load of fuel, had burned. One wing was torn away from the fuselage, and both engines were found apart from the wreckage. When ground searchers reached the remote site, they soon concluded there were no survivors and that many of the passengers and crew had been severely burned.

Search officials decided to set up a camp near a Northern Pacific

The tail of Flight 115 was the largest intact piece of the plane.
PHOTOGRAPH COURTESY OF BUTTE-SILVER BOW PUBLIC ARCHIVES.

Railway trestle on the Butte side of the ridge from which recovery teams would make the steep climb to the crash scene and bring the bodies back down to the trestle. A Northern Pacific work train was brought to the trestle area to ferry the bodies down the mountain to Butte funeral homes.

The official investigation report put the crash site about thirty feet from the top of the Continental Divide. An aerial photograph published in the *Standard* the next day captured the wreckage from above and also marked with an X the location of the Butte airport, which was clearly visible in the image. The report pinpointed the crash site at 8,250 feet, about two and one-half miles from the runway.

News accounts in the next few days detailed the grim task of identifying the victims and notifying next of kin. Northwest Airlines officials who had traveled to Butte said little publicly about the crash, although the *Standard* quoted one unnamed official this way: "We may never know what happened or why. . . . It looks like he [the pilot] just didn't have enough altitude, that's all."

But officials saw a pattern: counting the Butte crash, three Martin 202s

Searchers faced snow and rugged terrain, and the bleak task of recovering victims' bodies.
PHOTOGRAPH COURTESY OF BUTTE-SILVER BOW PUBLIC ARCHIVES.

operated by Northwest had crashed, with fatal consequences, in the span of twelve months. The first of the three crashes took place on March 7, 1950, in Minneapolis when a Martin 202 crashed into a house while attempting to land in stormy weather. The crash killed all thirteen onboard and two occupants of the house. The second crash of 1950 occurred in rural Minnesota on October 13 while a Northwest pilot undertook an instrument competency check. Six were killed after engine issues caused "dangerous flight characteristics" that led to the crash.

Six days after the Butte crash, Croil Hunter, Northwest's president and general manager, announced the temporary grounding of the airline's fleet of Martin 202 aircraft, a move that would allow for a complete inspection of the planes. Hunter said the inspections were a precaution and that "there is no evidence or any reason to believe that structural deficiencies contributed to our recent accidents." The inspections, he added, were intended "to assure the company and the public that there are no structural deficiencies in the plane." The planes were later returned to service after the airline reported finding no issues.

Yet clues that something was amiss were adding up. The worst crash involving a Northwest Martin 202 occurred on August 29, 1948, at Winona, Minnesota, when thirty-seven crew and passengers were killed after their plane lost a portion of its left wing. Investigators blamed fatigue in fittings used to attach the wing, along with severe turbulence, for the crash. The 202 model was the Martin Company's first commercial airliner, initially delivered in 1947. It was dogged by design issues that led to premature metal fatigue. The company eventually produced another version, the 202A, with a stronger airframe and other modifications.

The first hint at what may have led to the Butte crash emerged at a Civil Aeronautics Board hearing in Seattle about three weeks after the crash. The three-day hearing, featuring thirty-eight witnesses and eighty-five exhibits, included statements from several Northwest pilots who said the "letdown" procedure used to guide planes into Butte from the east was unsafe due to erratic radio signals from the beacons. The testimony also revealed the pilots sometimes deviated from the prescribed route and used an "on and off" technique when approaching the Mining City, relying on both instruments and visual observations.

In its final report released about eight months after the crash, the board methodically ruled out a number of possible factors. They found that the plane was flying level when it hit the mountain. There was no sign of any mechanical malfunction or fire prior to impact.

A review of weather conditions ruled out turbulence or a possible downdraft. Investigators determined that much of the flight had likely taken place in the clouds and with varying visibility. The plane was likely in a localized snowstorm as it approached the ridge, the report said, but the use of flight instruments would have greatly reduced the risk presented by those conditions.

The board also outlined the extensive testing of the navigational beacons before and after the crash and noted there was just one complaint about the devices prior to the crash. Tests found them to be operating properly and accurately on November 7, 1950. Investigators noted that the Western Airlines flight that followed just a few minutes behind Flight 115 reported no issues with the navigation markers and had no trouble finding a safe route to Butte.

The conclusions of the report took square aim at Lampman, the pilot, finding the likely cause of the crash was tied to a failure to follow flight procedures. "It seems probable that the pilot anticipated finding suitable weather for the last few miles to allow him to go through Homestake Pass visually," the board wrote. "The record in this case clearly shows that the captain demonstrated a complete lack of flight discipline by deviating from the prescribed instrument approach to Butte. It is obvious that had he followed the prescribed procedure, the accident would not have happened."

But more than five decades later, as Flight 115 became yet another colorful strand in the tapestry of Butte history, a local resident began to wonder if there might be more to the crash than the seemingly clear-cut conclusion of the Civil Aeronautics Board.

Kristi Dunks grew up in Butte and lived there for a time as an adult. A private pilot, Dunks also worked as an accident investigator for the National Transportation Safety Board before becoming a research analyst, focusing on safety programs, for the agency that investigates airline and civilian plane crashes.

Dunks made the climb to the crash site in 2004, a trek she described as being a steep, confusing hike. "I was just really interested, based on the work that I do and the history of the tragedy," she said. That trip led her to dig up the Civil Aeronautics Board crash report. From there, questions arose, prompted largely by the relative lack of information and evidence.

"We know what happened," Dunks said. "We know they were north of the course and they hit the mountain."

The plane's instruments were destroyed in the crash. The aircraft had no flight-data recorder, which didn't come into use until nearly a decade later. The devices, known popularly as "black boxes," provide information about altitude, flight speed, headings, and other operating conditions that help reconstruct the events leading to a crash. The crash also occurred before the advent of the cockpit voice recorder, which captures the conversations of the pilot and crew and can offer insight into human dynamics that might help explain a crash. Dunks also noted that there was no radar data tracking the course of the plane, leaving the board to draw conclusions about the plane's route largely on the basis of the accounts of the two witnesses on the ground on that stormy morning.

Given the lack of information, "we just can't say for sure what happened," Dunks said. What is clear is that the story of Flight 115 didn't end with the Civil Aeronautics Board crash report.

The wreckage of the plane remains scattered among the granite boulders high on the ridge. In 2002, the family of Lampman, the experienced flyer who worked as an aviation instructor before signing on as an airline pilot, placed a plaque at the site, dedicated to the passengers and crew.

A dozen years later, Debee Wachtel and her husband placed another memorial near the wreckage, noting the valiant efforts of searchers and those who recovered the bodies of the plane's occupants.

Wachtel is the daughter of Walter and Luceile Lundby. She and her brother, Dean Silber, were orphaned by the crash and adopted by relatives. A trip from California to Montana was an attempt to forge a link to the parents she never knew, she told a *Montana Standard* reporter. "I'm not looking for peace," she said. "I have peace. I just need to be at the place where my life changed."

Dunks is unlikely to forget the story of Flight 115. After preparing a public presentation on the crash and investigation that she shared in Butte, she was surprised that so many local residents offered memories about those days long ago. "Sixty-plus years after this accident, this tragedy is still felt by so many different people in so many different ways."

NUTTER PLANE CRASH, 1962

Montana governor Donald G. Nutter, like many politicians in the Cold War era, had clear ideas about the biggest threats facing the United States. Late in January 1962, Nutter taped an address titled "Americanism," in which he touted the virtues of free enterprise and a competitive society and vividly painted the dangers of political extremism, totalitarianism, and communism, salient concerns as the Soviet Union worked to establish a strong foothold in Cuba.

"You and I must recognize communism for what it is," the booming voice said, "a godless ideology which preys upon human misery, but offers no cure for it."

Such words played well with supporters of the former implement dealer and high-school basketball referee from Sidney, the farm town not far from the state's border with North Dakota. Nutter had easily defeated

Montana governor Donald D. Nutter, circa 1961.
PHOTOGRAPH COURTESY OF THE MONTANA HISTORICAL SOCIETY RESEARCH CENTER.

Democratic challenger Paul Cannon to win the state's highest office in November 1960.

He quickly carved a reputation as fiscal conservative, proposing cuts to the state's university system, consolidating state offices, and fighting tax increases at every turn. He ruffled feathers with his opposition to recognizing United Nations Day in the state. Some critics suspected Nutter had links to the ultra-conservative John Birch Society.

There was no reason to think he wouldn't get a warm welcome when he traveled to Cut Bank to address the local chamber of commerce, area barley growers, and others. Just months earlier, the *Cut Bank Pioneer Press* carried the headline, "Nutter's Mass Popularity Stronger Than Ever."

It was a Montana Air National Guard C-47 airplane that would carry Nutter, state agricultural commissioner Edward Wren, and Dennis Gordon, the governor's executive secretary, north from Helena toward Cut Bank on January 25, 1962.

The C-47 was the military version of the Douglas DC-3, a plane credited with revolutionizing aviation in the United States and abroad. Planes in use before the DC-3 were slow, noisy, limited in range, and prone to vibration. The twin-engine DC-3, first produced in 1935, quickly developed a reputation for rugged reliability and for being forgiving in flight and easy to repair. Its range, which allowed commercially desirable non-stop flights from New York to Chicago, would also allow passengers from New York to reach Los Angeles in a mere fifteen hours.

Its military cousin, the C-47 Skytrain, with an even sturdier build, became a World War II workhorse. With production of the civilian DC-3 halted during the war, military production revved up, and more than 10,000 C-47s rolled off assembly lines. The plane, used for transport of troops and supplies, could take off in less than 1,000 feet and land on airfields of greatly varied length and condition.

U.S. general Dwight Eisenhower would later credit the C-47, the jeep, bulldozer, and half-ton truck as the four pieces of equipment critical to the

A pair of C-47 Skytrains similar to the plane carrying Nutter, Wren, and Gordon.
PHOTOGRAPH COURTESY OF U.S. DEPARTMENT OF DEFENSE.

Allies' victory in World War II. More broadly, some aviation historians describe the DC-3 as the most important aircraft in the history of the world.

Along with a stout reputation, the DC-3/C-47 featured wings that were hailed as sterling examples of aviation innovation. Rather than the traditional rib-and-spar wing construction, the DC-3 wing was an arrangement of metal boxes, each riveted or bolted together. The resulting honeycomb construction was more aerodynamic and widely viewed as being incredibly sturdy, even fail-safe, some said. Whether fact or legend, numerous accounts claimed that the wing had remained functional after a steamroller was driven over it as part of a testing regime.

It was windy when the 1943 Air National Guard C-47 with Governor Nutter aboard departed Helena for Cut Bank. In fact, it was windy enough that the flight had been twice delayed in hope of calmer flying conditions. The forecast provided to the pilot and crew called for moderate to occasionally severe turbulence along the planned course. "Such turbulence," investigators would later note, "is a relatively common phenomenon in the flight area and it was not so unusual or severe as to restrict flying."

It is unlikely that Nutter, the broad-shouldered governor, was concerned about the flight. During World War II, he served as an Army Air Corps B-24 bomber pilot. He flew sixty-two missions and was awarded the Distinguished Flying Cross. An aviation weather forecast issued at 2 P.M. on January 25 called for moderate to occasionally severe turbulence over mountain ridges in the area, with "extreme turbulence" expected along the east slopes of the Continental Divide. The C-47 left Great Falls at 2:26 P.M. and arrived in Helena at 3 P.M. Hanson, the pilot, reported light to moderate turbulence on that first leg of the planned flight.

After taking off just after 3 P.M., the C-47 headed north, the state officials joined by a three-man Air National Guard crew, headed by pilot Major Clifford Hanson, co-pilot and flight engineer Major Joseph Devine, and a maintenance technician, Master Sergeant Charles Ballard. All three were based in Great Falls.

The plane was expected in Cut Bank shortly after 6 P.M. At about 4:30 P.M., a member of a logging crew working in the Wolf Creek area telephoned the Lewis and Clark Sheriff's Office to report a plane crash. The initial call noted the loggers found bodies in the burning wreckage but no survivors. There had been no distress signal from the plane.

Alex Stephenson, the Montana Highway Patrol supervisor, offered little hope in his description of the crash scene, reported by the *Great Falls Tribune*. The plane, he said, "was splattered all over the hill. There couldn't be any survivors."

Investigators later concluded that the plane had crashed at about 3:30 P.M. The main wreckage was found on the side of a mountain below a large mound of rocks. Despite deep snow, the fuselage was burned, along with several patches of nearby trees.

In the evening hours after the crash, searchers found a piece of metal from the C-47, about a foot square, on a highway about six miles from the crash scene. Additional search efforts yielded other pieces of the aircraft scattered over a two-mile area near the main wreckage.

Wolf Creek–area rancher Nick Wirth provided a description of the crash scene a few miles from his home, which he drove to after encountering the loggers. "We could see fire from the road," Wirth told the Associated Press. "The plane was demolished. . . . Most of the debris was in the notebook to car-door size. We were able to find only two bodies. Both were mangled and beyond recognition."

An additional observation from Wirth sparked hope. He said, "We found several parachutes that had been opened."

But the grim reality arrived quickly. Searchers, within hours, recovered bodies of all passengers on the plane. Dead were Nutter, Wren, Gordon, and the flight crew of Hanson, Devine, and Ballard. Agents from the FBI helped identify the bodies. Nutter was the second Montana governor to die in office. (The first was Frank C. Cooney, who died in 1935 from heart failure at the age of sixty-two.)

BODIES OF GOV. DON NUTTER, FIVE COMPANIONS RECOVERED

Tragic Plane Mishap Stuns State as Officals, Crew Die

By The Associated Press

Wolf Creek — At least five of the six victims who died in a fiery crash of a Montana Air National Guard plane atop a snow covered mountain peak west of here were located today. There was tentative identification of one body as that of Gov. Donald G. Nutter, one of those who died in the splintering crash.

Searchers who entered the rugged windswept area of doublweak reported sighting what appeared to be the sixth victim of the crash. The Thursday night tragedy has shocked all of Montana.

Two of the victims were found near where one of the C47's landed, but came to rest a mile or so [...]

Believed Nutter's death

About 100 yards away was an inner aboard the plane.

A part of a burned checkbook belonged to Edward C. Wren, 43, [...]

The other body was at a greater distance, and the shattering force of the crash threw the victims on opposite sides of the mountain on a snow covered ridge.

The body found almost in the plane wreckage tentatively was [...]

Gov. Donald G. Nutter

Ed C. Wren

Dennis B. Gordon

Nutter's Body Identified

By Mayo Ashley

Definite identification of one of the bodies found early a wallet as that of M. Sgt. Charles W. Ballard, flight engineer aboard the plane.

A piece of wrist bone, around which was wrapped a wrist watch, was found on one of the bodies about three-fourths the way up the mountain on which the crash occurred.

Deputy Sheriff Larry Lytle said the watch was engraved on its back, "Donald G. Nutter, Governor of Montana."

All six bodies had been recovered by noon and were placed in ambulances en route to Helena.

The body of Edward Wren was found near the base of the mountainside over which the plane bounced after splitting apart when it hit the peak. That of Dennis Gordon was nearby.

That of Governor Nutter and Sgt. C. W. Ballard were about three quarters of the way to the top.

The bodies of Pilot Bill Hanson and Capilat Andy Devine were in the wreckage originally discovered at the top of the mountain.

Army technicians strung telephone wires from the crash scene to Wolf Creek to aid with the investigation, which was to take place on the spot.

Babcock Aims To Attain Nutter's Goal

Montana's new chief executive, Tim M. Babcock, who assumed the governorship upon the death of Donald G. Nutter, said today he would work to carry out Nutter's goal of operating the state in the black.

State, National Weather

Forecast, Helena and vicinity: Occasional snow showers and colder tonight with a low of 10. High Saturday, 22.

The official Helena temperature at 2 p.m. was 47

Turbulent Winds Reported Before Plane Left Helena

IDENTIFICATION TEAM—Members of an identification team from Malmstrom Air Force Base are shown as they climbed the mountain to investigate the plane crash. (Independent Record Photo by Dave Carlson)

BODY IS FOUND—The body of one of the victims of the plane crash in which Gov. Donald G. Nutter was killed, was mangled beyond recognition. (Independent Record Photo by Dave Carlson)

Ill-Fated Pilot May Not Have Known Forecast

An official weather bureau forecast, issued at 2 o'clock Thursday afternoon and available to all pilots flying a wide area of Montana, warned of "extreme turbulence" along the east slope of the Continental Divide.

Whether Maj. Clifford E. Hanson, pilot of the ill-fated gubernatorial plane, availed himself of that forecast perhaps never will be determined.

Covered Wide Area

Generally, winds conditions were reported from Alberta all along the east slope of the divide, extending nearly to Helena. In addition, the pilot of a plane flying over the Bozeman vicinity at about 4 p.m. reported up and down drafts at the rate of 2,000 feet per minute. He was in a DC4.

Flew From Great Falls

Hansen, a Great Falls resident and an air traffic control specialist for the Federal Aviation Agency, had flown Gov. Donald G. Nutter and his party on other trips, notably one in 1962 to Minneapolis. Hansen and the two other crew members also killed in the crash—Joseph B. Devine and Charles W. Ballard, both of Great Falls—flew the plane from Great Falls to Helena to pick up the governor's party. Hansen reportedly did not get out of the plane at the Helena airport.

The Helena weather bureau's 8 p.m. forecast contained the following warning for the small aircraft: "Strong, gusty surface winds, Montana, east slope of Continental Divide, moderate to severe turbulence over mountain ridges and occasionally moderate turbulence to outwings of strong surface winds in the Great Falls area."

Visibility was Good

The forecast added that there was no particular cloudiness and that visibility was good. In the body of the forecast, the warning on turbulence was repeated thusly: "Extreme turbulence, surface to 10,000 feet mean sea level in vicinity of strong surface winds Montana, east slopes of divide." It added there was "moderate to occasionally severe" turbulence over the mountain ridges.

That forecast, prepared in Helena, was sent to the weather bureau at Great Falls.

At Wolf Creek

Reporter Tells of Scenes Covering Tragic Crash

By Mayo Ashley

It is ironic that Gov. Donald G. Nutter a staunch supporter throughout his political life of harmony and that [...]

SIXTEENTH GOVERNOR—Former Lt. Gov. Tim Babcock becomes Montana's 16th governor.

Wreckage Scattered

Tragic Story of Finding Six Bodies At Crash Scene Told by Writer

By Dave Carlson

[...]

Army Team Aids

[...]

The crash commanded the entire front page of the Helena *Independent Record*'s January 26, 1962, edition.
PHOTOGRAPH COURTESY OF HELENA *INDEPENDENT RECORD*.

Lieutenant Governor Tim Babcock, forty-two, a close friend of Nutter's and his 1960 running mate, was sworn in as Montana's governor. The crash investigation gained momentum.

A more detailed account from one of the loggers working near the crash site soon emerged. Harold Farrell, thirty-seven, of Missoula, was sitting in his truck when he spotted the plane, traveling fast, with its wings level, on a downward path.

"I thought at first it was a jet," he said in an Associated Press news story. "It was going so fast. The engine was wound up and we heard the whine first. It was coming down with its nose down quite steep, but it wasn't breaking up. I didn't see any pieces falling."

Farrell said he jumped out of the truck when he spotted the plane. "I had to run toward a creek to keep it in sight. I didn't see it hit but I saw the fireball explode when I got to the clearing." The logger, joined by two others, made his way to the fiery crash site twenty to thirty minutes later.

"We had no idea whose plane it was or what caused it," Farrell said, noting there were high clouds in the area but no visibility issues. "But there was an awful wind, probably 100 miles per hour in some places."

The wind and accompanying turbulence drove early speculation about the cause of the crash. A news story in the *Great Falls Tribune* the day after the crash told of "hurricane-force" winds in some areas along the Rocky Mountain Front the previous day.

While the highest gust reported in often blustery Great Falls was fifty-three miles per hour, the electric cooperative in the Augusta area, about thirty-five air miles north of the crash site, reported that more than six dozen power poles, each more than a foot thick, were snapped off by the wind. School officials in the ranch community canceled classes at noon because of the fierce wind.

Earlier on the day of the crash, pilots traversing the mountainous terrain near the crash scene reported updrafts and downdrafts at as much as 2,000 feet per minute, the *Tribune* reported. Encountering such air currents isn't unusual when flying over mountains, especially on the downwind side of ridges. But the resulting turbulence can reduce the margin for error even for experienced pilots.

Investigators sent pieces of the C-47 to Air Force laboratories for testing. A flight inspector from the Federal Aviation Administration traced the flight route from Helena to Cut Bank and found the plane to be on course "and following a route that would be expected of an experienced and prudent flyer." Flying in a DC-3, with more powerful engines than the C-47, the inspector, Robert Kelly, noted that the "lighter powered" Air National Guard plane "definitely could have had trouble with turbulence."

But a blaring headline in the Helena *Independent Record* on January 29, 1962, revealed a startling discovery. "Wing of Ill-Fated Plane Found One Mile from Main Wreckage," the headline read. A smaller subhead added, "High Wind May Have Ripped Part From C-47."

The accompanying news story detailed how an Air National Guard searcher had found a large portion of the right wing of the plane, mostly intact and only superficially damaged, on a steep, timbered slope. It appeared the wing had been torn from the plane just beyond the right engine.

The portion of the wing was shipped to Wright-Patterson Air Force Base in Dayton, Ohio, for a metallurgical analysis. The Air Force then outlined two scenarios shortly after the partial wing was found: turbulence alone caused the wing to be sheared from the plane, or structural failure of the wing itself caused the wing to come off when it encountered the turbulence.

Other revelations in that period garnered news coverage as well. The nineteen-year-old C-47 that carried Nutter and the others was the only plane of its type assigned to the Montana Air National Guard. An Associated Press news story noted that some aviation experts considered the C-47 obsolete.

Concerns about the C-47s were not a new development. At the Western Governors' Conference in the spring of 1961, attendees, including Nutter, petitioned the U.S. president and Congress to provide turbojet replacements for "outmoded" National Guard C-47 aircraft. Just a few days after the crash near Wolf Creek, a C-47 carrying the governor of Wyoming made a "forced" landing due to an oil leak. The two developments prompted a temporary national order to take the Guard C-47s out of service.

About a week later, a five-person Air Force board of inquiry issued its final report on the Montana crash. The primary cause, according to the report, was "metal fatigue failure" in the skin of the right wing. The failure caused the wing to break away from the plane. A contributing cause was "severe turbulence" that put additional stress on the weakened wing.

The wings of the Montana C-47 had been inspected within twenty-four months of the crash, officials said. But the report concluded that signs of damaged or weakened metal were likely covered by the wing's skin and not visible to flight crews or maintenance personnel.

The U.S. Air Force grounded all of its C-47s after the report was issued, allowing all of the aircraft to be examined for structural issues. Once the inspections were satisfactorily completed, there would be new rules regarding C-47 operations—flights through turbulence were to be avoided, and if turbulent conditions emerged unexpectedly, pilots were directed to reduce airspeed to the lowest safe levels to reduce stress on the aircraft.

The report, obtained through a Freedom of Information Act request, includes a significantly redacted three-page narrative section. It offers no information on injuries or the possible deployment of parachutes by the plane's passengers.

As the crash investigation gradually unfolded, official mourning and funeral planning began immediately. The casketed bodies of Nutter, Wren, and Gordon were placed in the capitol rotunda, allowing the public to pay their respects. A funeral was held in the House chamber.

Words of condolence poured in, including from Washington, D.C., and the Oval Office. President Dwight Eisenhower sent a note to Maxine

Nutter, the governor's widow, shortly after the crash. The Nutters had recently met with the Eisenhowers in Indio, California.

"We enjoyed so much meeting you both just two short weeks ago and were greatly impressed by the governor's vitality, enthusiasm, and dedication to the people of your state and our country," Eisenhower wrote. "His loss is a blow to all of us. We join in deepest sympathy."

Members of Montana's all-Democratic congressional delegation also weighed in. Senator Mike Mansfield recalled Nutter as being open with his opinions, a man "who always put his cards on the table, so there was never any doubt as to where he stood." Representative Lee Metcalf noted Nutter's early career as a basketball referee and his record of accomplishment. "Everything he tried, he did well," Metcalf said. "He was one of the best referees, he had a wonderful war record, and he was a good legislator." Representative Arnold Olson, in a House speech, described Nutter as "an able leader, a good Christian, and an honorable and decent man," adding that the deceased governor was also "an aggressive, outspoken fighter who never wavered in his beliefs."

An official state funeral for Nutter was held in Helena on January 28, just a few days after the crash, and another service was held in Sidney two days later. Nutter's copper-colored casket was ferried the 460 highway miles under escort by the Montana Highway Patrol. On the day of the funeral, schools and many businesses in Sidney were closed. Many businesses in Cut Bank also closed in honor of the late governor.

A funeral in the Sidney high school gymnasium drew an estimated 3,500 people. Nutter was remembered as a fearless man. "God gave him a powerful brain, clear eyes, and quick hands," a minister eulogized. "He had a real vigor, was tireless, a crusader, and had absolute integrity."

Nutter was buried in a Sidney cemetery; today a statue of the hometown hero stands in a city park. A plaque honoring Nutter and all of the victims of the crash was initially placed outside the governor's office in the capitol after the crash. A remodeling project prompted its removal, and it sat in storage until 2006, when it found a home outdoors near the capitol's south entrance.

At a ceremony for the plaque's re-installation, which included members of the Nutter, Devine, and Gordon families, Tim Babcock, who completed Nutter's term and was re-elected to a second term in 1964, recalled encouraging Nutter to seek the governorship, noting his military service, legislative experience, and "talent as a forceful speaker with strong convictions."

A few days after the crash, Babcock released the text of Nutter's "Americanism" speech. The taped version of the speech would be aired on a Helena radio station, and a text version appeared in the Helena *Independent Record*.

In the decades after the crash, Babcock would occasionally speak publicly about the emotional day that the plane carrying the governor lost its wing. Babcock had been bound for Billings, on a train, when he had received the news.

At a ceremony marking the fiftieth anniversary of the crash in 2012, then-governor Brian Schweitzer called January 25, 1962, "one of the darkest days in the history of Montana."

Babcock recalled losing his best friend. "I've looked on this day every day the past fifty years," he said. His wife, Betty, recalled the moment her husband was sworn into office: "He looked over at me and he said, 'You know, I bet this is the only time a governor went into office crying. We were all crying.'"

SOURCES

Great Falls Air Show Crash

Army Air Force. "Report of Major Accident, August 9, 1946, 2:05 P.M." Report released by the Air Force Historical Research Agency, Maxwell Air Force Base, Alabama.

Associated Press. "Army Planes Crash at State Fair; Montana Air Show Known Dead 6." *The New York Times*. August 10, 1946.

Great Falls Tribune. August 8–12, 1946.

Great Falls Tribune. "Rodeo Announcer Dies in Great Falls." April 17, 1980.

Krattiger, Larry. Personal interview. November 2019.

McFadden, Cyra. *Rain or Shine: A Family Memoir.* Knopf, 1986.

Post-Register, Idaho Falls, Idaho. "Rexburg Man Has Close Call in Plane Crash."
August 12, 1946.

Robison, Ken. Personal interview. November 2019.

Thomas McGuane. "King of the Rodeo." Review of *Rain or Shine: A Family
Memoir. The New York Times.* April 13, 1986.

Montana's Deadliest Plane Crash

Associated Press. "CAB Probes Butte Airplane Crash." *Montana Standard,* Butte
Montana. December 1, 1950.

Associated Press. "CAB Hearing on Butte Crash Ends." *Great Falls Tribune.*
December 3, 1950.

Benoit, Zach. "70th Anniversary of Billings' Deadliest Plane Crash." *Billings
Gazette.* December 8, 2015.

Civil Aeronautics Board. "Accident Investigation Report, Northwest Airlines Flight
115." June 22, 1951.

Dunks, Kristi. Personal interview. April 2019.

Great Falls Tribune. November 8–11, 1950.

Havre Daily News. George Killorn obituary. November 8, 1950.

Hoffman, Matt. "When Life Changed." *Montana Standard,* Butte, Montana.
August 18, 2014.

Independent Record, Helena, Montana. "Three Suits Are Filed in Federal Court
as Result of Crash." November 6, 1951.

Montana Standard, Butte, Montana. November 7–16, 1950.

West Seattle Herald. Lloyd Lampman obituary. November 9, 1950.

Nutter Plane Crash

Billings Gazette. February 9, 1962.

Great Falls Tribune. January 26 through April 1962.

Guide to Montana Governors' Records, 1889–1962. Archives West. archiveswest.
orbiscascade.org

Helena *Independent Record*. January 25 through April 1962; May 11, 1962; September 14, 2006; January 26, 2012.

Lucker, Jeff. "Reading a Machine: The DC-3 – A Solution to Many Problems." Historical Abstract. Princeton, New Jersey. 1984.

Rollins, Judith Beatrice. "Governor Donald G. Nutter and the Montana Daily Press." Chapter IV, master's thesis, University of Montana. 1963.

Sidney Herald, Sidney, Montana. June 10, 2014.

Tegler, Eric. "Why the DC-3 Is Such a Bad-Ass Plane." *Popular Mechanics*. August 2017.

United States Air Force. "Accident/Incident Report, Military Aircraft VC047A, Tail No. 42100861." Report released by Air Force Safety Center, Kirtland AFB, New Mexico.

INDEX

ABOUT THE AUTHOR

JAMES E. "BUTCH" LARCOMBE is a fourth-generation Montanan who grew up in Malta. He worked for more than thirty years as a reporter and editor for Montana newspapers and at *Montana Magazine*. A student of Montana history, he lives near Bigfork.